Isabelle Poirier
- 1995 -

PEOPLE AND PLACES IN THE BIBLE enables you to have at your fingertips all the proper names recorded in the Bible from Aaron to Zuzims!

ISBN 1-55748-030-3

Published by: **BARBOUR AND COMPANY, INC.**
164 Mill Street
Westwood, New Jersey 07675

(In Canada, THE CHRISTIAN LIBRARY,
960 The Gateway, Burlington, Ontario L7L 5K7)

EVANGELICAL CHRISTIAN PUBLISHERS ASSOCIATION **ECPA** MEMBER

Printed in the United States of America

PEOPLE AND PLACES
IN
THE BIBLE

By

JOHN FARRAR

BARBOUR BOOKS
164 Mill Street
Westwood, New Jersey 07675

PEOPLE AND PLACES
IN
THE BIBLE

AARON, Ay′-ron, *lofty, mountainous.*—The son of Amram and Jochebed, of the tribe of Levi. The first high-priest of the Jews. Exod. iv. 14; Luke i. 5.

AARONITES, Ay′-ron-ites, the descendants of Aaron, who went over to David to Hebron. 1 Chron. xii. 27.

ABADDON, A-bad′-don, *the destroyer.*—King of the locusts, and angel of the bottomless pit. Rev. ix. 11.

ABAGTHA, A-bag′-thah, *the father of the winepress.*—One of the chamberlains of king Ahasuerus. Esther i. 10.

ABANA, Ab′-a-nah, *stony.*—A river of Damascus, probably a branch of the Barrady, or Chrysorrhoas, which derives its source from the foot of Mount Libanus, eastward, runs round and through Damascus, and continues its course till lost in the wilderness. 2 Kings v. 12.

ABARIM, Ab′-a-rim, *passages.*—Mountains to the east of the river Jordan, of which Nebo and Pisgah were parts. Num. xxvii. 12.

ABBA, Ab′-bah, *father.*—Syriac. Mark xiv. 36.

ABDA, Ab′-dah, *a servant.*—The father of Adoniram, who was over king Solomon's tribute which he exacted from other nations. 1 Kings iv. 6.

ABDI, Ab′-dy, *my servant.*—The father of Kish. 2 Chron. xxix. 12.

ABDIEL, Ab′-de-el, *a servant of God.*—The father of Ahi, a descendant of Gad. 1 Chron. v. 15.

5

ABDON, Ab'-don, *a servant.*—1. The son of Hillel, of the tribe of Ephraim, and tenth judge of Israel. Judges xii. 13. 2. The son of Micah. 2 Chron. xxxiv. 20. 3. A son of Jehiel. 1 Chron. ix. 36. 4. A son of Jehiel and Maachah. 1 Chron. viii. 30. 5. The name of a city in the tribe of Asher. Josh. xxi. 30.

ABEDNEGO, A-bed'-ne-go, *servant of light.*—The Chaldee name given by the king of Babylon's officer to Azariah, one of Daniel's companions. Dan. i. 7.

ABEL, Ay'-bel, *vanity, vapour, mourning.*—The second son of Adam and Eve. Gen. iv. 2.

ABEL-BETH-MAACHAH, Ay'-bel-beth-may'-a-kah, *mourning of the house of Maachah.*—A town in Syria, situated to the north of Damascus, between Libanus and Antilibanus. 2 Sam. xx. 14, 15; 1 Kings xv. 20.

ABEL-MAIM, Ay'-bel-may'-im, *the mourning of the waters.*—A city in the tribe of Naphtali. 2 Chron. xvi. 4.

ABEL-MEHOLAH, Ay'-bel-me-ho'-lah, *mourning of weakness, of sickness.*—The country of the prophet Elisha, near to the river Jordan, about sixteen miles from Scythopolis, in the half-tribe of Manasseh. 1 Kings xix. 16.

ABEL-MIZRAIM, Ay'-bel-miz -ray-im, *the mourning of the Egyptians.*—The floor of Atad, beyond Jordan, where Joseph, his brethren, and the Egyptians mourned for the death of Jacob. Gen. l. 11.

ABEL-SHITTIM, Ay'-bel-shit'-tim, *mourning of the thorns.*—A city situate in the plains of Moab, beyond Jordan, opposite to Jericho. Num. xxv. 1; xxxiii. 49.

ABEZ, Ay'-bez, *an egg, muddy.*—A city in the tribe of Issachar. Josh. xix. 20.

ABI, Ay'-by, *my father.*—The mother of Hezekiah. 2 Kings xviii. 2.

ABIAH, A-by'-ah, *the Lord is my Father.*—The second son of the prophet Samuel, and brother of Joel. 1 Sam. viii. 2.

ABI-ALBON, A-be-al'-bon, *intelligent father.*—One of David's worthies. 2 Sam. xxiii. 31.

ABIASAPH, A-by'-a-saf, *a gathering or consuming father.*—One of the sons of Korah. Exod. vi. 24.

ABIATHAR, A-by'-a-thar, *excellent father.*—The father of Ahimelech, and tenth high-priest among the Jews, and fourth in descent from Eli. 2 Sam. viii. 17.

ABIB, Ay'-bib, *green fruits, ears of corn.*—The name of the first Hebrew sacred month, afterwards called Nisan: it contains 30 days, and answers to part of our March and April. Exod. xiii. 4.

ABIDAH, A-by'-dah, *father of knowledge.*—One of the sons of Midian. Gen. xxv. 4.

ABIDAN, Ab'-e-dan, *father of judgment.*—A son of one Gideoni, of the tribe of Benjamin. Num. vii. 60.

ABIEL, Ay'-be-el, *God my Father.*—The father of Kish and Ner, and grandfather of king Saul. 1 Sam. ix. 1.

ABI-EZER, A-be-e'-zer, *father of help.*—A Benjamite of the town of Anathoth, one of David's worthies. 1 Chron. xi. 28.

ABI-EZRITE, A-be-ez'-rite. — Joash, the father of Gideon. Judges vi. 11.

ABIGAIL, Ab'-e-gal, *the joy of the father.*—1. The sister of David. 1 Chron. ii. 16. 2. The wife of Nabal; 1 Sam. xxv. 3; afterwards married to David. 1 Sam. xxv. 42. A. M. 2944.

ABI-GIBEON, Ab'-e-gib'-eon, *the father of the cup.*—Father of Gibeon.

ABIHAIL, Ab-e-hay'-il, *the father of strength.*—The name of several eminent men among the Hebrews. 1 Chron. v. 14; Num. iii. 35; Esther ii. 15. Also the name of some women. 2 Chron. xi. 18, 19.

ABIHU, A-by'-hew, *he is my father.*—The son of Aaron the high-priest, destroyed with his brother Nadab, by fire sent from God. Lev. x. 1, 2.

ABIHUD, A-by'-hud, *the father of praise or confession.*—1 Chron. viii. 3.

ABIJAH, A-by'-jah, *the will of the Lord.*—1. The son of Jeroboam, the first king of the ten tribes. 1 Kings xiv. 1. A. M. 3046. 2. The son of Rehoboam, king of Judah: he succeeded his father, A. M. 3046. 2 Chron. xi. 20.

ABIJAM, A-by'-jam, *father of the sea.*—Same as ABIJAH. 1 Kings xiv. 31.

ABILENE, A-be-le'-ne, *father of the apartment, or of mourning.*—A small province of Syria, between Libanus and Antilibanus. Luke iii. 1.

ABIMAEL, A-bim'-a-el, *a father sent from God.*—Gen. x. 28.

ABIMELECH, A-bim'-me-lek, *father of the king.*—Title of the kings of Philistia, as Cæsar was of the Roman emperors. Also the name of one of the sons of Gideon; Judges ix. 1.

ABINADAB, A-bin'-na-dab, *father of willingness.*—1. The son of Jesse. 1 Sam. xvi. 8. 2. The son of Saul. 1 Sam. xxxi. 2. 3. The son-in-law of Solomon. 1 Kings iv. 11.

ABINOAM, A-bin'-no-am, *father of beauty or comeliness; my father is beautiful.*—The father of Barak. Judges iv. 6.

ABIRAM, A-by'-ram, *a high father, father of fraud.*—1. The eldest son of Hiel, the Bethelite. 1 Kings xvi. 34. 2. The son of Eliab; one that conspired with Korah and Dathan. Num. xvi. 1.

ABISHAG, Ab'-be-shag, *ignorance of the father.*—A young woman, a native of Shunem, in the tribe of Issachar, married to David in his old age. 1 Kings i. 3.

ABISHAI, A-bish'-a-i, *the present of my father, the father of the sacrifice.*—The son of Zeruiah, David's sister, and one of David's generals. 2 Sam. xxi. 17.

8

ABISHALOM, A-bish'-a-lom, *the father of peace, the recompence of the father.*—The father of Maachah, who was mother to Abijah, king of Judah. 1 Kings xv. 2.

ABISHUA, A-bish'-u-ah, *father of salvation, or of magnificence.*—The son of Phinehas. 1 Chron. vi. 4.

ABISHUR, Ab'-be-shur, *the father of the wall, or of uprightness.*—The son of Shammai, of the posterity of Judah. 1 Chron. ii. 28.

ABITAL, Ab'-be-tal, *the father of the dew.*—One of David's wives, and mother of Shephatiah. 1 Chron. iii. 3.

ABITUB, Ab'-be-tub, *father of goodness.*—The son of Hushim. 1 Chron. viii. 11.

ABIUD, A-by'-ud, *father of praise.*—The son of Bela. 1 Chron. viii. 3; Matt. i. 13.

ABNER, Ab'-ner, *father of light, son of the father.*—The son of Ner, uncle of king Saul, and general of his army. After Saul's death, he made Ishbosheth king, and for seven years supported the family of Saul, in opposition to David. In consequence of a quarrel between him and Ishbosheth, Abner went over to David, and his influence in the army produced a general submission to David, which cost him his life, for he soon fell by the hand of Joab. 1 Sam. xiv. 50.

ABRAHAM, Ay'-bra-ham, *the father of a great multitude;* and

ABRAM, Ay'-bram, *a high father, the father of elevation.*—The son of Terah, born at Ur, a city of Chaldea, A.M. 2008. The account of this patriarch occupies a large part of the book of Genesis, and is intimately connected with both the Jewish and Christian dispensations. For the particulars we must refer to Gen. xii.—xxv.

ABSALOM, Ab'-sa-lom, *father of peace.*—The son of David by Maachah, daughter of the king of Geshur, distinguished for his fine person, his vices, and his unnatural rebellion. Of his open revolt, his conduct in Jerusalem, his pursuit of the king his father, his defeat and death, see 2 Sam. xvi.—xviii.

9

ACCAD, Ak'-kad, *a pitcher, a spark.*—One of the four cities built by Nimrod. Gen. x. 10. Probably the present Akarkouff.

ACCHO, Ak'-ko, *close, pressed together.*—It was afterwards called Ptolemais, and now Akka, by the Arabs, and Acre by the Turks. It was given to the tribe of Asher. Judges i. 31.

ACELDAMA, A-kel'-da-mah, or A-sel'-da-mah, *the field of blood.*—A piece of ground, without the south wall of Jerusalem, on the other side of the brook Siloam. It was called the Potter's Field, because an earth or clay was dug in it, from which pottery was made. It was likewise called the Fuller's Field, because cloth was dried in it. It was called Aceldama, because purchased with the money which Judas brought back, the price of his betrayal of Christ. Zech. xi. 12, 13; Matt. xxvii. 8; Acts i. 19.

ACHAIA, A-kay'-yah, *grief, trouble.*—The name is used to denote the whole of Greece, as it existed as a Roman province; or Achaia Proper, a district in the northern part of the Peloponnesus, on the bay of Corinth, and in which the city of that name stood. It appears to have been used in the former sense in 2 Cor. xi. 10; and in the latter, Acts xix. 21.

ACHAICUS, A-kay'-e-kus, *sorrowing, sad.*—A native of Achaia. 1 Cor. xvi. 17.

ACHAN or ACHAR, Ay'-kan, Ay'-kar, *he that troubles or bruises.*—1. The son of Carmi, of the tribe of Judah. See his history, Josh. vii. 1—26. 2. One of Esau's descendants. Gen. xxxvi. 27.

ACHAZ, Ay'-kaz.—Mentioned Matt. i. 9.

ACHBOR, Ak'-bor, *a rat, bruising.*—1. The father of Baal-hanan, king of Edom. Gen. xxxvi. 38. 2. An officer of king Josiah. 2 Kings xxii. 12.

ACHIM, Ay'-kim, *confirming, revenging.*—Matt. i. 14.

ACHISH, Ay'-kish, *thus it is, how is this?*—A king of Gath, to whom David fled for shelter from Saul. 1 Sam. xxi. 10. There was another king of Gath of this name in the days of Solomon. 1 Kings ii. 39, 40.

ACHMETHA, Ak'-me-thah.—Or Ecbatana, a city of Media. Ezra vi. 2.

ACHOR, Ay'-kor, *trouble.*—A valley between Jericho and Ai. So called from the trouble brought upon the Israelites by the sin of Achan. Josh. vii. 24.

ACHSAH, Ak'-sah, *adorned, bursting of the veil.*— The daughter of Caleb and the wife of Othniel. Josh. xv. 16—19; Judges i. 12—15.

ACHSHAPH, Ak'-shaf, *poison, tricks, one that breaks, the brim of any thing.*—A city of Palestine, near Mount Tabor, in the tribe of Asher. Josh. xii. 20.

ACHZIB, Ak'-zib, *a liar, one that runs.*—A city of Palestine, in the tribe of Asher. Josh. xix. 29.

ADA, ADAH, Ay'-dah, *an assembly.*—1. One of La-mech's wives, the mother of Jabal and Jubal. Gen. iv. 19. 2. The name of a daughter of Elon, the Hittite, and wife of Esau. Gen. xxxvi. 4.

ADAIAH, Ad-a-i'-ah, *the witness of the Lord.*—The name of several men among the Hebrews. 1 Chron. vi. 41; viii. 21; ix. 12; 2 Kings xxii. 1; Neh. xi. 12.

ADALIA, Ad-a-ly'-ah, *one that draws water, poverty, cloud, death.*—The fifth son of Haman, who was hanged, with the rest of his brethren, by the command of Ahas-uerus. Esther ix. 8.

ADAM, Ad'-am, *earthy, taken out of red earth.*—The first man, and father of the human race. Gen. i. 26. Also, the name given to man in general. Gen. v. 1, 2; Josh. xiv. 15; 2 Sam. xii. 19; Eccles. iii. 21; Jer. xxxii. 20; Hosea vi. 7; Zech. xiii. 7. The second Adam, the Lord Jesus Christ. The name of two cities.

ADAMA, Ad'-a-mah, *red earth.*—The same as ADMAH.

ADAMAH, Ad'-a-mah, *red earth.*—The name of a city in the tribe of Naphtali. Josh. xix. 36.

ADAMI, Ad'-da-my, *my man, red, earthy.*—A city of Palestine. Josh. xix. 33.

11

ADAR, Ay'-dar, *high, eminent.*—1. The twelfth month of the ecclesiastical, and the sixth of the civil, year among the Hebrews, answering to part of February and March. Ezra vi. 15. 2. The son of Ishmael. Gen. xxv. 15. 3. A king of Edom. Gen. xxxvi. 39. 4. The name of a place. Josh. xv. 3.

ADBEEL, Ad'-be-el, *vapour, a cloud of God, a vexer of God.*—The third son of Ishmael, and head of the tribe of the Ishmaelites. Gen. xxv. 13.

ADDAN, Ad'-dan, *lord, foundation.*—A city in the empire of Babylon. Ezra ii. 59.

ADDAR, Ad'-dar, *one that commands.*—A son of Bela, a descendant from the patriarch Benjamin. 1 Chron. viii. 3.

ADDI, Ad'-dy, *my witness.*—The father of Melchi. Luke iii. 28.

ADDON, Ad'-don, *basis, foundation, lord.*—The name of a place. Neh. vii. 61.

ADER, Ay'-der, *high.*—The name of one that took the city of Gath. 1 Chron. viii. 15.

ADIEL, Ay'-de-el, *the witness of the Lord.*—The name of a person mentioned 1 Chron. iv. 36.

ADIN, Ay'-din, *adorned, dainty.*—One who returned from the Babylonish captivity. Ezra ii. 15.

ADINA, Ad'-de-nah, *adorned.*—The son of Shiza. 1 Chron. xi. 42.

ADINO, Ad'-de-no, *dainty.*—One of David's captains. 2 Sam. xxiii. 8.

ADITHAIM, Ad-e-thay'-im, *assemblies, testimonies.*—A city belonging to the tribe of Judah. Josh. xv. 36.

ADLAI, Ad'-la-i, *my witness, my ornament.*—Principal herdsman to king David. 1 Chron. xxvii. 29.

ADMAH, Ad'-mah, *earthy, red earth.*—One of the five cities which were destroyed by fire from heaven, and buried under the waters of the Dead Sea. Gen. x. 19.

ADMATHA, Ad'-ma-thah, *a cloud of death, a mortal vapour.*—One of the principal officers in the court of Ahasuerus. Esther i. 14.

ADNA, Ad'-nah, *rest, testimony, eternal.*—A Levite. Ezra x. 30.

ADNAH, Ad'-nah, *rest, testimony, eternal.*—1. A valiant man of the tribe of Manasseh, who left his party to follow David. 1 Chron. xii. 20. 2. The name of a general of Jehoshaphat. 2 Chron. xvii. 14.

ADONI-BEZEK, Ad'-o-ni-be'-zek, *the lightning of the Lord, the lord of Bezek.*—The king of the city of Bezek, in the land of Canaan. Judges i. 5, &c. A bloody and oppressive tyrant, whom the Israelites subdued.

ADONIJAH, Ad-o-ny'-jah, *the Lord is my master.*—1. The fourth son of David and Haggith, was born at Hebron. 1 Kings i. 5, 6, &c. 2. The name of a Levite. 2 Chron. xvii. 8. And of another. Neh. x. 16.

ADONIKAM, A-don'-e-kam, *the Lord is raised, my Lord hath raised me.*—One that returned from Babylon with 666 of his family. Ezra ii. 13.

ADONIRAM, Ad-o-ny'-ram, *my Lord is most high, the Lord of might and elevation.*—The principal receiver of Solomon's tribute. 1 Kings v. 14.

ADONI-ZEDEC, Ad'-o-ni-ze'-dek, *justice of the Lord.*—The king of Zedek or Jerusalem. Josh. x. 1—27. A.M. 2553.

ADORAIM, Ad-o-ray'-im, *strength or power of the sea.*—A city of Palestine, in the tribe of Judah, built by Rehoboam. 2 Chron. xi. 9.

ADORAM, A-do'-ram, *their beauty, their power, their praise.*—1. The chief treasurer of Rehoboam. 1 Kings xii. 18. 2. The principal treasurer to king David. 2 Sam. xx. 24. See also HADORAM.

13

ADRAMMELECH, A-dram'-me-lek, *the cloak or glory of the king.*—The son of Sennacherib, king of Assyria. Isai. xxxvii. 38; 2 Kings xix. 37.   Also the name of one of the gods of Sepharvaim.

ADRAMYTTIUM, Ad-ra-mit'-te-um, *the court of death.* —A city on the western coast of Mysia, in Lesser Asia, over against the Isle of Lesbos. Acts xxvii. 2.   Now called *Edremit.*

ADRIA, Ay'-dre-a.—The name of a city which gives name to the Adriatic Sea, now the Gulf of Venice. Acts xxvii. 27.

ADRIEL, Ay'-dre-el, *the flock of God.*—The son of Barzillai: he married Merab, the daughter of Saul, who was first promised to David. 1 Sam. xviii. 19.

ADULLAM, A-dul'-lam, *their testimony, their prey, their ornament.*—A city belonging to the tribe of Judah, situated in the southern part of this tribe, near the Dead Sea. Josh. xv. 35.   Memorable from the cave in this neighbourhood where David retired from Achish, king of Gath. 1 Sam. xxii. 1.

ADULLAMITE, A-dul'-lam-ite.—A citizen of Adullam, named Hirah. Gen. xxxviii. 1.

ADUMMIM, A-dum'-mim, *earthly or bloody things.*— A mountain and city in the tribe of Benjamin. Josh. xv. 7; xviii. 17.

ÆNEAS, E'-ne-as, *praised.*—A man who was miraculously healed. Acts ix. 33. (In Virgil, E-ne'-as.)

ÆNON, E'-non.—A village of Palestine, near Jordan. John iii. 23.

AGABUS, Ag'-ga-bus, *a locust, the feast of the father.* —A prophet, and, as the Greeks say, one of the seventy disciples of our Saviour. He foretold a famine which came to pass in the fourth year of the emperor Claudius. Acts. xi. 28.   A.D. 43.

AGAG, Ay'-gag, *roof, floor.*—A common name of the princes of Amalek, one of whom was very powerful as early as the time of Moses. Num. xxiv. 7.

14

AGAGITE, Ay'-gag-ite.—Of the race of Agag. Such Haman was called, probably because he was an Amalekite. Esther iii. 1.

AGAR, Ay'-gar, *a stranger, that fears.*—Mount Sinai. Gal. iv. 24, 25. See HAGAR.

AGEE, Ag'-e-e, *a valley, deepness.*—A Hararite, the father of Shammah, one of David's worthies. 2 Sam. xxiii. 11.

AGRIPPA, A-grip'-pa, *one who at his birth causes great pain.*—1. He was surnamed Herod; was the son of Aristobulus and Mariamne, and grandson of Herod the Great; was born A. M. 3997, three years before the birth of our Saviour, and seven years before the vulgar æra. Acts xii. 1, 2. 2. A son of the former. Acts xxv. 13, 14, &c.; and Acts xxvi.

AGUR, Ay'-gur, *a stranger, gathering.*—The thirtieth chapter of Proverbs begins, "The words of *Agur*, the son of Jakeh." Some suppose Solomon describes himself by this appellation.

AHAB, Ay'-hab, *the brother of the father.*—1. A king of Israel, the son and successor of Omri. A wicked prince, who exceeded all his predecessors in crime. 1 Kings xvi. 29. He married Jezebel, the daughter of Ethbaal, king of Zidon, who introduced the abominations and idols of her country, Baal and Ashtaroth. 2. The son of Kolaiah, one of the false prophets, who seduced the Israelites at Babylon. Jer. xxix. 21, 22.

AHARAH, A-har'-ah, *a sweet brother, an odoriferous meadow.*—A son of Benjamin. 1 Chron. viii. 1.

AHAREL, A-har'-el, *another host, another sorrow, the sleep of the brother.*—The son of Harum. 1 Chron. iv. 8.

AHASAI, A-has'-a-i.—One of the Jews that returned from Babylon, chosen to dwell in Jerusalem. Neh. xi. 13.

AHASBAI, A-has'-ba-i, *trusting in me, brother compassing.* In Syriac, *brother of age.*—The father of Eliphelet, one of David's worthies. 2 Sam. xxiii. 34.

AHASUERUS, A-has-u-e'-rus, *prince, chief.*—1. The king of Persia, who advanced Esther to be queen, and at

15

her request delivered the Jews from the destruction plotted for them by Haman. Esther i. 1. 2. A name given in Scripture to Cambyses, the son of Cyrus; Ezra iv. 6; and to Astyages, king of the Medes. Dan. ix. 1.

AHAVA, A-hay'-va, *essence, generation.*—A river of Assyria, where Ezra gathered together those captives that he brought with him into Judea. Ezra viii. 15.

AHAZ, Ay'-haz, *one that takes and possesses.*—1. A king of Judah, the son of Jotham, remarkable for his vices and impieties. After the customs of the heathen, he made his children to pass through fire, he shut up the temple, and destroyed its sacred vessels. Such was his impiety, that he was not allowed burial in the sepulchres of the kings of Israel. 2 Kings xvi.; 2 Chron. xxviii. 2. The father of Jehoadah. 1 Chron. viii. 36.

AHAZIAH, A-ha-zy'-ah, *possession, vision of the Lord.*—1. The son of Ahab, king of Israel. 1 Kings xxii. 51, &c. 2. The king of Judah, the son of Jehoram and Athaliah. He succeeded his father in the kingdom of Judah, A. M. 3119. 2 Kings viii. 26, &c.

AHBAN, Ah'-ban.—The son of Abishur. 1 Chron. ii. 29.

AHER, Ay'-her.—A descendant of Benjamin. 1 Chron. vii. 12.

AHI, Ay'-hy, *my brother, my brethren.*—1. A descendant of Gad. 1 Chron. v. 15. 2. A descendant of Asher. 1 Chron. vii. 34.

AHIAH, A-hy'-ah, *brother of the lord.*—1. The son of Shisha, and secretary to King Solomon. 1 Kings iv. 3. 2. The son of Ahitub, the high-priest, and his successor. 1 Sam. xiv. 3.

AHIAM, A-hy'-am, *brother of the nation.*—One of David's captains. 2 Sam. xxiii. 33.

AHIAN, A-hy'-an, *brother of wine.*—1 Chron. vii. 19.

AHIEZER, A-he-e'-zer, *brother of help.*—The son of Ammishaddai, chief of the tribe of Dan. Num. i. 12.

16

AHIHUD, A-hy'-hud, *brother of vanity.*—1. A son of Naaman, and descendant of Benjamin. 1 Chron. viii. 7. 2. A son of Shelomi, of the tribe of Asher. Num. xxxiv. 27.

AHIJAH, A-hy'-jah, *brother of the Lord.*—1. The prophet of the Lord, who dwelt in Shiloh. 1 Kings xi. 29. 2. The son of Baasha, king of Israel. 3. The son of Pelon, one of those brave officers who had a command in David's army. 1 Chron. xi. 36. 4. Keeper of the temple treasury. 1 Chron. xxvi. 20. 5. Son of Esrom, a descendant of Judah. 1 Chron. ii. 25.

AHIKAM, A-hy'-kam, *a brother that raises up.*—The son of Shaphan, and father of Gedaliah. 2 Kings xxii. 12.

AHILUD, A-hy'-lud, *a brother born.*—The father of Jehoshaphat, who was David's secretary. 2 Sam. viii. 16.

AHIMAAZ, A-him'-a-az, *brother of the council.*—The son of Zadok, the high-priest. He succeeded his father, A. M. 3000. 2 Sam. xv. 27.

AHIMAN, A-hy'-man, *a brother prepared.*—A giant of the race of Anak, who dwelt at Hebron. Num. xiii. 22.

AHIMELECH, A-him'-me-lek, *my brother is a king.* —He was the son of Ahitub, and brother of Ahia, whom he succeeded in the high-priesthood. He is called Abiathar. Mark ii. 26 ; 1 Sam. xxii. 9.

AHIMOTH, A-hy'-moth, *brother of death.*—A son of Elkanah, a descendant of Levi. 1 Chron. vi. 25.

AHINADAB, A-hin'-a-dab, *a willing brother, a brother of a vow, brother of the prince.*—The son of Iddo, a governor of Mahanaim, beyond Jordan. 1 Kings iv. 14.

AHINOAM, A-hin'-no-am, *the beauty and comeliness of the brother.*—1. The daughter of Ahimaaz, and wife of king Saul. 1 Sam. xiv. 50. 2. Wife of David, and mother of Amnon. 1 Sam. xxx. 5, and 17—20.

AHIO, A-hy'-o, *his brother, his brethren.*—1. Son of Abinadab. 2 Sam. vi. 3. 2. Son of Beriah. 1 Chron. viii. 14.

AHIRA, A-hy′-rah, *brother of iniquity, or of the shepherd.*
—The son of Enan, chief of the tribe of Naphtali. Num.
i. 15.

AHIRAM, A-hy′-ram, *brother of craft or protection.*—
A son of Benjamin. Num. xxvi. 38.

AHISAMACH, A-his′-sa-mak, *a brother of strength or
of support.*—The father of Aholiab, the famous artificer,
employed by Moses in building the tabernacle. Exod.
xxxi. 6.

AHISHAHAR, A-hish′-a-har, *the brother of the morning.*
—A son of Bilhan, a descendant of Benjamin. 1 Chron.
vii. 10.

AHISHAR, A-hy′-shar, *brother of the prince.*—High
steward of Solomon's household. 1 Kings iv. 6.

AHITHOPHEL, A-hit′-o-fel, *brother of ruin or folly.*—A
native of Gillo, who having been David's counsellor, joined
in the rebellion of Absalom, and assisted him with his
advice. Because his counsel was refused, he hanged
himself. 2 Sam. xvi., xvii. A. M. 2981; B.C. 1023.

AHITUB, A-hy′-tub, *brother of goodness.*—1. The son
of Phinehas, and grandson of the high-priest Eli. His
father having been slain in an engagement with the
Philistines, he succeeded his grandfather. 1 Sam. iv. 11;
xxii. 11. A.M. 2888.   2. The son of Amariah, and father
of the high-priest Zadok. 1 Chron. vi. 8.

AHLAB, Ah′-lab, *which is of milk, fat.*—A city of
Palestine, in the tribe of Asher. Judges i. 31.

AHLAI, Ah′-lay, *beseeching, sorrowing, beginning, brother to me.*—1. A descendant of Jerahmeel. 1 Chron. ii. 31.
2. One of David's captains. 1 Chron. xi. 41.

AHOAH, A-ho′-ah, *a thistle, a thorn, a fish-hook, bro-
therhood.*—The third son of Bela, and grandson of Benjamin. 1 Chron. viii. 4.

AHOLAH, A-ho′-lah, *his tabernacle, his tent.*—Samaria
is represented by this name. Ezek. xxiii. 4.

18

AHOLIAB, A-ho'-le-ab, *the tent or tabernacle of the father.*—An individual of the tribe of Dan, who assisted in building the tabernacle. Exod. xxxv. 34.

AHOLIBAH, A-hol'-le-bah, *my tent or my tabernacle in her.*—A feigned name to represent Jerusalem. Ezek. xxiii. 4.

AHOLIBAMAH, A-ho-lib'-a-mah, *my tabernacle is exalted.*—1. The wife of Esau. Gen. xxxvi. 2. 2. A descendant of Esau, name of a duke. 1 Chron. i. 52.

AHUMAI, A-hew'-ma-i, *a meadow of waters, brother of waters.*—A descendant of Judah, a Zorathite. 1 Chron. iv. 2.

AHUZAM, A-hew'-zam, *their taking possession, vision.*—The son of Naarah, a descendant of Judah. 1 Chron. iv. 6.

AHUZZATH, A-huz'-zath, *possession, apprehension, vision.*—The friend of Abimelech, king of Gerar. Gen. xxvi. 26.

AI, Ay'-i, *mass, heap.*—A town of Palestine, situate west of Bethel, and at a small distance north-west of Jericho. It is called by the LXX, Gai, and by Josephus, Ajah. Gen. xii. 8; Josh. vii. 2, &c.

AIAH, Ay-i'-ah, *a raven, a vulture ; alas, where is it ?*—The mother of Rizpah, Saul's concubine. 2 Sam. xxi. 8.

AIATH, A-i'-ath, *an hour.*—A city of Palestine, in the tribe of Simeon. Isai. x. 28.

AIJALON, or AJALON, Ad'-ja-lon, *a chain, strength, a stag.*—A city of the Canaanites : the valley adjoining to which is memorable in sacred history from the miracle of Joshua in arresting the course of the sun and moon. Josh. x. 12, 13. Aijalon was afterwards a Levitical city. Judges i. 35. It is probable there were other towns of this name.

AIN, Ay'-in, *an eye, a fountain.*—A city. Num. xxxiv. 11.

AKKUB, Ak'-kub, *the print of the foot where any creature has gone, supplantation.*—1. The son of Elioenai.

19

1 Chron. iii. 24. 2. A porter of the temple. 1 Chron. ix. 17. 3. A teacher of the law. Neh. viii. 7.

AKRABBIM, Ak-rab′-bim, *scorpions.*—A city of the Amorites. Num. xxxiv. 4.

ALAMETH and ALEMETH, Al′-a-meth and Al′-e-meth, *hiding, youth, worlds, upon the dead.*—1. A city. 1 Chron. vi. 60. 2. A son of Becher. 1 Chron. vii. 8. 3. A son of Jehoadah. 1 Chron. viii. 36.

ALAMMELECH, A-lam′-me-lek, *God is King.*—A city of Palestine in the tribe of Asher. Josh. xix. 26.

ALEXANDER, A-leks-an′-der, *one that assists men.*— 1. King of Macedon, commonly called the Great; son and successor of Philip. He is denominated in the prophecies of Daniel as a leopard with four wings, signifying his great strength and the rapidity of his conquests. Dan. vii. 6. And by a one-horned he-goat running over the earth so swiftly as not to touch it, attacking a ram with two horns, overthrowing him, and trampling upon him, without any being able to rescue him. Dan. viii. 4—7. In the statue beheld by Nebuchadnezzar, the belly of brass was the emblem of Alexander. He succeeded his father, A.M. 3668; and in the 20th year of his reign was chosen general of the Greeks, who marched against the Persians. He subdued the whole of Asia and the Indies with incredible success and rapidity, and at length died in the thirty-third year of his age, the victim of intemperance. 2. Alexander, the son of Simon the Cyrenian. Mark xv. 21. 3. One who was in the council which summoned Peter and John before them. Acts iv. 6. 4. A Jew of Ephesus, who addressed the rabble. Acts xix. 33. 5. An artificer in copper. 1 Tim. i. 20.

ALEXANDRIA, Al-eks-an′-dre-a, *the city of Alexander.* —A famous city of Egypt, built by Alexander the Great, situated between the Mediterranean Sea and the Lake Mœris. Acts xviii. 24; xxvii. 6.

ALIAH, A-ly′-ah, *high.*—A descendant of Esau. 1 Chron. i. 51.

ALIAN, A-ly'-an, *high.*—A descendant of Esau. 1 Chron. i. 40.

ALLON, Al'-lon, *an oak, strong.*—1. The name of a man. 1 Chron. iv. 37. 2. The name of a city in Palestine. Josh. xix. 33.

ALLON-BACHUTH, Al'-lon-bak'-kuth, *the oak of weeping.*—An oak or grove where Deborah was buried. Gen. xxxv. 8.

ALMODAD, Al-mo'-dad, *the measure of God.*—The son of Joktan, a descendant of Shem. Gen. x. 26.

ALMON, Al'-mon, *hidden.*—A city. Josh. xxi. 18.

ALMON-DIBLATHAIM, Al'-mon-dib-la-thay'-im, *a hiding in a heap of figs.*—The fortieth encampment of the Israelites in the wilderness. Num. xxxiii. 46.

ALOTH, Ay'-loth.—A place in Palestine. 1 Kings iv. 16.

ALPHA, Al'-fah, *the first letter in the Greek alphabet, Omega being the last.*—Both are titles appropriated to Christ, Rev. i. 8; xxi. 6; denoting his perfection and eternity.

ALPHÆUS, Al-fe'-us, *thousand, chief.*—1. The father of St. James the less. Matt. x. 3; Luke vi. 15. The husband of Mary who is supposed to have been sister of the holy virgin, for which reason James is called the brother of our Lord. 2. The father of Levi, or St. Matthew. Mark ii. 14.

ALVAH, Al'-vah, *his rising higher.*—A duke of Edom. Gen. xxxvi. 40.

ALVAN, Al'-van.—Son of Shobal, the Horite. Gen. xxxvi. 23.

AMAD, Ay'-mad, *a people of witness, people everlasting.* —A city of Palestine. Josh. xix. 26.

AMAL, Ay'-mal, *labour, iniquity.*—A descendant of Asher. 1 Chron. vii. 35.

AMALEK, Am'-a-lek, *a people that licks up or uses ill.* —The son of Eliphaz, by Timna, his concubine, and the grandson of Esau. Gen. xxxvi. 12. The Arabians have a tradition respecting an Amalek, who they say was the son of Ham, and grandson of Noah. Moses speaks of the Amalekites long before the son of Eliphaz was born, viz., in the days of Abraham, when Chedorlaomer, king of Elam, devastated their country. Gen. xiv. 7.

AMALEKITES, A-mal'-e-kites.—The descendants of Amalek, who dwelt in Arabia Petræa, called in Balaam's prophecy, " the first of nations," the avowed enemies of the Israelites. Gen xiv. 7.

AMAM, Ay'-mam, *mother, fear of them, people.*—A city belonging to the tribe of Judah. Josh. xv. 26.

AMANA, Am'-a-nah, *integrity and truth.*—A mountain mentioned in Solomon's Song. Ch. iv. 8.

AMARIAH, Am-a-ry'-ah, *the Lord says, the excellency of the Lord.*—1. The eldest son of Meraioth. 1 Chron. vi. 7, 11; and father of the high-priest Ahitub. 2. One who returned from the Babylonish captivity. Ezra x. 42. 3. The grandfather of the prophet Zephaniah. Zeph. i. 1.

AMASA, A-may'-sah, *a forgiving people, the burden of the people.*—1. The son of Ithra and Abigail, David's sister, whom Absalom, when he rebelled against his father, appointed general of his army. 2 Sam. xvii. 25. 2. The son of Hadlai. 2 Chron. xxviii. 12.

AMASAI, A-mas'-a-i, *strong.*—The son of Elkanah. 1 Chron. vi. 25.

AMASHAI, A-mash'-a-i, *the gift or present of the people.*—One who returned from the Babylonish captivity. Neh. xi. 13.

AMAZIAH, Am-a-zy'-ah, *the strength of the Lord.*—1. One of the kings of Judah, the son of Joash, whom he succeeded, A. M. 3165. 2 Chron. xxiv. 27. 2. The priest of the golden calves which were in Bethel. Amos vii. 10.

AMI, Ay'-my, *mother, fear, people.*—The head of a great family which returned from Babylon. Ezra ii. 57, 58.

AMITTAI, A-mit'-tay, *true, fearing.*—The father of the prophet Jonah. Chap. i. 1; 2 Kings xiv. 25.

AMMAH, Am'-mah, *my people.*—A hill where Asahel, the brother of Joab, was slain by Abner, not far from Gibeon. 2 Sam. ii. 24.

AMMI, Am'-my, *my people.*—A name given to the ten tribes. Hosea ii. 1.

AMMIEL, Am'-me-el, *the people of God, God with me.*—1. One of the twelve deputed to view the land of Canaan. Num. xiii. 12. 2. The father of Bathshua. 1 Chron. iii. 5. 3. The father of Machir. 2 Sam. ix. 4. 4. The son of Obed-edom. 1 Chron. xxvi. 5.

AMMIHUD, Am-my'-hud, *people of praise.*—1. Father of Elishama. Num. i. 10. 2. The father of Shemuel. Num. xxxiv. 20. 3. The father of Pedahel. Num. xxxiv. 28. 4. The father of Talmai, king of Geshur. 2 Sam. xiii. 37.

AMMINADAB, Am-min'-a-dab, *prince of the people, a people that vows.*—1. The son of Aram, the father of Naashon and Elisheba, the wife of Aaron. Exod. vi. 23. 2. The brother of Korah. 1 Chron. vi. 22. 3. Or Abinadab, a son of Saul, slain with him in the battle of Gilboa. 1 Sam. xxxi. 2. 4. A Levite, and inhabitant of Kirjathjearim, where the ark was deposited after it was brought back from the land of the Philistines. 1 Sam. vii. 1. 5. The chariots of AMMINADIB are mentioned, Cant. vi. 12, as being extremely light. He is thought to have been some skilful charioteer, whose horses were remarkably swift.

AMMISHADDAI, Am-me-shad'-day-i, *the people of the Almighty.*—The father of Ahiezer, a prince of the tribe of Dan. Num. i. 12.

AMMIZABAD, Am-miz'-a-bad, *the dowry of the people.*—The son of Benaiah, who was one of the principal officers in David's army. 1 Chron. xxvii. 6.

AMMON, Am'-mon, *a people, the son of my people.*—1. Ammon, or Hammon, or Jupiter-Ammon, a name given to Jupiter in Libya, where was a celebrated temple of that deity, visited by Alexander the Great. 2. The son of Lot, by his youngest daughter. Gen. xix. 38. The father of the Ammonites.

AMMONITES, Am′-mon-ites.—The descendants of Ammon, the son of Lot. They took possession of a country called by their name after having driven out the Zamzummims, who were its ancient inhabitants. They had kings, were uncircumcised, and seem to have been employed in husbandry. Jer. ix. 25, 26; Deut. ii. 19, &c.

AMNON, Am′-non, *faithful and true, foster-father.*— 1. The eldest son of David by Ahinoam, his second wife. His history is recorded 2 Sam. xiii. 1, &c.   2. The son of Shimon. 1 Chron. iv. 20.

AMOK, Ay′-mok, *a valley.*—A priest, mentioned Neh. xii. 7.

AMON, Ay′-mon, *faithful, true.*—1. The governor of Samaria, who kept the prophet Micaiah in · custody. 1 Kings xxii. 26.   2. The fourteenth king of Judah; the son of Manasseh and Meshullemeth.   2 Kings xxi. 19. 3. One of the Nethinims. Neh. vii. 59.

AMORITES, Am′-o-rites, *bitter, rebels, talkative, babblers.*—The descendants of Hamor, Gen. xxxiii. 19, called Emmor. Acts vii. 16.   The fourth son of Canaan. Gen. x. 16.   The name Amorite is frequently used for the Canaanites in general.

AMOS, Ay′-mos, *loading, weighty.*—1. The fourth of the minor prophets, who in his youth had been a herdsman in Tekoa.   2. The father of the prophet Isaiah. Chap. i. 1. 3. The son of Nahum, and father of Mattathias, mentioned in the genealogy of our Saviour. Luke iii. 25.

AMPHIPOLIS, Am-fip′-po-lis, *encompassed by the sea.* —A city lying between Macedon and Thrace. Acts xvii. 1. Now called *Emboli.*

AMPLIAS, Am′-ple-as, *large, extensive.*—An individual highly esteemed by St. Paul. Rom. xvi. 8.

AMRAM, Am′-ram, *an exalted people, handfuls of corn.* —1. The son of Kohath, of the tribe of Levi, the father of Aaron, Miriam, and Moses. Exod. vi. 18.   2. The son of Bani, one who returned from Babylon. Ezra x. 34.

AMRAMITES, Am′-ram-ites.—The family of Kohath. Num. iii. 27.

AMRAPHEL, Am'-ra-fel, *one that speaks of hidden things or of ruin.*—The king of Shinar, confederate with Chedorlaomer, king of the Elamites, and two other kings, to make war against the kings of Sodom and Gomorrah. Gen. xiv. 1, &c.

AMZI, Am'-zy, *strong, mighty.*—A Levite, who served in the temple. 1 Chron. vi., 46.

ANAB, Ay'-nab, *a grape, a knot.*—A city in the mountain of Judah. Josh. xi. 21.

ANAH, Ay'-nah, *one who answers or sings, poor, afflicted.*—The son of Zibeon, the Hivite, and father of Aholibamah, Esau's wife. Gen. xxxvi. 24.

ANAHARATH, An-a-hay'-rath, *dryness, burning, wrath.* —A city belonging to the tribe of Issachar. Josh. xix. 19.

ANAIAH, An-a-i'-ah.—One of the assistants of Ezra in reading the law. Neh. viii. 4.

ANAK, Ay'-nak, *a collar, an ornament.*—A giant, who was the son of Arba, who gave the name to Kirjath-arba, or Hebron. Josh. xiv. 15. He had three sons. Josh. xv. 14; Num. xiii. 22.

ANAKIMS, An'-a-kims.—The descendants of Anak. Deut. i. 28.

ANAMMELECH, A-nam'-me-lek, *answer, song of the king.*—An idol of the Sepharvites, who are said to burn their children in honour of Adrammelech and Anammelech. 2 Kings xvii. 31.

ANAN, Ay'-nan, *a cloud, prophecy.*—One of those who sealed the covenant with Nehemiah. Neh. x. 26.

ANANI, An-ay'-ny.—The son of Elioenai. 1 Chron. iii. 24.

ANANIAH, An-a-ny'-ah, *the cloud or deliverance of the Lord.*—1. A city of Palestine, where the Benjamites dwelt. Neh. iii. 23. 2. A Jew who returned from the captivity, and was employed in building the walls of Jerusalem. Neh. xi. 32.

ANANIAS, An-a-ny'-as, *the cloud of the Lord.*—1. The son of Nebedæus, high-priest of the Jews. Acts xxii. 12.

2. One of the first Christians, who died instantly in consequence of lying to the Holy Ghost. Acts v. 1. 3. A disciple of Christ, dwelling in Damascus, whom the Lord in a vision directed to go to Saul. Acts ix. 10.

ANATH, Ay'-nath, *an answer, a song, affliction, poverty.*—The father of Shamgar, a judge of Israel. Judges iii. 31.

ANATHEMA MARAN-ATHA, A-nath'-e-ma, maran-ath'-a.—The former word signifies *accursed;* and the latter, *the Lord cometh.* 1 Cor. xvi. 22.

ANATHOTH, An'-a-thoth, *answer, affliction.*—1. The son of Becher, and grandson of Benjamin. 1 Chron. vii. 8. 2. A city in the tribe of Benjamin, about three miles from Jerusalem. Josh. xxi. 18. It was one of the cities of refuge. 1 Chron. vi. 60.

ANDREW, An'-drue, *a stout and strong man.*—An apostle of Jesus Christ, a native of Bethsaida, and brother of Peter. He was at first a disciple of John the Baptist, whom he left to follow Jesus after the testimony of John. John i. 40. See Matt. iv. 18.

ANDRONICUS, An-dro-ny'-kus, *a man excelling others.*—Rom. xvi. 7.

ANEM, Ay'-nem, *an answer, a song of them.*—A city belonging to the tribe of Issachar, given to the Levites. 1 Chron. vi. 73.

ANER, Ay'-ner, *an answer.*—1. A city of Manasseh, given to the Levites. 1 Chron. vi. 70. 2. One of the Canaanites who joined forces with Abraham in the pursuit of Chedorlaomer, Amraphel, and their allies, who had plundered Sodom, and carried off Lot. Gen. xiv. 13.

ANIAM, Ay'-ne-am, *the strength of people, the ship of people.*—The son of Shemidah. 1 Chron. vii. 19.

ANIM, Ay'-nim, *answerings, singings.*—A city of Judah. Josh. xv. 50.

ANNA, An'-nah, *gracious, merciful.*—The daughter of Phanuel, a prophetess and widow, of the tribe of Asher. Luke ii. 36, 37.

26

ANNAS, An'-nas, *one that answers, that afflicts.*—The son of Seth, and high-priest of the Jews. He was father-in-law to Caiaphas. John xviii. 13.

ANTIOCH, An'-te-ok, *instead of a chariot.*—There were sixteen cities of this name; but only two are mentioned in Scripture. 1. The capital of Syria, on the river Orontes. It was built by Seleucus Nicator, about 300 years before Christ. Here the disciples of Christ were first called Christians. Acts xi. 26. 2. Antioch in Pisidia. St. Paul and Barnabas preached here, and the Jews here raised a tumult against them. Acts xiii. 14.

ANTIPAS, An'-te-pas, *against all.*—Antipas-Herod, or Herod-Antipas, was the son of Herod the Great, and Cleopatra of Jerusalem. The same that married his brother's wife Herodias, and who imprisoned and beheaded John the Baptist for testifying against his sin. Matt. xiv. 3, 4; Mark vi. 17, 18; Luke iii. 19, 20. The same that ridiculed Christ, by dressing him in a gorgeous robe. Luke xxiii. 11. 2. The faithful martyr mentioned Rev. ii. 13.

ANTIPATRIS, An-tip'-a-tris, *against his own father.*— A town in Palestine, anciently called Caphar-Saba, but named Antipatris by Herod, in honour of his father Antipater. Acts xxiii. 31.

ANTOTHIJAH, An-to-thy'-jah, *answers or songs of the Lord.*—The son of Shashak. 1 Chron. viii. 24.

ANUB, Ay'-nub, *a grape.*—The son of Coz. 1 Chron. iv. 8.

APELLES, A-pel'-lees, *to exclude, to separate.*—A disciple approved in Christ. Rom. xvi. 10.

APHARSACHITES, A-far'-sa-kites.—A people sent by the kings of Assyria to inhabit the country of Samaria in the room of those Israelites who had been removed beyond the Euphrates. Ezra v. 6.

APHEK, Ay'-fek, *a stream, vigour.*—The name of several cities. 1. In the tribe of Judah, where the Israelites encamped when the ark was brought from Shiloh.

27

1 Sam. iv. 1, 2, &c.   2. In the valley of Jezreel. 1 Sam. xxix. 1.   3. In the tribe of Asher. Josh. xix. 30.   4. A city of Syria. 1 Kings xx. 26.

APHEKAH, A-fe′-kah.—A city of Palestine, in the tribe of Judah, supposed to be the same as Aphek. Josh. xv. 53.

APHIAH, A-fy′-ah, *speaking, blowing.*—The great-grandfather of Kish, the father of Saul. 1 Sam. ix. 1.

APHRAH, Af′-rah, *dust.*—A city of Palestine, called Beth-Aphrah. Micah i. 10.

APHSES, Af′-sees.—One of the twenty-four appointed by king David, for the service of the temple. 1 Chron. xxiv. 15.

APOLLONIA, Ap-ol-lo′-ne-a, *destruction.*—A city of Macedonia, through which Paul passed in his way to Thessalonica. Acts xvii. 1.

APOLLOS, A-pol′-los, *one that destroys or lays waste.* —A Jew of Alexandria, who came to Ephesus during the absence of St. Paul, who was gone to Jerusalem. Acts xviii. 24.   He was an eloquent man, and mighty in the Scriptures.

APOLLYON, A-pol′-le-on, *one that exterminates or destroys.*—It is a Greek word, answering to the Hebrew Abaddon. Rev. ix. 11.

APPAIM, Ap′-pa-im, *a countenance or face; the nostrils, bakers.*—A son of Nadab, of the posterity of Judah. 1 Chron. ii. 30.

APPHIA, Af′-fe-a, *that is fruitful.*—Philemon 2.

APPII FORUM, Ap′-pe-i fo′-rum, *the village of Appius.* —A place about 50 miles from Rome, near the modern town of Piperno, on the road to Naples.   To this place some Christians from Rome came to meet Paul. Acts xxviii. 15.

AQUILA, Ak′-wil-la, *an eagle.*—A native of Pontus, in Asia-Minor, and converted by the instrumentality of St. Paul to the Christian religion.   He was by trade a tent-maker, and the apostle wrought and lodged with him at Corinth. Acts xviii. 2, 3.

AR, Ar, *awakening, uncovering.*—The capital of Moab, situated in the hills on the south of the river Arnon. It was also called Rabbah, and Rabbath-Moab: now El-Rabba. Num. xxi. 15.

ARA, Ay'-rah, *cursing, seeing.*—A son of Jether, a descendant from the patriarch Asher. 1 Chron. vii. 38.

ARAB, Ay'-rab, *multiplying, sowing sedition, a window, a locust.*—A city belonging to the tribe of Judah. Josh. xv. 52.

ARABAH, Ar'-ra-bah.—A city belonging to the tribe of Benjamin. Josh. xviii. 18.

ARABIA, A-ra'-be-a, *evening, a place wild and desert, mixtures,* because this country was inhabited by different kinds of people.—A vast country of Asia, extending 1500 miles from north to south, and 1200 from east to west, containing a surface equal to four times that of France. It is divided by geographers into three separate regions, called Arabia Petræa, Arabia Deserta, and Arabia Felix. 1 Kings x. 15; Gal. i. 17

ARAD, Ay'-rad, *a wild ass, a dragon.*—A city lying to the south of Judah, in Arabia Petræa. Num. xxi. 1; xxxiii. 40. Also the name of the king of the place.

ARAH, Ay'-rah, *the way or traveller.*—1. The son of Ullah, and grandson of Asher. 1 Chron. vii. 39. 2. A person whose descendants returned from Babylon. Ezra ii. 5.

ARAM, Ay'-ram, *magnificence, one that deceives.*—1. The fifth son of Shem. Gen. x. 22. 2. The son of Esrom, and father of Amminadab. Ruth iv. 19; Matt. i. 4.

ARAN, Ay'-ran, *an ark, their malediction.*—A son of Dishan, and descendant of Esau. Gen. xxxvi. 28.

ARARAT, Ar'-ra-rat, *the curse of trembling.*—A mountain of Asia, in Armenia, on which the ark rested after the cessation of the deluge. Gen. viii. 4.

ARAUNAH, A-raw'-nah, *ark, song, curse.*—A Jebusite, whose threshing-floor was situated on that part of Mount Zion where the temple of Jerusalem was afterwards built. 2 Sam. xxiv. 16, 18.

ARBA, Ar'-bah, *four*.—The name of a giant among the Anakims, who built Kirjath-Arba. Gen. xxiii. 2.

ARCHELAUS, Ar-ke-la'-us, *the prince of the people*.—The son of Herod the Great, by Maltace, his fifth wife. Matt. ii. 22.

ARCHEVITES, Ar'-ke-vites.—A people who petitioned Artaxerxes against the re-building of Jerusalem. Ezra iv. 9.

ARCHI, Ar'-ky.—A city of Palestine, in the tribe of Manasseh. Josh. xvi. 2.

ARCHIATAROTH, Ar-ke-at'-a-roth, *the longitude of crowns or circles*.—The same as Ataroth-addar. Josh. xvi. 2, 5.

ARCHIPPUS, Ar-kip'-pus, *governor of horses*.—One spoken of by Paul in the epistle to the Colossians. Chap. iv. 17.

ARCTURUS, Ark-tew'-rus, *a gathering together*.—A star near the tail of the Great Bear. Job ix. 9; xxxviii. 32.

ARD, Ard, *one that commands*.—1. The youngest son of Benjamin. Gen. xlvi. 21. 2. The son of Bela. Num. xxvi. 40.

ARDON, Ar'-don, *ruling, the judgment of malediction*.—A son of Caleb, the son of Hezron. 1 Chron. ii. 18.

ARELI, A-re'-ly, *the light or vision of God*.—A son of the patriarch Gad. Gen. xlvi. 16.

AREOPAGITE, A-re-op'-a-gite.—The title given to a member of the Areopagus. Acts xvii. 34.

AREOPAGUS, A-re-op'-a-gus.—The hill of Mars: a place where the magistrates of Athens held their supreme council: from ἀρεῖος, of Mars, and παγος, a hill. Acts xvii. 19, &c.

ARETAS, Ar-e'-tas, *one that is virtuous*.—A king of Arabia. Acts ix. 23, &c.; 2 Cor. xi. 32, 33.

ARGOB, Ar'-gob, *a turf of earth, curse of the well.*—A canton lying beyond Jordan, in the half-tribe of Manasseh, in the country of Bashan. In the region of Argob, there were 66 cities. Deut. iii. 13, 14.

ARIDAI, A-rid'-a-i.—The ninth son of Haman, who was hanged with his nine brethren. Esther ix. 9.

ARIDATHA, A-rid'-a-tha.—The sixth son of Haman. Esther ix. 8.

ARIEH, A-ry'-eh.—An officer of Pekah, king of Israel. 2 Kings xv. 25.

ARIEL, Ay'-re-el, *the altar, light, lion of God.*—The capital city of Moab, frequently mentioned in Scripture. Ezra viii. 16. It is also taken for the altar of burnt-offerings, or for the city of Jerusalem. Isai. xxix. 1, 2, 7; Ezek. xliii. 15, 16.

ARIMATHÆA, Ar-re-ma-the'-ah, *a lion dead to the Lord.*—A city of Palestine, in the tribe of Ephraim. It is also called Rumah, Arumah, and Ramath, where the prophet Samuel lived. Luke xxiii. 51.

ARIOCH, Ay'-re-ok, *long, your drunkenness, your lion.* —King of Ellasar. Gen. xiv. 1.

ARISAI, A-ris'-ai.—The eighth son of Haman. Esther ix. 9.

ARISTARCHUS, A-ris-tar'-kus, *the best prince.*— Spoken of by St. Paul in his epistle to the Colossians, and often mentioned in the Acts of the Apostles. He was a Macedonian, and a native of Thessalonica. Col. iv. 10; Acts xix. 29; xx. 4; xxvii. 2.

ARISTOBULUS, A-ris-to-bew'-lus, *the best counsellor.* —A person mentioned Rom. xvi. 10

ARKITES, Ark'-ites.—A people of ancient Canaan. Gen. x. 17.

ARMAGEDDON, Ar-ma-ged'-don, *the mountain of Megiddo, of the Gospel, of fruits.*—A place spoken of
31

Rev. xvi. 16, situated in the great plain at the foot of Carmel, where the good prince Josiah received his mortal wound.

ARMENIA, Ar-me′-ne-a.—A province of Asia, supposed to take its name from Aram. Isai. xxxvii. 38.

ARMONI, Ar′-mo-ny.—The son of Saul and Rizpah: he was hanged with his brethren by the Gibeonites. 2 Sam. xxi. 8.

ARNAN, Ar′-nan, *rejoicing, their ark, the light of the sun.*—One of the posterity of the patriarch Judah. 1 Chron. iii. 21.

ARNON, Ar′-non, *rejoicing, their ark, the light of the sun, the light eternal.*—A river, or brook, springing in the mountains of Gilead, and discharging itself into the Dead Sea. Num. xxi. 24.

AROD, Ay′-rod, *ruling, descending.*—A son of the patriarch Gad, and father of the Arodites. Num. xxvi. 17.

ARODI, Ar′-o-dy, *ruling, descending, domineering lion.* —One of the sons of the patriarch Gad. Gen. xlvi. 16.

AROER, Ar′-o-er, *heath, tamarisk, the nakedness of the skin or of the enemy.*—A city in the tribe of Gad, situated on the northern banks of the brook Arnon. Deut. ii. 36. There appear to have been several cities of this name. See Josh. xiii. 25; Judges xi. 33; 1 Sam. xxx. 28.

ARPAD or ARPHAD, Ar′-pad or Ar′-fad, *the light of redemption.*—A city of Syria. 2 Kings xviii. 34; xix. 13; Isai. x. 9.

ARPHAXAD, Ar-faks′-ad, *one that heals or releases.*— The son of Shem, and father of Salah. Gen. xi. 12.

ARTAXERXES, Ar-taks-erks′-ees, *the silence of light.* —Or Ahasuerus, a king of Persia, the husband of Esther. Artaxerxes Longimanus, supposed by Dr. Prideaux to be the Ahasuerus of Esther. The son of Xerxes, and grandson of Darius Hystaspis. He reigned king of Persia, from A. M. 3531 to 3579. It was he that permitted Ezra to

32

return into Judea, and afterwards Nehemiah. Ezra vii., viii.; Neh. ii. 11.

ARTEMAS, Ar'-te-mas, *whole, sound.*—A disciple who was sent by St. Paul into Crete, in the room of Titus. Tit. iii. 12.

ARUBOTH, Ar'-u-both.—A city or country belonging to the tribe of Judah. 1 Kings iv. 10.

ARUMAH, A-rew'-mah, *high, exalted, cast away.*—A city near Shechem, where Abimelech dwelt. Judges ix. 41.

ARVAD, Ar'-vad.—A city of Phœnicia, situated in a small island south of Tyre, and about a league from the continent. Ezek. xxvii. 11.

ARZA, Ar'-zah.—Governor of Tirzah. 1 Kings xvi. 9.

ASA, Ay'-sah, *physician, cure.*—The son and successor of Abijam, king of Judah: he began to reign A. M. 3049, and B. C. 955. He reigned forty-one years at Jerusalem, and did right in the sight of the Lord. 1 Kings xv. 8.

ASAHEL, As'-a-hel, *the work or creature of God.*—The son of Zeruiah, and brother of Joab. He was killed by Abner in the battle of Gibeon. 2 Sam. ii. 18, 19.

ASAIAH, As-a-i'-ah, *the Lord hath wrought.*—1. A servant of king Josiah, who was sent by that prince to consult Huldah, the prophetess, concerning the book of the law. 2 Chron. xxxiv. 20. 2. A prince of the tribe of Simeon. 1 Chron. iv. 36. 3. A prince of the tribe of Levi. 1 Chron. vi. 30.

ASAPH, Ay'-saf, *one that assembles together.*—1. A celebrated musician in the time of David; was the son of Berachiah, and of the tribe of Levi. 1 Chron. vi. 39. Several of the Psalms are ascribed to him. 2. The father of Joah, who was secretary to king Hezekiah. 2 Kings xviii. 18.

ASARELAH, As-a-re'-lah, *the blessedness of God.*—A son of Asaph, a singer in the Jewish temple. 1 Chron. xxv. 2.

ASENATH, As'-e-nath.—The daughter of Poti-pherah, priest of On, and wife of Joseph. Gen. xli. 45.

33

ASHAN, Ay'-shan, *vapour, smoke.*—A city in the tribe of Judah. Josh. xv. 42.

ASHBEL, Ash'-bel, *an old fire.*—The second son of Benjamin. 1 Chron. viii. 1; Gen. xlvi. 21.

ASHDOD, Ash'-dod, *inclination, a wild open place.*—Azoth, according to the Vulgate; or Azotus, according to the Greek. A city assigned by Joshua to the tribe of Judah, but possessed a long time by the Philistines, and rendered famous by the temple of their god Dagon. It lies upon the Mediterranean Sea, about nine or ten miles north of Gaza. Josh. xv. 47.

ASHDOTH-PISGAH, Ash'-doth-piz'-gah, *inclination, eminence.*—A city of Palestine, in the tribe of Reuben. Deut. iii. 17.

ASHER, Ash'-er, *blessedness.*—The son of Jacob and Zilpah his wife, Leah's servant. The province allotted to this tribe was a maritime one, stretching along the coast, from Sidon on the north, to mount Carmel on the south. Gen. xxx. 13.

ASHIMAH, Ash'-e-mah, *the fire of the sea, the offence.*—The name of an idol worshipped by the people of Hamath. 2 Kings xvii. 30.

ASHKENAZ, Ash'-ke-naz, *a fire that distils or spreads.*—The eldest son of Gomer. Gen. x. 3.

ASHNAH, Ash'-nah.—A city in the tribe of Judah. Josh. xv. 33.

ASHPENAZ, Ash'-pe-naz.—A governor of Nebuchadnezzar's eunuchs. Dan. i. 3.

ASHTAROTH, Ash'-ta-roth, *flocks, riches.*—The city of Og, king of Bashan. Josh. ix. 10.

ASHTORETH, Ash'-to-reth, *flocks, riches.*—Or Astarte, a goddess of the Zidonians. 1 Kings xi. 33.

ASHURITES, Ash'-ur-ites.—The people of Assyria. 2 Sam. ii. 9.

ASIA, Ay'-she-a, *muddy, boggy.*—One of the four great divisions of the earth. It is also used in a more restricted sense for Asia Minor, or Anatolia. In the New Testament it always signifies the Roman Proconsular Asia, in which the seven Apocalyptic churches were situated. Acts ii. 9.

ASIEL, Ay'-se-el, *the work of God.*—One of the posterity of the patriarch Simeon. 1 Chron. iv. 35.

ASKELON, As'-ke-lon, *weight, balance, fire of infamy.*—A city in the land of the Philistines, situated between Azoth and Gaza, upon the coast of the Mediterranean Sea, about 520 furlongs from Jerusalem. The tribe of Judah, after the death of Joshua, took the city of Askelon, being one of the five governments belonging to the Philistines. Judges i. 18.

ASMAVETH, As'-ma-veth, *a strong death, the strength of death.*—One of king David's worthies. See AZMAVETH.

ASNAH, As'-nah.—One who returned from the captivity. Ezra ii. 50.

ASNAPPER, As-nap'-per, *unhappiness, fruitless.*—The king of Assyria, who sent the Cutheans into the country belonging to the ten tribes. Ezra iv. 10. Many take this prince to be Shalmaneser, but others, with more probability, take him for Esar-haddon.

ASPATHA, As'-pa-thah.—The third son of Haman, who was hung. Esther ix. 7.

ASRIEL, As'-re-el, *the beatitude of God.*—1. The son of Gilead. Num. xxvi. 31. 2. The son of Manasseh. Josh. xvii. 2.

ASSHUR, Ash'-ur, *one that is happy.*—The son of Shem, who gave his name to Assyria. Gen. x. 11, 12.

ASSHURIM, A-shew'-rim, *layers in wait.*—A son of Dedan, the grandson of the patriarch Abraham and Keturah. Gen. xxv. 3.

ASSIR, As'-ser, *prisoner, fettered.*—1. The son of Jeconiah, king of Judah. 1 Chron. iii. 17. 2. The son of Korah. Exod. vi. 24; 1 Chron. vi. 22.

ASSOS, As'-sos, *approaching.*—A seaport town, situated on the south-west part of the province of Troas, and over against the island of Lesbos. Acts xx. 13, 14.

ASSUR, As'-sur.—Assyria is so called. Ezra iv. 2; Psalm lxxxiii. 8

ASSYRIA, As-sir'-e-a, *happy.*—A kingdom of Asia, probably comprehending those provinces of Turkey and Persia which are now called Curdistan, Dearbec, and Iraca Arabic. Very different accounts have been given of it by ancient authors. The name occurs frequently in Scripture. Gen. ii. 14.

ASTAROTH, As'-ta-roth, *sheep.*—A goddess of the Zidonians. Deut. i. 4. It is the plural form of Astarte.

ASTARTE, As-tar'-te.—A goddess of the Phœnicians, Philistines, 1 Sam. xxxi. 10; and of the Zidonians. 1 Kings xi. 5.

ASUPPIM, A-sup'-pim, *gatherings.*—The treasury-place of the temple of Jerusalem. 1 Chron. xxvi. 15.

ASYNCRITUS, A-sin'-kre-tus, *incomparable.*—An individual mentioned by St. Paul, Rom. xvi. 14.

ATAD, Ay'-tad, *a thorn.*—The threshing-floor, where the sons of Jacob, and the Egyptians who accompanied them, mourned for that patriarch. Gen. l. 10, 11.

ATARAH, At'-a-rah, *a crown.*—One of the wives of Jerahmeel, the mother of Onam. 1 Chron. ii. 26.

ATAROTH, At'-a-roth, *crowns, counsel of making full.*—The names of two cities, one in the tribe of Gad, beyond Jordan, Num. xxxii. 3, 34; the other on the frontiers of Ephraim. Josh. xvi. 7.

ATER, Ay'-ter, *the left hand.*—One whose descendants, to the number of 98, returned from Babylon. Ezra ii. 16.

ATHACH, Ay'-thak, *thy hour, thy time.*—A city in the tribe of Judah. 1 Sam. xxx. 30.

ATHAIAH, Ath-a-i′-ah, *the hour or time of the Lord.* —A son of Uzziah, the son of Zechariah, of the tribe of Judah. Neh. xi. 4.

ATHALIAH, Ath-a-ly′-ah, *the time of the Lord.*—The daughter of Omri, king of Samaria, and wife of Jehoram, king of Judah. See 2 Kings xi.

ATHENS, Ath′-ens, *without increase, of Minerva.*—A principal city of ancient Greece : it was first called Attica, from Acteus ; then Cecropia, from Cecrops, its first king, A.M. 2422. Its latitude is 38° 5′ north, longitude 23° 57′ east. Acts xvii. 16.

ATHLAI, Ath′-lay, *my hour, my time.*—The son of Bebai ; one who, among others, divorced his wife, because she was not an Israelite. Ezra x. 28.

ATROTH, At′-roth.—The name of a city. Num. xxxii. 35.

ATTAI, At′-tay.—A grandson of Sheshan. 1 Chron. ii. 35.

ATTALIA, At-ta-ly′-a, *that increases or sends.*—A city of Pamphylia, in Asia, situated on a bay, whither St. Paul and Barnabas went to preach the Gospel, A.D. 45. Acts xiv. 25.

AUGUSTUS, Aw-gus′-tus, *increased, majestic.*—Emperor of Rome, and successor of Julius Cæsar. This is the emperor who appointed the enrolment mentioned Luke ii. 1, which obliged Joseph and the Virgin Mary to go to Bethlehem, the place where Jesus was born.

AVA, Ay′-vah.—The name of a city. 2 Kings xvii. 24.

AVEN, Ay′-ven, *iniquity, sorrow, riches.*—1. A city of Egypt, afterwards called Heliopolis and On. Ezek. xxx. 17. 2. A plain in Syria, the same as the valley of Baal, where stood the magnificent temple dedicated to the sun : it is also called the valley of Lebanon, Josh. xi. 17 : see also Amos i. 5. 3. Bethel was so called, because of the wickedness committed there.

AVIM, Ay′-vim, *wicked, perverse.*—A city in the tribe of Benjamin. Josh. xviii. 23.

AVIMS, Ay′-vims, *wicked men.*—A people descended from Hevius, the son of Canaan. Deut. ii. 23.

AVITH, Ay'-vith, *wicked, perverse.*—The capital of Hadad, king of Edom. Gen. xxxvi. 35.

AZALIAH, Az-a-ly'-ah, *departure of God.*—Father of Shaphan. 2 Kings xxii. 3.

AZANIAH, Az-a-ny'-ah, *hearkening to the Lord, the weapons of the Lord.*—The father of Jeshua, a Levite. Neh. x. 9.

AZAREEL, A-zay'-re-el, *the help of God.*—1. One of king David's worthies, who resorted to him at Ziklag. 1 Chron. xii. 6. 2. One who returned from the captivity. Ezra x. 41.

AZARIAH, Az-a-ry'-ah, *assistance, he that hears the Lord.*—The name of several persons among the Jews. 1. The king of Judah, son of Amaziah. 2 Kings xv. 1. 2. The son of Nathan. 1 Kings iv. 5. 3. A prophet who delivered a message to Asa. 2 Chron. xv. 1—7. 4. The son of Obed, one to whom the high-priest Jehoiada discovered that Joash was living. 2 Chron. xxiii. 1, 2, &c. 5. The name of two sons of Jehoshaphat the king. 2 Chron. xxi. 2. 6. The son of Hoshaiah. Jer. xliii. 2. 7. A Jew, who was called Abednego, in Babylon. Dan. i. 7.—Azariah is also the name of several high-priests among the Jews. 1. The successor of Ahimaaz. 1 Chron. vi. 9. 2. The son of Johanan. 1 Chron. vi. 10. 3. High-priest in the reign of Hezekiah. 2 Chron. xxxi. 10. 4. One who lived under Uzziah. 2 Chron. xxvi. 17.

AZAZ, Ay'-zaz.—The father of Bela. 1 Chron. v. 8.

AZAZIAH, Az-a-zy'-ah.—A Levite, zealous for the law. 2 Chron. xxxi. 13.

AZBUK, Az'-buk.—The father of Nehemiah. Neh. iii. 16.

AZEKAH, A-ze'-kah, *strength of walls.*—A city of Judah. Josh. x. 10; xv. 35; Jer. xxxiv. 7.

AZEL, Ay'-zel, *he departed.*—A descendant from king Saul. 1 Chron. viii. 38.

AZEM, Ay'-zem.—A city in the tribe of Simeon. Josh. xix. 3.

AZGAD, Az'-gad, *a strong army, strength of felicity.*—One who returned from captivity. Ezra ii. 12.

AZIEL, Ay'-ze-el, *strength of the Lord.*—A musician. 1 Chron. xv. 20.

AZIZA, A-zy'-zah, *strength.*—One who returned from captivity. Ezra x. 27.

AZMAVETH, Az'-ma-veth.—1. A city in the tribe of Judah. Neh. vii. 28. 2. The son of Beroni, one of David's gallant men. 2 Sam. xxiii. 31. 3. The son of Jehoadah, of the tribe of Benjamin. 1 Chron. viii. 36. 4. The son of Adriel. 1 Chron. xi. 33.

AZMON, Az'-mon, *bone of a bone.*—A city in the southern borders of Canaan. Num. xxxiv. 4.

AZNOTH-TABOR, Az'-noth-tay'-bor, *the ears of Tabor, of choice, purity, contrition.*—A city which Eusebius places in the plain not far from Diocesarea. Josh. xix. 34.

AZOR, Ay'-zor, *a helper, entry, a court, converted.*— The son of Eliakim. His name is found in the genealogy of Christ. Matt. i. 13.

AZOTH, or **AZOTUS,** Ay'-zoth, A-zo'-tus.—The same as ASHDOD. Acts viii. 40.

AZRIEL, Az'-re-el, *the help of God.*—One of king David's worthies, of the tribe of Manasseh. 1 Chron. v. 24.

AZRIKAM, Az'-re-kam, *help, rising up, revenging.*— 1. A person who was massacred by Zichri. 2 Chron. xxviii. 7. 2. One of Ezra's assistants in reading the law. Neh. xi. 15. 3. A descendant of king David. 1 Chron. iii. 23. 4. A descendant of king Saul. 1 Chron. ix. 44.

AZUBAH, A-zew'-bah, *forsaken.*—1. The wife of Caleb. 1 Chron. ii. 18. 2. The wife of Asa, king of Judah, and mother of Jehoshaphat. 1 Kings xxii. 42.

AZUR, Ay'-zur, *he that assists.*—1. The father of the false prophet Hananiah. Jer. xxviii. 1. 2. The father of Jaazaniah. Ezek. xi. 1.

AZZAH, Az'-zah, *strong.*—A country of the Avims. Deut. ii. 23.

AZZAN, Az'-zan, *the strength.*—The father of Paltiel, prince of the tribe of the children of Issachar. Num. xxxiv. 26.

39

AZZUR, Az'-zur, *helper.*—One who sealed the covenant with Nehemiah. Neh. x. 17.

B

BAAL, Bay'-al, *Bel* or *Belus,* denoting *Lord.*—A divinity among several ancient nations, as the Canaanites, Phœnicians, Sidonians, Carthaginians, Babylonians, Chaldeans, and Assyrians. The term Baal, which is itself an appellative, served at first to denote the true God, among those who adhered to the true religion. But when various nations degenerated into idolatry, they retained this name with some epithet annexed to it, as *Baal-Berith, Baal-Gad, Baal-Moloch, Baal-Peor,* &c. It occurs frequently in Scripture.

BAALAH, Bay'-al-ah, *her idol, a spouse.*—The city called Kirjathjearim. Josh. xv. 9; 1 Chron. xiii. 6.

BAALATH, Bay'-al-ath, *proud lord.*—A city in the tribe of Dan. Josh. xix. 44.

BAALATH-BEER, Bay'-al-ath-be'-er.—A city lying in the south of the tribe of Simeon. Josh. xix. 8.

BAAL-BERITH, Bay'-al-be'-rith, *idol of the covenant.* —An idol of the Shechemites. Judges viii. 33; ix. 4, 46.

BAAL-GAD, Bay'-al-gad', *the idol of the troop, the Lord is master of the troop.*—A city situated at the foot of Mount Hermon. Josh. xi. 17.

BAAL-HAMON, Bay'-al-hay'-mon, *one that rules a multitude, a populous place.*—The name of a place where Solomon had a vineyard. Cant. viii. 11.

BAAL-HANAN, Bay'-al-han'-an.—The son of Achbor, who succeeded Saul in the kingdom of Edom. Gen. xxxvi. 38; 1 Chron. i. 49.

BAAL-HAZOR, Bay'-al-hay'-zor, *lord of court, possessor of grace.*—A city in the tribe of Ephraim, where Absalom kept his flocks. 2 Sam. xiii. 23.

BAAL-HERMON, Bay'-al-her'-mon, *the possessor of destruction, of a thing devoted to God.*—A city northward of the tribe of Issachar. 1 Chron. v. 23.

BAALE, Bay'-al-e, *my Lord.*—The place ·from whence David fetched the ark. 2 Sam. vi. 2.

BAALI, Bay'-a-ly, *my Lord.*—Hosea ii. 16.

BAALIM, Bay'-al-im, *lords.*—The plural of Baal. Judges ii. 11, &c.

BAALIS, Bay'-a-lis, *a rejoicing, proud lord.*—The king of the Ammonites, who sent Ishmael, the son of Nethaniah, to kill Gedaliah, who had been set over the remnant of the Jews, who were not sent captive to Babylon. Jer. xl. 14.

BAAL-MEON, Bay'-al-me'-on, *the idol, the master of the house.*—A city in the tribe of Reuben. Num. xxxii. 38.

BAAL-PEOR, Bay'-al-pe'-or, *master of the opening.*— Peor is supposed to have been a part of Abarim: Baal-Peor may then have been a temple of an idol belonging to the Moabites on that mountain which the Israelites worshipped when they encamped at Shittim; this brought a plague upon them, of which 24,000 died. Chemosh, the abomination of Moab, to whom Solomon erected an altar, 1 Kings xi. 7, is supposed to have been the same deity. Others suppose Baal-Peor to have been Priapus; others, Saturn; others, Pluto; and others again, Adonis. Num. xxv. 3.

BAAL-PERAZIM, Bay'al-per'-a-zim, *master of divisions.*—The place where David put to flight the Philistines; 2 Sam. v. 20; about three miles south-west of Jerusalem.

BAAL-SHALISHA, Bay'-al-shal'-e-shah, *the third idol, the third husband.*—A place situated about fifteen miles north of Diaspolis. 2 Kings iv. 42.

BAAL-TAMAR, Bay'-al-tay'-mar, *master of the palm-tree.*—The place where the children of Israel fought those of the tribe of Benjamin, near Gibeah. Judges xx. 33.

BAAL-ZEBUB, Bay'-al-ze'-bub, *the master of flies.*— An idol of the Ekronites. 2 Kings i. 2. This deity is called the prince of the devils. Matt. xii. 24.

BAAL-ZEPHON, Bay'-al-ze'-fon, *the idol of the north, secret, or the god of the watch-tower.*—Probably the temple of some idol, which served at the same time for a place of observation for the neighbouring sea and country and a beacon to travellers by either. Exod. xiv. 2, 9.

BAANA, Bay′-a-nah, *in affliction, answering.*—The son of Ahilud, governor of Taanach, Megiddo, and Beth-shean. 1 Kings iv. 12.

BAANAH, Bay′-a-nah, *in the answer, in affliction.*—1. An officer belonging to Ishbosheth, the son of Saul. 2 Sam. iv. 2.   2. One of king Solomon's purveyors. 1 Kings iv. 16.

BAARA, Bay′-a-rah, *a flame, a purging.*—A wife of Shaharaim. 1 Chron. viii. 8.

BAASEIAH, Bay-a-sy′-ah, *making or pressing together.*—One of the ancestors of Asaph, a singer in the temple of Jerusalem. 1 Chron. vi. 40.

BAASHA, Bay′-a-shah, *in the work, he that demands, he that lays waste.*—The son of Ahijah, commander-in-chief of the armies belonging to Nadab, the son of Jeroboam, the king of Israel. 1 Kings xv. 27, &c.

BABEL, Bay′-bel, *confusion, mixture.*—The tower and city founded by the descendants of Noah, in the plains of Shinar. The different tribes descended from Noah were here collected; and from this point were dispersed, through the confusion of their language. Gen. xi. 9.

BABYLON, Bab′-be-lon, *confusion, mixture.*—2 Kings xxiv. 1. The capital of Chaldea, built by Nimrod, Gen. x. 10, in the place where the tower of Babel was begun. It was under Nebuchadnezzar that Babylon, then become the seat of universal empire, is supposed to have acquired that extent and magnificence which rendered it the wonder of the world.

BABYLONIANS, Bab-be-lo′-ne-ans.—The inhabitants of the kingdom of Babylon. Ezra iv. 9.

BACA, Bay′-kah, *mulberry trees.*—A village near Galilee. Psalm lxxxiv. 6.

BACHRITES, Back′-rites.—Descendants of Becher. Num. xxvi. 35.

BACHUTH-ALLON, Bak′-uth-al′-lon, *the oak of weeping.*—The place where the nurse of Rebekah was buried. Gen. xxxv. 8.

BAHURIM, Ba-hew′-rim, *choice, valiant, warlike.*—A city of Palestine, in the tribe of Benjamin. 2 Sam. iii. 16; xvi. 5.

BAJITH, Bay′-jith, *a house.*—The name of a heathen temple. Isai. xv. 2.

BAKBAKKAR, Bak-bak′-kar.—The name of a Levite who returned from captivity. 1 Chron. ix. 15.

BAKBUKIAH, Bak-buk-i′-ah.—One who officiated in the worship of God in the temple at Jerusalem. Neh. xi. 17.

BALAAM, Bay′-lam, *the old age or ancient of the people, without the people.*—A prophet of the city of Pethor, or Bosor, upon the Euphrates, whose intercourse with Balak, king of the Moabites, who sent for him to curse the Israelites, is recorded at large by Moses, Num. xxii. to xxiv.

BALADAN, Bal′-la-dan, *one without rule or judgment, ancient in judgment.*—The Scripture name for a king of Babylon. Isai. xxxix. 1; 2 Kings xx. 12. He is called by profane authors, *Belesus, Nabonassar,* or *Nanybrus.*

BALAH, Bay′-lah, *old, worn.*—A city in the tribe of Simeon. Josh. xix. 3.

BALAK, Bay′-lak, *one who lays waste, who laps.*—The son of Zippor, king of the Moabites, mentioned Num. xxii. 2, &c.; Rev. ii. 14.

BAMAH, Bay′-mah, *eminence.*—One of the altars of the Heathen. Ezek. xx. 29.

BAMOTH, Bay′-moth, *the high places.*—A place mentioned Num. xxi. 19, 20.

BAMOTH-BAAL, Bay′-moth-bay′-al, *the high places of Baal.*—A city beyond Jordan, given to the tribe of Reuben. Josh. xiii. 17.

BANI, Bay′-ny.—1. One of king David's worthies. 2 Sam. xxiii. 36. 2. A Levite who returned from Babylon. Neh. iii. 17. 3. A person who assisted in reading the law. Neh. viii. 7. 4. One who returned from the captivity. Ezra ii. 10.

BARABBAS, Ba-rab'-bas, *son of the father of confusion.*
—A notorious robber, guilty also of sedition and murder,
who was preferred to Jesus Christ by the Jews. John
xviii. 40.

BARACHEL, Bar'-a-kel, *who blesses God.*—The father
of Elihu. Job xxxii. 2.

BARACHIAS, Bar-a-ky'-as, *who blesses God.*—The
father of Zacharias, mentioned Matt. xxiii. 35, as slain
between the temple and the altar.

BARAK, Bay'-rak, *thunder, in vain.*—The son of
Abinoam, chosen by God to deliver the Israelites from that
bondage under which they were held by Jabin, king of
the Canaanites. Judges iv. 6, &c.

BARHUMITES, Bar-hew'-mites.—The inhabitants of
Bahurim. 2 Sam. xxiii. 31.

BARIAH, Ba-ry'-ah.—One of the posterity of king
David. 1 Chron. iii. 22.

BAR-JESUS, Bar-je'-sus, *son of Jesus.*—A Jewish sorcerer in the Isle of Crete. Acts xiii. 6. St. Luke calls him
Elymas.

BAR-JONA, Bar-jo'-nah, *the son of a dove, or of Jonas.*
—Simon Peter is thus called, Matt. xvi. 17.

BARKOS, Bar'-kos.—One whose children were Nethinims. Ezra ii. 53.

BARNABAS, Bar'-na-bas, *the son of consolation.*—A
disciple of Jesus Christ, and companion of St. Paul in his
labours. He was a Levite, born in the island of Cyprus,
whose proper name was Joses: the apostles added to it
Barnabas. Acts iv. 36, 37.

BARSABAS, Bar'-sa-bas, *son of return, of rest.*—1.
Joseph Barsabas, surnamed Justus, was one of the first
disciples of Jesus Christ, and probably one of the seventy.
Acts i. 23. 2. This was also the surname of Judas, one of
the principal disciples, mentioned Acts xv. 22, &c.

BARTHOLOMEW, Bar-thol'-o-mew, *a son that suspends the waters.*—One of the twelve apostles, and thought to be the same person who is called Nathanael, one of the first disciples of Christ. Matt. x. 3.

BARTIMÆUS, Bar-te-me'-us, *the son of Timeus, or of the honourable.*—A blind man of Jericho, who sat near the public road when our Saviour passed that way on his journey to Jerusalem. Mark x. 46—52.

BARUCH, Bay'-ruk, *who is blessed, who bends the knee.*—1. The son of Neriah, and grandson of Maaseiah: he was of illustrious birth, and of the tribe of Judah. See Jer. xxxvi. 4.   2. Baruch, the son of Zabbai, a person who assisted to build the walls of Jerusalem. Neh. iii. 20. 3. One who signed the covenant. Neh. x. 6.   4. The father of one chosen by lot to dwell in Jerusalem. Neh. xi. 5.

BARZILLAI, Bar-zil'-la-i, *son of contempt, made of iron.*—1. A native of Rogelim, in the land of Gilead, and an old friend of David, who assisted him in his troubles when he was forced away from Jerusalem by his son Absalom. 2 Sam. xvii. 27.   2. A native of Meholath, in the tribe of Simeon. 2 Sam. xxi. 8.   3. A person mentioned Neh. vii. 63.

BASHAN, Bay'-shan, *in the tooth, in the change or sleep.*—One of the most fertile cantons in Canaan, bounded on the west by the river Jordan, on the east by the mountains of Gilead, on the south by the brook of Jabbok, and on the north by the land of Geshur. Og, king of the Amorites, possessed this country when Moses made the conquest thereof. Deut. iii. 1.

BASHAN-HAVOTH-JAIR, Bay'-shan-hay'-voth-jay'-ir.—The country of Argob, settled by Jair. Deut. iii. 14.

BASHEMATH, Bash'-e-math, *perfumed, in desolation.*—A daughter of Elon the Hittite, married to Esau, the son of Isaac. Gen. xxvi. 34.

BASMATH, Bas'-math.—A daughter of Solomon. 1 Kings iv. 15.

45

BATHRABBIM, Bath-rab′-bim.—The name of a tower. Cant. vii. 4.

BATH-SHEBA, Bath′-she-bah, *the seventh daughter, or daughter of an oath.*—The daughter of Eliam, and the wife of Uriah the Hittite. See 2 Sam. xi. 1—27; xii. 1—25.

BATHSHUA, Bath′-shu-ah.—The same as Bathsheba. 1 Chron. iii. 5.

BAVAI, Bav′-a-i.—The son of Henadad, and one that returned from the captivity. Neh. iii. 18.

BAZLITH, Baz′-lith.—One whose children were Nethinims. Neh. vii. 54.

BAZLUTH, Baz′-luth.—One whose descendants returned from the captivity. Ezra ii. 52.

BDELLIUM, Del′-le-um, *a resinous gum, or a precious stone.*—Gen. ii. 12; Num. xi. 7.

BEALIAH, Be-a-ly′-ah, *the god of an idol, or in an assembly.*—One of the thirty brave men in David's army. 1 Chron. xii. 5.

BEALOTH, Be′-a-loth.—A city of Palestine. Josh. xv. 24.

BEBAI, Beb′-a-i, *void or empty.*—One whose descendants returned from the captivity, to the number of 623. Ezra ii. 11.

BECHER, Be′-ker, *the first-begotten, or first-fruits.*— 1. The son of Ephraim, chief of the family of the Bachrites. Num. xxvi. 35. 2. A son of Benjamin. Gen. xlvi. 21.

BECHORATH, Be-ko′-rath, *first-fruits.*—The great-grandfather of Kish, the father of king Saul. 1 Sam. ix. 1.

BEDAD, Be′-dad, *alone, in friendship.*—A king of Moab. Gen. xxxvi. 35.

BEDAN, Be′-dan, *door, bar, alone.*—Some suppose him to have been Jair, who judged Israel twenty-two years. 1 Sam. xii. 11.

BEDEIAH, Be-dy'-ah, *the only lord.*—One who returned from the captivity, and had married a heathen wife. Ezra x. 35.

BEELIADA, Be-el-i'-a-da, *an open field.*—One of David's sons. 1 Chron. xiv. 7.

BEELZEBUB, Be-el'-ze-bub.—See BAALZEBUB.

BEER, Be'-er, *a well.*—The name of a place about four leagues from Jerusalem. Judges ix. 21.

BEERA, Be-e'-rah.—The son of Zophah, a descendant of Asher. 1 Chron. vii. 37.

BEERAH, Be-e'-rah.—A head of the tribe of Reuben, who was carried into captivity by Tilgath-pilneser. 1 Chron. v. 6.

BEER-ELIM, Be-er-e'-lim, *the well of the princes.*—Mentioned by Isaiah, chap. xv. 8; and thought to be the same with that mentioned Num. xxi. 18.

BEERI, Be-e'-ry.—1. A Hittite, father-in-law to Esau. Gen. xxvi. 34. 2. The father of the prophet Hosea. Chap. i. 1.

BEER-LAHAI-ROI, Be'-er-la-hay'-i-roy, *the well of him who lives and sees me.*—A well situated between Kadesh and Bered. Gen. xvi. 14.

BEEROTH, Be-e'-roth.—1. A city belonging to the Gibeonites; which was afterwards yielded to the tribe of Benjamin. Josh. ix. 17. 2. One of the stations of the Israelites in the wilderness. Deut. x. 6.

BEER-SHEBA, Be-er'-she-ba, *the well of an oath, or the well of seven.*—The place where Abraham made an alliance with Abimelech, king of Gerar. It was about 70 miles south of Hebron. The limits of the land are often expressed, from Dan to Beersheba. 2 Sam. xvii. 11.

BEESHTERAH, Be-esh'-te-rah.—A city in the south of Palestine. Josh. xxi. 27.

BEHEMOTH, Be'-he-moth.—An animal described Job xl. 15.

BEKAH, Be'-kah.—A Jewish coin, value half a shekel, about 1s. 1½d. Exod. xxxviii. 26.

BEL, Bel, *ancient, nothing, subject to change.*—Also BELUS, a name which many Heathens, and particularly Babylonians, called their chief idol. But whether under this appellation, they worshipped Nimrod, their first Baal or lord, or Pul, king of Assyria, or some other monarch, or the sun, or all in one, is uncertain. Isai. xlvi. 1.

BELA, Be'-la, *destroying.*—The son of Beor, king of Dinhabah, in the eastern part of Edom. Gen. xxxvi. 32.

BELAH, Be'-lah, *destroying.*—A son of the patriarch Benjamin. Gen. xlvi. 21.

BELIAL, Be'-le-al, *wicked, worthless.*—A name given to the inhabitants of Gibeah, who abused the Levite's wife. Judges xix. 22. In latter times it denotes the devil. 2 Cor. vi. 15.

BELSHAZZAR, Bel-shaz'-zar, *master of the treasure.*—The last king of Babylon, and the grandson of Nebuchadnezzar. Dan. v. 1.

BELTESHAZZAR, Bel-te-shaz'-zar, *who lays up treasures in secret, who secretly endures pain and pressure.*—A name given to Daniel at the court of Nebuchadnezzar. Dan. i. 7.

BEN, Ben, *a son.*—One of the porters of the temple at Jerusalem. 1 Chron. xv. 18.

BENAIAH, .Ben-ay'-yah, *son of the Lord, the Lord's building.*—1. The son of Jehoiada, one of David's worthies, and captain of his guard. 2 Sam. viii. 18. 2. A son of Pahath-Moab, who returned from Babylon, and had married against law. Ezra x. 30. See verses 25, 35.

BEN-AMMI, Ben-am'-mi, *the son of my people.*—The father of the Ammonites, and son of Lot. Gen. xix. 38.

BENE-BERAK, Ben-eb'-e-rak, *son of lightning.*—A place in Palestine, situated in the tribe of Dan. Josh. xix. 45.

BENE-JAAKAN, Ben-e-jay'-a-kan, *the sons of sorrow.*
—The twenty-eighth encampment of the Israelites. Num.
xxxiii. 31.

BEN-HADAD, Ben-hay'-dad, *the son of noise or clamour.*
—1. The son of Tabrimon, king of Syria, who came to the
assistance of Asa, king of Judah, against Baasha, king of
Israel. 1 Kings xv. 18. 2. King of Syria, son of the
preceding: he made war upon Ahab, but was defeated:
he also declared war against Jehoram. 2 Kings vi. 24.
3. The son of Hazael: he succeeded his father as king of
Syria. 2 Kings xiii. 24.

BEN-HAIL, Ben-hay'-il, *the son of strength.*—One of
those whom Jehoshaphat sent to the several cities of his
dominions to instruct the people, and reclaim them from
idolatry. 2 Chron. xvii. 7.

BEN-HANAN, Ben-hay'-nan, *the son of grace.*—One of
the posterity of the patriarch Judah. 1 Chron. iv. 20.

BENINU, Ben'-e-nu, *our sons.*—One who joined in
covenant with Nehemiah to renounce idolatry. Neh.
x. 13.

BENJAMIN, Ben'-ja-min, *the son of the right hand.*—
1. The youngest son of Jacob and Rachel, who was born
A.M. 2272. Gen. xxxv. 16, 17, &c. 2. The name of one
who assisted in repairing the walls of Jerusalem. Neh.
iii. 23. 3. A person of distinction who returned from
captivity. Neh. xii. 34.

BENO, Be'-no.—A descendant of Levi. 1 Chron.
xxiv. 26.

BEN-ONI, Be-no'-ny, *son of my grief.*—The name which
Rachel gave her son, whom Jacob named Benjamin. Gen.
xxxv. 18.

BEN-ZOHETH, Ben-zo'-heth, *the son of separation.*—
One of the posterity of Judah. 1 Chron. iv. 20.

BEON, Be'-on, *in affliction.*—A city beyond Jordan.
Num. xxxii. 3.

49

BEOR, Be'-or, *burning or mad.*—1. The father of Balaam. Num. xxii. 5. 2. The father of Bela, king of Dinhabah, in Edom. Gen. xxxvi. 32.

BERA, Be'-ra, *a well, a declaring.*—A king of Sodom, who lived in the time of Abraham. He was tributary to Chedorlaomer, king of Elam. Gen. xiv. 2.

BERACHAH, Ber'-a-kah, *blessing, or bending the knee.*—One who repaired to king David at Ziklag. 1 Chron. xii. 3.

BERACHIAH, or BERECHIAH, Ber-a-ky'-ah, or Ber-e-ky'-ah, *speaking well of the Lord.*—1. One of the posterity of Levi. 1 Chron. vi. 39. 2. A descendant of Judah. 1 Chron. ix. 16. 3. A descendant of king David. 1 Chron. iii. 20. 4. The father of Meshullam, one who repaired the walls of Jerusalem. Neh. iii. 4, 30.

BERAIAH, Be-ra-i'-ah, *the choosing of the Lord.*—A descendant of Benjamin. 1 Chron. viii. 21.

BEREA, Be-re'-ah, *heavy, weighty.*—A city of Macedonia, where St. Paul preached the Gospel with great success. Acts xvii. 10.

BERED, Be'-red, *hail.*—A place mentioned Gen. xvi. 14.

BERI, Be'-ry, *my corn.*—A descendant of Asher. 1 Chron. vii. 36.

BERIAH, Be-ry'-ah, *in fellowship or envy.*—The son of Asher, the father of Heber. Gen. xlvi. 17.

BERITH, Be'-rith, *covenant.*—A deity worshipped by the Canaanites. Judges ix. 46.

BERNICE, Ber-ny'-se, *one that brings victory.*—The daughter of Agrippa, surnamed the Great, king of the Jews, and sister to young Agrippa, also king of the Jews. She heard the discourses which Paul delivered before Festus. Acts xxv. 23.

BERODACH BALADAN, Be-ro'-dak bal'-a-dan, *the son of death.*—The son of Baladan, king of Babylon, who sent ambassadors to Hezekiah, king of Judah, with letters and presents, when he heard he had been sick. 2 Kings xx. 12.

BEROTHAH, Be-ro'-thah, *wells.*—A city of Syria, supposed to be Beroth. Ezek. xlvii. 16.

BEROTHAI, Ber'-o-thay, *wells, or cypress-trees.*— A city of Syria. 2 Sam. viii. 8.

BESAI, Be'-say, *a despising, or dirty.*—A Nethinim. Neh. vii. 52.

BESODEIAH, Be-so-dy'-ah, *the counsel of the Lord.*— The father of Meshullam. Neh. iii. 6.

BESOR, Be'-sor, *glad news.*—A brook which falls into the Mediterranean, between Gaza and Rhinocolura. 1 Sam. xxx. 9.

BETAH, Be'-tah, *confidence.*—A city of Syria, taken by David from Hadadezer. 2 Sam. viii. 8.

BETEN, Be'-ten, *the belly.*—A city of Canaan, on the borders of the tribe of Asher. Josh. xix. 25.

BETHABARA, Beth-ab'-ba-rah, *the house of passage, of anger.*—A place beyond Jordan, where John baptized. John i. 28.

BETH-ANATH, Beth'-a-nath, *the house of affliction.*— A city on the borders of Naphtali. Josh. xix. 38.

BETH-ANOTH, Beth'-a-noth, *the house of affliction.*— A city in the tribe of Judah. Josh. xv. 59.

BETHANY, Beth'-a-ne, *the house of song, of affliction, of obedience, the grace of God.*—A considerable place, situated on the ascent of the Mount of Olives, about two miles from Jerusalem. John xi. 18. It was here Martha and Mary lived, with their brother Lazarus, whom Jesus raised from the dead. It is at present a very inconsiderable place.

BETH-ARABAH, Beth-ar'-ra-bah, *the house of sweet smell.*—1. A city belonging to the tribe of Judah. Josh. xv. 6, 61. 2. A city belonging to the tribe of Benjamin. Josh. xviii. 22.

BETH-ARAM, Beth'-ar-am, *the house of height.*—A city of Palestine, in the tribe of Gad. Josh. xiii. 27. Now called *Livias.*

51

BETH-ARBEL, Beth-ar′-bel, *the house of ambush.*—A place in Armenia. Hosea x. 14.

BETH-AVEN, Beth-ay′-ven, *the house of vanity, of strength.*—The same as BETHEL. This city, on the revolt of the ten tribes, belonged to the kingdom of Israel, and was one of the cities in which Jeroboam set up the golden calves; whence the prophet calls it, in derision, BETHAVEN, *the house of vanity,* Hosea iv. 15, instead of BETHEL, *the house of God.*

BETH-AZMAVETH, Beth-az′-ma-veth, *the house of death's strength.*—A place mentioned Neh. vii. 28.

BETH-BAAL-MEON, Beth-bay′-al-me′-on, *an idol of the dwelling-place.*—A city in the tribe of Reuben. Josh. xiii. 17.

BETHBARAH, Beth-bay′-rah, *the chosen house.*—A place beyond Jordan. Judges vii. 24. Thought to be the same as BETHABARA.

BETH-BIREI, Beth-bir′-re-i, *the house of my Creator.*—A city in the tribe of Simeon. 1 Chron. iv. 31.

BETH-CAR, Beth′-kar, *the house of the lamb.*—A city in the tribe of Dan. 1 Sam. vii. 11.

BETH-DAGON, Beth-day′-gon, *the house of fish, of corn, of the god Dagon.*—1. A city in the tribe of Judah. Josh. xv. 41. 2. In the tribe of Asher. Josh. xix. 27.

BETH-DIBLATHAIM, Beth-dib-la-thay′-im, *the house of dry figs.*—A city in the land of Canaan. Jer. xlviii. 22.

BETH-EDEN, Beth-e′-den, *the house of pleasure.*—Amos. i. 5. Marginal reading.

BETH-EL, Beth′-el, *the house of God.*—A city which lay to the west of Ai, about eight miles to the north of Jerusalem, in the confines of the tribe of Ephraim and Benjamin. Here Jacob slept and had his vision. Gen. xxviii. 19.

BETH-EMEK, Beth-e′-mek, *the house of deepness.*—A frontier city of the tribe of Asher. Josh. xix. 27.

BETHER, Be′-ther, *division, in the turtle, in the trial.*—Mountains of Bether. Cant. ii. 17. Probably BETH-HORON.

BETHESDA, Beth-es′-da, *the house of effusion, of pity.*—The name of a public pool, or bath, at Jerusalem, which had five porticos or piazzas round it. John v. 2, &c.

BETH-EZEL, Beth-e′-zel, *a neighbour's house.*—Micah i. 11.

BETH-GADER, Beth-gay′-der.—One of the descendants of Caleb. 1 Chron. ii. 51.

BETH-GAMUL, Beth-gay′-mul, *the house of recompence, of the weaned, of the camel.*—A city in the tribe of Reuben. Jer. xlviii. 23.

BETH-HACCEREM, Beth-hak′-se-rem, or Beth-hak′-ke-rem, *the house of the vineyard.*—A city situated on an eminence between Jerusalem and Tekoa. Jer. vi. 1; Neh. iii. 14.

BETH-HARAN, Beth-hay′-ran, *the house of a hill.*—A fenced city of Gilead. Num. xxxii. 36.

BETH-HOGLA, Beth-hog′-lah.—1. A city in the tribe of Judah. Josh. xv. 6. 2. A city belonging to the tribe of Benjamin. Josh. xviii. 21.

BETH-HORON, Beth-ho′-ron, *the house of wrath, of the hole, of liberty.*—The name of two cities in the tribe of Ephraim, the upper and the nether, built by a female called Sherah. 1 Chron. vii. 24.

BETH-JESHIMOTH, Beth-jesh′-e-moth, *the house of desolation.*—A city in the tribe of Reuben. Josh. xiii. 20.

BETH-LEBAOTH, Beth-leb′-a-oth, *the house of lionesses.*—A city in the tribe of Simeon. Josh. xix. 6. Called Lebaoth. Josh. xv. 32.

BETH-LEHEM, Beth'-le-hem, *the house of bread, of war.*—A city in the tribe of Judah; and also called Ephrath, Gen. xlviii. 7; or Ephratah, Micah v. 2; and the inhabitants Ephrathites, Ruth i. 2; 1 Sam. xvii. 12. In this place David was born, and spent his early years as a shepherd. Here also the scene of the beautiful narrative of Ruth is laid. But its highest honour is, that here our divine Lord condescended to be born of woman.

BETH-LEHEM EPHRATAH, Beth'-le-hem eff'-ra-tah. —Micah v. 2. See the preceding article.

BETH-LEHEM JUDAH, Beth'-le-hem ju'-dah.— Judges xvii. 7. See BETHLEHEM.

BETH-MAACHAH, Beth-may'-a-kah, *house of bruising.*—A city of Palestine. 2 Sam. xx. 14.

BETH-MARCABOTH, Beth-mar'-ca-both, *the house of bitterness, wiped out.*—A city of Palestine, in the tribe of Simeon. Josh. xix. 5.

BETH-MEON, Beth-me'-on, *the house of the dwelling-place.*—A city belonging to the Moabites in the tribe of Reuben. Jer. xlviii. 23.

BETH-NIMRAH, Beth-nim'-rah, *the house of rebellion.* —A city in the tribe of Gad, in the land of Gilead. Num. xxxii. 36.

BETH-PALET, Beth-pay'-let, *the house of expulsion.*— A city in the most southern part of the tribe of Judah. Josh. xv. 27.

BETH-PAZZEZ, Beth-paz'-zez, *the house of dividing asunder.*—A city in Palestine, in the tribe of Issachar. Josh. xix. 21.

BETH-PEOR, Beth-pe'-or, *the house of gaping.*—A city of Moab, given to the tribe of Reuben. Deut. iv. 46.

BETHPHAGE, Beth'-fa-je, *the house of the month, or of early figs.*—A small village in Mount Olivet, and somewhat nearer Jerusalem than Bethany. Matt. xxi. 1.

BETH-RAPHA, Beth'-ra-fah, *the house of health.*—A descendant of the patriarch Judah. 1 Chron. iv. 12.

BETH-REHOB, Beth'-re-hob, *the house of liberty.*—The same as REHOB. A city of Syria, possessed by the Danites. 2 Sam. x. 6.

BETHSAIDA, Beth-say'-e-dah, *the house of fruits, of hunters.*—A city not mentioned in the Old Testament, though frequently occurring in the New. It belonged to the tribe of Naphtali, at the north end of the lake of Gennesaret, just where the Jordan runs into it. Peter and Andrew here followed the occupation of fishermen. John i. 44.

BETH-SHAN, Beth'-shan, *the house of the tooth, of change, or of sleep.*—A city belonging to the half tribe of Manasseh, on the west of Jordan, and not far from the river. 1 Sam. xxxi. 10.

BETH-SHEMESH, Beth'-she-mesh, *the house of the sun.*—1. A city of the tribe of Judah, belonging to the priests. Josh. xxi. 16. 2. A city in the tribe of Issachar. Josh. xix. 22. 3. A city in the tribe of Naphtali. Josh. xix. 38; Judges i. 33.

BETH-SHITTAH, Beth-shit'-tah, *house of thorns.*—Gideon pursued the Midianites to this place. Judges vii. 22.

BETH-TAPPUAH, Beth-tap'-pu-ah, *the house of an apple-tree.*—A city and mountain in the tribe of Judah. Josh. xv. 53.

BETHUEL, Be-thew'-el, *filiation of God.*—The son of Nahor and Milcah. He was Abraham's nephew, and father of Rebekah, the wife of Isaac. Gen. xxii. 22, 23.

BETHUL, Be'-thul, *the virgin of the Lord.*—A city in the tribe of Simeon. Josh. xix. 4.

BETH-ZUR, Beth'-zur, *the house of a rock.*—A city belonging to the tribe of Judah, being south of Edom. Josh. xv. 58.

BETONIM, Bet'-o-nim.—A city in the tribe of Gad. Josh. xiii. 26.

BEULAH, Be-yew'-lah, or Bew'-lah, *married.*—A name given to the Jewish church. Isai. lxii. 4.

BEZALEEL, Be-zal'-e-el, *in the shadow of God.*—The principal artificer of the tabernacle. Exod. xxxi. 2.

BEZEK, Be'-zek, *lightning, in chains.*—A city in the tribe of Judah. Judges i. 4—7.

BEZER, Be'-zer, or BOZRA, or BOSTRA, *munition, or vine branches.*—1. A city beyond Jordan, given by Moses to Reuben. Deut. iv. 43. 2. A descendant of Asher. 1 Chron. vii. 37.

BICHRI, Bik'-ry, *first-born, or first-fruits.*—A Benjamite, the father of Sheba, remarkable for his rebellion against David. 2 Sam. xx. 1, 2.

BIDKAR, Bid'-kar, *in compunction or sharp pain.*—Captain of the guards to Jehu, king of Israel. 2 Kings ix. 25.

BIGTHA, Big'-thah, *giving meat.*—A chamberlain to king Ahasuerus. Esther i. 10.

BIGTHAN, Big'-than.—Esther ii. 21. See BIGTHA.

BIGTHANA, Big'-tha-nah.—Esther vi. 2. See BIGTHA.

BIGVAI, Big'-va-i, *in my body.*—1. One of Ezra's companions from Babylon. Ezra viii. 14. 2. One who returned from captivity. Ezra ii. 2.

BILDAD, Bil'-dad, *old friendship, or old love.*—The Shuhite, one of Job's friends, thought by some to have descended from Suah, the son of Abraham, by Keturah. Job ii. 11, &c.

BILEAM, Bil'-e-am, *the ancient of the people, the devourer.*—A city in the tribe of Manasseh. on the other side of Jordan. 1 Chron. vi. 70.

BILGAH, Bil'-gah, *ancient countenance.*—The chief of the fifteenth band of priests established by David. 1 Chron. xxiv. 14.

BILGAI, Bil'-ga-i.—A prince who sealed the covenant. Neh. x. 8.

BILHAH, Bil'-hah, *one who is old, troubled, confused.*— Rachel's handmaid, given by her to Jacob, her husband, as a concubine. Gen. xxx. 3, 4.

BILHAN, Bil'-han.—1. A son of Ezar, a descendant of Esau. Gen. xxxvi. 27. 2. A son of Jediael, a descendant of Benjamin. 1 Chron. vii. 10.

BILSHAN, Bil'-shan.—One who returned from the captivity. Ezra ii. 2.

BIMHAL, Bim'-hal.—A descendant of Asher. 1 Chron. vii. 33.

BINEA, Bin'-e-ah, *the son of the Lord.*—A descendant of Saul. 1 Chron. viii. 37.

BINNUI, Bin'-nu-i, *building.*—1. One of the princes who repaired the walls of Jerusalem, after the captivity. Neh. iii. 24. 2. A Levite, the father of Noadiah. Ezra viii. 33.

BIRSHA, Bir'-shah, *in evil, a son that beholds.*—King of Gomorrah, who was at war with Chedorlaomer and his allies. Gen. xiv. 2, &c.

BIRZAVITH, Bir'-za-vith.—A descendant of Asher. 1 Chron. vii. 31.

BISHLAM, Bish'-lam.—An officer of the king of Persia. Ezra iv. 7.

BITHIAH, Bith-i'-ah, *daughter of the lord.*—A female of the tribe of Judah. 1 Chron. iv. 18.

BITHRON, Bith'-ron, *division, in his examination, daughter of the song, of anger, of liberty.*—A place in Palestine, on the east side of Jordan. 2 Sam. ii. 29.

BITHYNIA, Bith-in'-ne-ah, *violent precipitation.*—A large country in Asia-Minor, bounded on the north by the Euxine Sea. Acts xvi. 7.

BIZTHA, Biz'-thah.—A chamberlain of Ahasuerus. Esther i. 10.

BLASTUS, Blas'-tus, *one that sprouts or brings forth.*— Chamberlain to Herod, king of Judea. Acts xii. 20.

BOANERGES, Bo-an-er'-jees, *sons of thunder.*—A name given to James and John. Mark iii. 17.

BOAZ or BOOZ, Bo'-az or Bo'-oz, *in strength, in the goat.*—1. The son of Salmon and Rachab. Ruth iv. 20, &c.; Matt. i. 5. 2. The name of one of those brazen pillars which Solomon erected in the porch of the temple, the other column being called Jachin. 1 Kings vii. 21.

BOCHERU, Bok'-ke-rew, *first-born.*—A descendant of Saul. 1 Chron. viii. 38.

BOCHIM, Bo'-kim, *the place of weeping, mourning, or mulberry-trees.*—The situation is doubtful, some placing it near Jerusalem, others at Shiloh. Judges ii. 1.

BOHAN, Bo'-han.—A descendant of Reuben. Josh. xv. 6.

BOSCATH, Bos'-kath, *in poverty.*—A place in the tribe of Judah. 2 Kings xxii. 1.

BOSOR, Bo'-sor, *taking away.*—The father of Balaam. 2 Pet. ii. 15. Also called Beor, Num. xxii. 5.

BOSRAH, or BOZRAH, Bos'-rah, or Boz'-rah, *in tribulation or distress.*—1. The metropolis of Idumea, in the half-tribe of Manasseh. Gen. xxxvi. 33. 2. The same as Bezer in the wilderness. It was given to the Levites, and was a place of refuge. Josh. xx. 8.

BOZEZ, Bo'-zez, *mud, in the flower.*—The name of a rock which Jonathan the son of Saul climbed when he went to attack the Philistines. 1 Sam. xiv. 4.

BUKKI, Buk'-ky, *void.*—A high-priest of the Jews, the son of Abishua, and the father of Uzzi. 1 Chron. vi. 5.

BUKKIAH, Buk-ky'-ah, *the dissipation of the lord.*— One of the musicians of the temple of Jerusalem. 1 Chron. xxv. 4.

BUL, Bull, *changeable, perishing.*—The eighth month of the ecclesiastical year of the Jews, and the second month of the civil year.

BUNAH, Bew'-nah, *building or understanding.*—A descendant of the patriarch Judah. 1 Chron. ii. 25.

BUNNI, Bun'-ny, *building me.*—A Levite who returned from the Babylonish captivity. Neh. ix. 4.

BUZ, Buz, *despised, plundered.*—1. The son of Nahor and Milcah, and brother to Huz. Gen. xxii. 21. 2. The son of Abihail, and father of Jahdo. 1 Chron. v. 14.

BUZI, Bew'-zy, *my contempt.*—The father of Ezekiel. Chap. i. 3.

BUZITE, Bew'-zite.—A descendant of Buz. Elihu, one of Job's friends, was a Buzite. Job xxxii. 2.

C

CABBON, Kab'-bon, *as though understanding.*—A city mentioned Josh. xv. 40.

CABUL, Kay'-bul, *displeasing, dirt.*—The name which Hiram, king of Tyre, gave to the twenty cities in the land of Galilee, of which Solomon made him a present, in acknowledgment for his services in building the temple. 1 Kings ix. 13.

CÆSAR, Se'-zar, *one cut out.*—A title borne by all the Roman emperors till the destruction of that empire. In Scripture the reigning emperor is generally mentioned by the name of CÆSAR, without expressing any other distinction. Matt. xxii. 21; Acts xxv. 10.

CÆSAREA, Se-zar-re'-a, *a bush of hair.*—A city and port of Palestine, built by Herod the Great, and thus called in honour of Augustus Cæsar. It is often mentioned in Scripture. Here Herod was smitten; here Cornelius resided, Acts x.; also Philip and his four maiden daughters.

CÆSAREA PHILIPPI, Se-za-re'-a fil-lip'-py.—This place was first called Laish or Lishim. Judges xviii. 7.

After it was subdued by the Danites, it received the name of Dan, and is by heathen writers called Paneas. Philip, the youngest son of Herod the Great, made it the capital of his tetrarchy. Mark viii. 27.

CAIAPHAS, Kay'-e-a-fas, *a searcher.*—High-priest of the Jews, successor to Simon, son of Cameth. He was high-priest A. M. 4037, the year of Jesus Christ's death. John xviii. 24.

CAIN, Kane, *possession.*—The oldest son of Adam and Eve. He was the first man that had been a child, and the first man born of a woman. He was the murderer of his brother Abel. See Gen. iii. and iv.

CAINAN, Kay-i'-nan, *possessor, one that laments.*— 1. The son of Enos, born A.M. 325. Gen. v. 9. 2. The son of Arphaxad. Luke iii. 36.

CALAH, Kay'-lah, *good opportunity, as the verdure.*— A city of Assyria, built by Ashur. Gen. x. 12.

CALCOL, Kal'-col, *nourishing, or as consuming all things.*—A son of Terah, a descendant of Judah. 1 Chron. ii. 6.

CALEB, Kay'-leb, *a dog, a crow, a basket.*—1. The son of Jephunneh, of the tribe of Judah, one of those who accompanied Joshua when he went to view the land of Canaan. Num. xiii. 6. 2. The name of a canton in the tribe of Judah. 1 Sam. xxx. 14. 3. The son of Hezron. 1 Chron. ii. 18. 4. The son of Hur, and grandson of the former Caleb. 1 Chron. ii. 50.

CALEB EPHRATAH, Kay'-leb ef'-fra-tah.—A place so called by the conjunction of the names of Caleb and his wife Ephratah. 1 Chron. ii. 24.

CALNEH, Kal'-neh, *our consummation, or as murmuring.*—A city in the land of Shinah, built by Nimrod, and the last city mentioned, Gen. x. 10, as belonging to his kingdom. It is believed to be the same as CALNO. Isai. x. 9.

CALNO, Kal'-no, *consummation.*—See CALNEH. Isai. x. 9.

CALVARY, Kal'-va-re, *the place of a skull.*—Called in Hebrew, Golgotha; supposed to be thus denominated from the similitude it bore to the figure of the skull of a man's head, or from its being a place of burial. A small eminence to the north of Mount Zion, and the west of Jerusalem. The place where Christ was crucified. Luke xxiii. 33.

CAMBYSES, Kam-by'-sees.—The son of Cyrus, king of Persia. He succeeded his father A. M. 3475, and is the Ahasuerus mentioned in Ezra iv. 6.

CAMON, Kay'-mon, *his resurrection.*—A city belonging to the tribe of Manasseh, on the other side Jordan. Judges x. 5.

CANA, Kay'-nah, *zeal, possession, nest, cave.*—1. A town of Galilee, where Jesus performed his first miracle. John ii. 1, &c. 2. Or Kanah, a place belonging to the tribe of Asher. Josh. xix. 28.

CANAAN, Kay'-nan, *a merchant, a trader.*—1. The son of Ham. Gen. ix. 25. 2. The country lying between the Mediterranean Sea, and the mountains of Arabia. It was afterwards called Palestine and the Land of Promise. At the time of the Christian era, Palestine was divided into five provinces, Judea, Samaria, Galilee, Perea, and Idumea. It is in this country most of the remarkable occurrences of Scripture took place.

CANDACE, Kan-day'-se, or Kan'-da-se, *who possesses contrition.*—The name of an Ethiopian queen. Acts viii. 27.

CANNEH, Kan'-neh, *a wall.*—Ezek. xxvii. 23. See CALNEH.

CAPERNAUM, Ka-per'-na-um, *the field of repentance, city of comfort.*—A city celebrated in the Gospels, being the place where Jesus principally resided during the time of his ministry. It stood on the sea-coast; that is, on the coast of the sea of Galilee, in the borders of Zabulon and Nephthalim. Matt. iv. 13.

CAPHTOR, Kaf'-tor, *sphere, a buckle, a hand, doves, those that seek and inquire.*—The island of Caphtor, whence came the Caphtorims, otherwise called the Cherethims, or Cherethites, or Philistines. Gen. x. 14; Deut. ii. 23; Jer. xlvii. 4; Amos ix. 7. It is generally supposed to be Cappadocia. Calmet thinks it was Crete.

CAPHTORIM, Kaf'-to-rim.—A son of Mizraim. Gen. x. 14.

CAPPADOCIA, Kap-pa-do'-she-a, *a sphere*.—A country having the Euxine Sea on the north, Armenia on the east, Phrygia and Pamphilia on the west, and Cilicia on the south. It is mentioned Acts ii. 9; also by St. Peter, who addresses his first Epistle to the dispersed throughout Pontus, Galatia, Cappadocia, Bithynia, and Asia.

CARCAS, Kar'-kas, *the covering of a lamb.*—A chamberlain of Ahasuerus. Esther i. 10.

CARCHEMISH, or CHARCHEMISH, Kar'-ke-mish, *a lamb, as taken away.*—A town lying upon the Euphrates, and belonging to the Assyrians. Isai. x. 9; 2 Chron. xxxv. 20.

CARMEL, Kar'-mel, *a circumcised lamb, harvest, vineyard of God.*—1. A city in the tribe of Judah, situated on a mountain of the same name, in the southern part of Palestine. Josh. xv. 55; 1 Sam. xxv. 2, 5. 2. The name of a mountain to the south of Ptolemais. 1 Kings xviii. 19.

CARMI, Kar'-my, *my vineyard, the knowledge, or the lamb of the waters.*—1. The fourth son of Reuben. Num. xxvi. 6. 2. The father of Achan. Josh. vii. 1, 18.

CARPUS, Kar'-pus, *fruit, or fruitful.*—A disciple of St. Paul, who dwelt at Troas. St. Paul lodged with him. 2 Tim. iv. 13.

CARSHENA, Kar-she'-na.—A servant of Ahasuerus. Esther i. 14.

CASIPHIA, Ka-sif'-fe-a, *money or covetousness.*—A place near the Caspian Sea, between Media and Hyrcania. Ezra viii. 17.

CASLUHIM, Kas'-lu-him, *hopes, or life, or as pardoned.*—One of the sons of Misraim. Gen. x. 14; 1 Chron. i. 12.

CASTOR, Kas′-tor, *a beaver.*—Castor and Pollux, in the heathen mythology, were two brothers, sons of Jupiter and Leda, who sprung from the same egg. The vessel in which St. Paul embarked when he went to Rome, had the sign of Castor and Pollux. Acts xxviii. 11.

CEDRON, Se′-dron, or Ke′-dron.—A brook between Jerusalem and Mount Olivet. John xviii. 1. Called Kidron, 2 Sam. xv. 23.

CENCHREA, Sen′-kre-a, *millet, small pulse.*—A sea-port town belonging to Corinth, in the Archipelago. Acts xviii. 18.

CEPHAS, Se′-fas, *a stone or rock.*—Jesus changed Peter's name, John i. 42, from Simon into Cephas, a Syriac word, signifying a stone, which, by the Greeks was rendered Πετρος, and by the Latins, Petrus; both signifying the same.

CHALCOL, Kal′-kol, *who nourishes, sustains the whole.* —A person celebrated for wisdom. 1 Kings iv. 31.

CHALDEA, Kal-de′-a, *as demons, as robbers.*—A country of Asia, known in the most ancient times by the name of Shinar. The metropolis was Babylon. Jer. l. 10.

CHALDEANS, Kal-de′-ans.—The inhabitants of Chaldea, or Babylonians. Job i. 17.

CHANES, Kay′-nees.—The same as HANES. A garrison on the borders of Egypt. Isai. xxx. 4.

CHARASHIM, Kar′-a-shim.—A valley in Judea. 1 Chron. iv. 14.

CHARRAN, Kar′-ran, *a singing, the heat of wrath.*— The country of Mesopotamia in Asia. Acts vii. 4.

CHEBAR, Ke′-bar, *strength or power.*—A river of Chaldea. Ezek. i. 1. It is thought to have arisen near the mouth of the Tigris, and to have run through Mesopotamia to the south-west, and emptied itself into the Euphrates.

CHEDORLAOMER, Ked-or-lay'-o-mer, *as a generation of servitude.*—A king of the Elamites; who were either Persians, or a people bordering on the Persians. Gen. xiv. 1.

CHELAL, Ke'-lal.—An Israelite who returned from Babylon. Ezra x. 30.

CHELLUH, Kel'-lu.—The name of a place. Ezra x. 35.

CHELUB, Ke'-lub.—A descendant from Asher. 1 Chron. iv. 11.

CHELUBAI, Ke-lew'-bay.—A son of Hezron. 1 Chron. ii. 9.

CHEMARIMS, Kem'-a-rims, *black, or blackness.*—A word only occurring once in the Bible. Zeph. i. 4. Probably meaning priests of Baal.

CHEMOSH, Ke'-mosh, *as handling, as taking away.*—An idol of the Moabites. Num. xxi. 29.

CHENAANAH, Ke-nay'-a-nah, *broken in pieces.*—The name of an artificer of king Ahab. 1 Kings xxii. 11.

CHENANI, Ken'-a-ny.—The name of a Levite. Neh. ix. 4.

CHENANIAH, Ken-a-ny'-ah, *preparation, rectitude of the Lord.*—A chief of the Levites, and master of the temple music. 1 Chron. xv. 22.

CHEPHAR-HAAMMONAI, Ke'-far-ha-am'-mo-nay. —A city of the Gibeonites, given to the tribe of Benjamin. Josh. xviii. 24.

CHEPHIRAH, Kef-i'-rah.—See CHEPHAR-HAAMMONAI.

CHERAN, Ke'-ran, *anger.*—A descendant of Esau. Gen. xxxvi. 26.

CHERETHIMS, Ker'-e-thims, *who cuts, tears away.*—Philistines so named. Ezek. xxv. 16.

CHERETHITES, Ker'-eth-ites. — See CHERETHIMS. David had foreign guards, called Cherethites and Pelethites. 2 Sam. xv. 18.

CHERITH, Ke'-rith, *calling, piercing, slaying.*—A brook which falls into the Jordan below Bethshan. 1 Kings xvii. 3, 5.

CHERUB, Tsher'-ub, CHERUBIM, Tsher'-u-bim, in Syriac, *to till or plough.*—The figures placed in the holy of holies, at each end of the mercy-seat. Exod. xxv. 19.

CHERUB, Ke'-rub.—One of the Israelites who returned from Babylon, and was unable to prove his genealogy. Ezra ii. 59.

CHESALON, Kes'-a-lon.—A city in the tribe of Judah. Josh. xv. 10.

CHESED, Ke'-sed, *a devil, a destroyer.*—The son of Nahor and Milcah. Gen. xxii. 22. Also father of the Casedim, or Casdim, or Chaldeans.

CHESIL, Ke'-sil.—A city in the tribe of Judah. Josh. xv. 30.

CHESULLOTH, Ke-sul'-loth.—A place situated on the side of Mount Tabor. Josh. xix. 18.

CHEZIB, Ke'-zib.—A place mentioned Gen. xxxviii. 5, and thought to have been the same as Achzib. Josh. xv. 44.

CHIDON, Ky'-don.—The thrashing-floor of Chidon is the place where Uzzah was struck dead. 1 Chron. xiii. 9.

CHILEAB, Kil'-le-ab, *totality or perfection of the father.* The son of king David and Abigail. 2 Sam. iii. 3.

CHILION, Kil'-le-on, *finished, complete.*—The son of Elimelech and Naomi, of Bethlehem-judah. Ruth i. 2, 5.

CHILMAD, Kil'-mad, *teaching or learning.*—A city of Arabia. Ezek. xxvii. 23.

CHIMHAM, Kim'-ham, *as they, like to them.*—1. The son of Barzillai, the Gileadite. 2 Sam. xix. 37, 38. 2. The name of a place near Bethlehem. Jer. xli. 17.

CHINNEROTH, or CHINNERETH, Kin′-ner-oth, or Kin′-ner-eth.—A city of the tribe of Naphtali, to the south of which lay a great plain, reaching to the Dead Sea. Josh. xi. 2; xii. 3; xix. 35. The same as TIBERIAS.

CHIOS, Ky′-os, *open or opening.*—An island in the Archipelago, over against Smyrna. Acts xx. 15.

CHISLEU, Kis′-lew, *rashness, confidence.*—The third month of the Jewish civil year, and the ninth of their sacred year, answering to a part of November and December. Neh. i. 1. It contains 30 days.

CHISLON, Kis′-lon, *hope or trust.*—The father of Elidad. Num. xxxiv. 21.

CHISLOTH-TABOR, Kis′-loth-tay′-bor, *fears or purity.* —A city of Palestine, in the tribe of Zebulun. Josh. xix. 12.

CHITTIM, Kit′-tim, *those that bruise, gold, staining.*— Probably the same as Macedonia, peopled by Kittim, the son of Javan, and grandson of Noah. Gen. x. 4. Others think the coasts and islands of the Mediterranean. Num. xxiv. 24.

CHIUN, Ky′-un.—An Egyptian god, whom some think to be Saturn. Amos v. 26.

CHLOE, Klo′-e, *green herb.*—A Christian female of Corinth, who informed St. Paul of the divisions which then prevailed there on account of Cephas, Apollos, and himself. 1 Cor. i. 11.

CHORAZIN, Ko-ray′-zin, *the secret, here is a mystery.* —A town of Judea, situated on the lake of Galilee, and not far from Capernaum. Matt. xi. 21; Luke x. 13.

CHOZEBA, Ko-ze′-ba.—A town in the tribe of Judah. 1 Chron. iv. 22.

CHUB, Kub.—Calmet supposes it to be the habitation of the Cubeans, placed by Ptolemy in the Marcotis. Ezek. xxx. 5.

CHUN, Kun.—A city of ancient Syria. 1 Chron. xviii. 8.

CHUSHAN-RISHATHAIM, Kush′-an-rish-a-thay′-im, *Ethiopian, blackness of iniquities.*—King of Mesopotamia. Judges iii. 8.

CHUZA, Kew′-zah, *the prophet, Ethiopian.*—Steward to Herod. Luke viii. 3.

CILICIA, Sil-ish′-e-a, *which rolls or overturns.*—A country in the south of Asia Minor, at the east of the Mediterranean Sea: the capital was Tarsus. Acts xxi. 39.

CLAUDA, Klaw′-dah, *a broken voice, a lamentable voice.* —An island near Crete. Acts xxvii. 16.

CLAUDIA, Klaw′-de-a.—A Roman lady. 2 Tim. iv. 21.

CLAUDIUS, Klaw′-de-us.—1. A Roman emperor: he succeeded Caius Caligula, A. D. 41. In the ninth year of his reign he published an edict, expelling all Jews from Rome. Acts xviii. 2. 2. Claudius Felix, successor of Cumanus, in the government of Judea. Acts xxiii. 26. 3. Claudius Lysias, a tribune of the Roman troops, which kept guard at the temple at Jerusalem. Acts xxiii. 26.

CLEMENT, Klem′-ent, *mild, good, merciful.*—A person mentioned Phil. iv. 3.

CLEOPAS, Kle′-o-pas, *the whole glory.*—According to Eusebius and Epiphanius, he was brother of Joseph, both being sons of Jacob. He was the father of Simeon, of James the less, of Jude, and Joseph or Joses. Cleopas married Mary, sister to the blessed virgin. He was, therefore, uncle to Jesus Christ, and his sons were first cousins to him. Luke xxiv. 18.

CNIDUS, Ni′-dus.—A city and promontory of Asia. Acts xxvii. 7.

COL-HOZEH, Kol-ho′-zeh.—A ruler in Jerusalem. Neh. iii. 15.

COLOSSE, Ko-los′-se, *punishment, correction.*—A city of Phrygia Minor, which stood on the river Lyceus, at an equal distance between Laodicea and Hierapolis. Col. i. 2; iv. 13.

COLOSSIANS, Ko-losh'-e-ans.—The inhabitants of Colosse.

CONIAH, Ko-ny'-ah, *the strength or stability of the Lord.* —Jer. xxii. 28.

CONONIAH, Ko-no-ny'-ah, *the strength of the Lord.*— The name of a Levite. 2 Chron. xxxi. 12.

COOS, Ko'-os.—An island in the Archipelago. Acts xxi. 1.

CORINTH, Kor'-inth, *which is satisfied, beauty.*—A celebrated city, the capital of Achaia, seated on the isthmus which connects Peloponnesus with Attica, Acts xviii. 1, &c. To the Christians in this city, Paul addressed two letters.

CORINTHIANS, Ko-rin'-the-ans. — Inhabitants of Corinth.

CORNELIUS, Kor-ne'-le-us, *a horn.*—A centurion of a cohort belonging to the legion surnamed Italian. Acts x. 1—3, &c.

COSAM, Ko'-sam.—The son of Elmodam, and one of our Saviour's ancestors. Luke iii. 28.

COZ, Koz, *a thorn.*—A descendant of Asher. 1 Chron. iv. 8.

COZBI, Koz'-by, *a liar, as sliding away.*—The daughter of Zur, a prince of the Midianites. Num. xxv. 6—15.

CRESCENS, Kres'-sens, *growing, increasing.*—A person named 2 Tim. iv. 10.

CRETANS, or **CRETIANS,** Kre'-tans, or Kre'-she-ans. —Inhabitants of Crete. Titus i. 12.

CRETE, Kreet, *carnal, fleshy.*—An island in the Mediterranean, now called Candia, of which Titus was bishop. Titus i. 5.

CRISPUS, Kris'-pus, *curled.*—The chief of the Jewish synagogue at Corinth, who was converted to Christianity. Acts xviii. 8; 1 Cor. i. 14.

CUSH, Kush, *blackness, Ethiopians.*—The eldest son of Ham. Gen. x. 6—8. Ethiopia is frequently in Scripture called Cush. The first country which bore this name was encompassed by the river Gihon, which encircles a great part of the province of Chuzestan, in Persia. In process of time, the increasing family spread over the vast territory of India and Arabia, the whole of which tract, from the Ganges to the borders of Egypt, became the land of Cush, or Asiatic Ethiopia.

CUSHAN, Kew'-shan, *Ethiopia, black, heat.*—Hab. iii. 7.

CUSHI, Kew'-shy, *black.*—1. The name of a person mentioned 2 Sam. xviii. 21. 2. The father of Shelemiah. Jer. xxxvi. 14. 3. The father of the prophet Zephaniah. Chap. i. 1.

CUTHAH, Kew'-thah, *black.*—Probably the same as Cush. 2 Kings xvii. 24.

CYPRUS, Sy'-prus, *fair, fairness.*—A large island in the Mediterranean, situated between Cilicia and Syria. Acts xiii. 4.

CYRENE, Sy-re'-ne, *a wall, coldness, a meeting, a floor.*—A city of Lybia, in Africa. Acts ii. 10.

CYRENIUS, Sy-re'-ne-us, *who governs.*—The governor of Syria. Luke ii. 2.

CYRUS, Sy'-rus, *as miserable, as heir, the belly.*—The son of Cambyses the Persian, and of Mandane, daughter of Astyages, king of the Medes. See 2 Chron. xxxvi. 22, 23 ; Ezra i. 1, 2.

D

DABBASHETH, Dab'-ba-sheth, *flowing with honey, causing infamy.*—A town belonging to the tribe of Zebulun. Josh. xix. 11.

DABERATH, Dab'-be-rath, *word, thing, bee, submissive.*—A town mentioned Josh. xix. 12.

DALAIAH, Da-la-i'-ah, *the poor of the Lord.*—A descendant of king David. 1 Chron. iii. 24.

DALMANUTHA, Dal-ma-new'-thah, *a bucket, leanness, branch.*—A place on the western side of the lake of Tiberias, near Magdala. Mark viii. 10.

DALMATIA, Dal-may'-she-a, *deceitful lamps, vain brightness.*—A part of old Illyria, lying along the gulf of Venice. Titus preached here. 2 Tim. iv. 10.

DAMARIS, Dam'-a-ris, *a little woman.*—A female mentioned Acts xvii. 34.

DAMASCUS, Da-mas'-kus, *a sack full of blood, similitude of burning.*—A celebrated city of Asia, and anciently the capital of Syria; one of the most venerable places in the world for its antiquity. Gen. xv. 2; 2 Cor. xi. 32.

DAN, Dan, *judgment, he that judges.*—1. The fifth son of Jacob. Gen. xxx. 6. 2. A city called after Dan, situated at the foot of Mount Libanus. 1 Kings xii. 29.

DANIEL, Dan'-e-el, *judgment of God.*—1. A prophet descended from the royal family of David, and carried captive to Babylon when very young, in the fourth year of Jehoiakim, king of Judah, A.M. 3398. He was a very extraordinary prophet, favoured of God, and honoured of men beyond all his contemporaries. His prophecies are remarkably clear and explicit. 2. A son of David by Abigail. 1 Chron. iii. 1. 3. A priest who attended Ezra to Judea, A.M. 3550. Ezra viii. 2.

DAN-JAAN, Dan-jay'-an.—A city in Palestine. 2 Sam. xxiv. 6.

DANNAH, Dan'-nah.—A city in Palestine, in the tribe of Judah. Josh. xv. 49.

DARA, Day'-rah, *generation, house of the shepherd, companion, race of wickedness.*—A descendant from the patriarch Judah. 1 Chron. ii. 6.

DARDA, Dar'-dah, *the dwelling-place of knowledge.*—A wise man mentioned 1 Kings iv. 31.

DARIUS, Da-ry'-us, *he that inquires and informs himself.*—The name of several princes, some of whom are mentioned in Scripture. 1. DARIUS the *Mede*, Dan. v. 31; ix. 1; xi. 1. He was the son of Astyages, king of the Medes, and brother of Mandane, the mother of Cyrus. 2. DARIUS, the son of *Hystaspes*, who is supposed to be the Ahasuerus of Scripture, and the husband of Esther.

3. DARIUS CODOMANUS. He was of the royal family of the Persians, but remote from the crown. He was raised to the throne by the famous eunuch Bagoas. He is that Darius with whom Alexander the Great contended in war. See Dan. vii. 5, 6; ii. 39, 40; viii. 5—7, 20—22.

DARKON, Dar'-kon, *of generation, or the possession.*— One who returned from the Babylonish captivity. Ezra ii. 56.

DATHAN, Day'-than, *laws, rites.*—One of those who conspired against Moses and Aaron. Num. xvi. 1, &c.

DAVID, Day'-vid, *beloved, dear.*—The son of Jesse, of the tribe of Judah, and town of Bethlehem. He was born, according to Usher, A.M. 2919. He was the most celebrated king of Israel. His history is recorded in the books of Samuel.

DEBIR, De'-ber, otherwise called Kirjath-sepher.— 1. A city in the tribe of Judah, near Hebron. Josh. x. 39; xii. 13; xv. 15. 2. A town beyond Jordan. Josh. xiii. 26. 3. A king of Eglon. Josh. x. 3.

DEBORAH, Deb'-o-rah, *a word, a bee.*—1. Rebekah's nurse. Gen. xxxv. 8. 2. A prophetess, the wife of Lapidoth, who judged Israel, and dwelt under a palm-tree, between Ramoth and Bethel. Judges iv. 5, &c.

DECAPOLIS, De-kap'-o-lis, *ten cities.*—A country in Palestine, so called because it contained ten principal cites, some situated on the west, and some on the east, side of Jordan. Matt. iv. 25.

DEDAN, De'-dan, *their breasts, friendship, uncle.*—The son of Raamah. Gen. x. 7. Or a descendant of Abraham. Gen. xxv. 3.

DEDANIM, Ded'-a-nim.—Descendants of Dedan. Isai. xxi. 13.

DEHAVITES, De-hay'-vites.—A people mentioned Ezra iv. 9, and thought to be the same with those spoken of 2 Kings xvii. 24.

71

DEKAR, De'-kar.—Father of one of Solomon's household. 1 Kings iv. 9.

DELAIAH, De-lay-i'-ah, *the poor of the Lord.*—1. The son of Elioenai, of David's family. 1 Chron. iii. 24. 2. One of Jehoiakim's counsellors, Jer. xxxvi. 12.

DELILAH, Del'-e-lah, *poor, head of hair, bucket.*—A beautiful woman, who lived in the valley of Sorek, with whom Samson was in love. Judges xvi. 4, &c.

DEMAS, De'-mas, *popular.*—A disciple of Paul, Col. iv. 14; but who afterwards forsook him. 2 Tim. iv. 10.

DEMETRIUS, De-me'-tre-us, *belonging to Ceres, to corn.*—There were two kings of this name, mentioned in the book of Maccabees. Two individuals of this name are mentioned in Scripture. 1. A silversmith of Ephesus, Acts xix. 24. 2. A pious man mentioned 3 John 12.

DERBE, Der'-be, *a sting.*—A city of Lycaonia. Acts xiv. 6.

DEUEL, De-yew'-el, *the knowledge of God.*—The son of Eliasaph. Num. i. 14.

DIANA, Dy-ay'-nah, *luminous, perfect.*—A celebrated goddess of the Heathens, who was honoured principally at Ephesus. Acts xix.

DIBLAIM, Dib'-la-im, *a cluster of figs.*—Gomer's daughter, whom Hosea married.

DIBON, Dy'-bon, *understanding, abundance of building.*—A city given to the tribe of Gad. Num. xxxii. 3, 34.

DIBON-GAD, Dy'-bon-gad, *abundance of sons, happy and powerful.*—A place mentioned Num. xxxiii. 45.

DIBRI, Dib'-ry.—A descendant of Gad. Lev. xxiv. 11.

DIDYMUS, Did'-e-mus, *a twin.*—The surname of Thomas. John xxi. 2.

DIKLAH, Dik'-lah.—The seventh son of Joktan. Gen. x. 27.

DILEAN, Dil'-e-an.—A city in the tribe of Judah. Josh. xv. 38.

DIMNAH, Dim'-nah, *dung.*—A city in the tribe of Zebulun. Josh. xxi. 35.

DIMON, Dy'-mon, *where it is red.*—A place in the land of Moab. Isai. xv. 9

DIMONAH, Dy-mo'-nah.—A town in the south of Judah. Josh. xv. 22.

DINAH, Dy'-nah, *judgment, who judges.*—The daughter of Jacob and Leah. Gen. xxx. 21.

DINAITES, Dy'-na-ites.—A people mentioned Ezra iv. 9, who opposed the re-building of Jerusalem.

DINHABAH, Din'-ha-bah, *she gives judgment.*—A city of Edom, where Bela the son of Beor, a descendant of Esau, reigned. Gen. xxxvi. 32.

DIONYSIUS, Dy-o-nish'-e-us, *divinely touched.*—A member of the Areopagus at Athens, and a convert of St. Paul. Acts xvii. 34. He was made afterwards first bishop of Athens.

DIOTREPHES, Dy-ot'-re-feez, *nourished of Jupiter.*—A worthless domineering man at Corinth. 3 John 9.

DISHAN, or DISHON, Dy'-shan, or Dy'-shon.—Descendants of Esau. Gen. xxxvi. 21.

DIZAHAB, Diz'-a-hab.—The name of a place. Deut. i. 1.

DODAI, Dod'-a-i.—One of David's captains. 1 Chron. xxvii. 4.

DODANIM, Dod'-a-nim.—A descendant of Javan. Gen. x. 4.

DODAVAH, Dod'-a-vah.—The father of Eliezer. 2 Chron. xx. 37.

DODO, Do'-do.—A descendant of Issachar. Judges x. 1.

DOEG, Do'-eg, *who acts with uneasiness, a fisherman.*—An Edomite chief herdsman to king Saul. 1 Sam. xxii. 18.

DOPHKAH, Dof'-kah, *a knocking.*—One of the encampments of the Israelites in the wilderness. Num. xxxiii. 12.

DOR, Dor, *generation, habitation.*—The capital of a country in the land of Canaan, called in Hebrew, Nephat-Dor. Josh. xii. 23.

DORCAS, Dor'-kas, *the female of a roebuck.*—A pious and benevolent woman. Acts ix. 36.

DOTHAN, Do'-than, *law, custom.*—A town twelve miles north of Samaria. Gen. xxxvii. 17.

DRUSILLA, Drew-sil'-lah, *watered by the dew.*—The third daughter of Agrippa the Great. She first married Azizus, king of the Emesenes; but in a short time left him, to marry Claudius Felix, governor of Judea. Acts xxiv. 24.

DUMAH, Dew'-mah, *silence, resemblance.*—1. A city of Palestine, in the tribe of Judah. Isai. xxi. 11. 2. A son of Ishmael, who perhaps gave the name to the above place. Gen. xxv. 14.

DURA, Dew'-rah, *generation, habitation.*—A plain in the neighbourhood of Babylon. Dan. iii. 1.

E

EBAL, E'-bal, *a heap, collection of old age.*—1. A descendant of Esau. Gen. xxxvi. 23. 2. A celebrated mountain in the tribe of Ephraim, over against Gerizim. Deut. xi. 29, &c.; xxvii.; xxviii.

EBED, E'-bed, *a servant or labourer.*—A person mentioned Judges ix. 26.

EBED-MELECH, E-bed'-me-lek, *the king's servant.*—An Ethiopian in the court of king Zedekiah. Jer. xxxviii. 7, &c.

EBEN-EZER, Eb-en-e'-zer, *the stone of help.*—1. The name of that field where the Israelites were defeated by the

Philistines. 1 Sam. iv. 1.   2. A memorial-stone set up by
Samuel to commemorate a victory over the Philistines.
1 Sam. vii. 12.

EBER, E'-ber, *one that passes, anger, wrath.*—A descendant of Shem. Gen. x. 21.

EBIASAPH, E-by'-a-saf, *a father that gathers together.*
—A son of Korah. 1 Chron. ix. 19.   Also a son of
Elkanah. 1 Chron. vi. 23.

EBRONAH, E-bro'-nah, *passing over, or being angry.*—
The thirty-first encampment of the Israelites. Num.
xxxiii. 34.

ECCLESIASTES, Ek-kle-ze-as'-tees, *the preacher.*—A
canonical book of the Old Testament, of which Solomon
was the author.

ED, Ed, *witness.*—An altar erected by the Israelites.
Josh. xxii. 34.

EDAR, E'-dar, *a flock.*—A place mentioned Gen.
xxxv. 21.

EDEN, E'-den, *pleasure or delight.*—The residence of
our first parents in a state of purity and innocence.   The
name has been given to several places which from their
situation were pleasant or delightful.   Amos (chap. i. 5)
speaks of an Eden in Syria, in the valley of Damascus:
some have therefore concluded that this was the original
Eden.   Others have fixed its site on the eastern part of
Mount Libanus.   But the opinion which has been most
generally received on this subject, is that which places the
garden on the lower Euphrates, between the junction of
that river with the Tigris and the Persian Gulf.

EDER, E'-der.—A city of Judah. Josh. xv. 21.

EDOM, E'-dom, *red, earthy, red earth.*—Gen. xxxvi. 1.
1. The name of Esau.   2. A province of Arabia which
derives its name from Esau or Edom, who there settled
in the mountains of Seir, in the land of the Horites, south-
east of the Dead Sea.

EDOMITES, E'-dom-ites.—Inhabitants of Edom. Gen.
xxxvi. 9.

EDREI, Ed'-re-i, *a very great mass, cloud, death of the wicked.*—1. A town situated beyond Jordan, in the tribe of Manasseh. Josh. xiii. 12. 2. A town in the tribe of Naphtali. Josh. xix. 37.

EGLAH, Eg'-lah, *heifer, chariot, round.*—The sixth wife of David, and mother of Ithream. 2 Sam. iii. 5.

EGLAIM, Eg'-la-im, *drops of the sea.*—A city beyond Jordan, to the east of the Dead Sea, in the land of Moab. Isai. xv. 8.

EGLON, Eg'-lon, *a heifer, a chariot.*—1. A king of Moab, who oppressed the Israelites. Judges iii. 14, 21. It is thought to have been a common name of the kings of Moab, as Abimelech was of the Philistines. 2. A city whose king was Debir. Josh. x. 3. 3. The name of a city in the tribe of Judah. Josh. xv. 39.

EGYPT, E'-jipt, *that binds or straitens, that troubles or oppresses.*—A country called in the Hebrew Scriptures, Mizraim. It is situated between the twenty-fourth and thirty-third degrees of north latitude, and between the twenty-ninth and thirty-fourth of east longitude, being six hundred miles long, and three hundred broad. It is bounded on the south by Ethiopia, on the north by the Mediterranean Sea, on the east by the Red Sea, and on the west by Libya. Exod. iii. 20.

EHI, E'-hy, *my brother.*—The sixth son of Benjamin. Gen. xlvi. 21.

EHUD, E'-hud, *he that praises.*—The son of Gera, a Benjamite. Judges iii. 15.

EKER, E'-ker, *barren, feeble.*—A descendant of Judah. 1 Chron. ii. 27.

EKRON, Ek'-ron, *barrenness, torn away.*—A city and government of the Philistines. It fell by lot to the tribe of Judah. Josh. xv. 45. Afterwards it was given to the tribe of Dan. Josh. xix. 43.

EKRONITES, Ek'-ron-ites.—Inhabitants of Ekron. Josh. xiii. 3.

ELADAH, El'-a-dah, *the eternity of God.*—A descendant of Ephraim the patriarch. 1 Chron. vii. 20.

ELAH, E'-lah, *an elm, oak, or oath, or imprecation.*—1. A ruler of Edom. Gen. xxxvi. 41. 2. The son of Baasha, king of Israel. 1 Kings xvi. 6—11. 3. The name of a valley, where David slew the giant Goliath. 1 Sam. xvii. 19.

ELAM, E'-lam, *a young man, a virgin, secret, an age.*—The eldest son of Shem, who settled in a country to which he gave his name. Gen. x. 22. It is frequently mentioned in Scripture, lying to the south-east of Shinar.

ELASAH, El'-a-sah, *the doings of God.*—One of the sons of Pashur. Ezra x. 22.

ELATH, E'-lath, *a hind, strength, an oak.*—1. A place in the wilderness where the Israelites sojourned. Deut. ii. 8. 2. A part of Idumea, on the Red Sea, the emporium of Syria in Asia. It was taken by David, who there established an extensive trade. Solomon also built ships there. 2 Chron. viii. 17, 18.

EL-BETH-EL, El-beth'-el, *the God of Bethel.*—A place where Jacob built an altar, in the land of Canaan. Gen. xxxv. 7.

ELDAAH, El'-da-ah, *the knowledge of God.*—A grandson of Abraham. Gen. xxv. 4.

ELDAD, El'-dad, *loved of God.*—One of the seventy elders of Israel. Num. xi. 24—26.

ELEAD, E'-le-ad, *witness of God.*—One of the grandsons of Ephraim, who was killed in the city of Gath. 1 Chron. vii. 21.

ELEALEH, E-le-ay'-leh, *ascension, or burnt-offering of God.*—A town belonging to the tribe of Reuben. Num. xxxii. 37.

ELEASAH, E-le-ay'-sah, *the doings of God.*—The son of Helez. 1 Chron. ii. 39.

ELEAZAR, E-le-ay'-zar, *help or court of God.*—1. The third son of Aaron, and his successor in the priesthood.

Exod. vi. 23.   2. The son of Abinadab, to whose care the
ark was entrusted when it was sent back by the Philistines.   1 Sam. vii. 1.   3. The son of Dodo, one of David's
worthies.   1 Chron. xi. 11—18.   4. The son of Eliud.
Matt. i. 15.

EL-ELOHE-ISRAEL, El el-o'-he iz'-ra-el, *God the God
of Israel.*—The name of an altar erected by Jacob. Gen.
xxxiii. 20.

ELEPH, E'-lef, *learning.*—A city of Palestine. Josh.
xviii. 28.

ELHANAN, El-hay'-nan, *grace, gift, or mercy of God.*
—The son of Dodo, one of David's warriors. 2 Sam. xxi.
19; 1 Chron. xi. 26.

ELI, E'-ly, *the offering or lifting up.*—1. A high-priest
of the Hebrews, of the race of Ithamar, who succeeded
Abdon, and governed the Hebrews, both as priest and
judge, during forty years. 1 Sam. i. 3.   2. Eli, or Heli.
Luke iii. 23.

ELIAB, E-ly'-ab, *God my father.*—1. The son of Helon,
prince of the tribe of Zebulun. Num. i. 9.   2. The son
of Jesse, David's brother. 1 Sam. xvi. 6.   3. One who
joined David at Ziklag. 1 Chron. xii. 9.   4. The son of
Elkanah, a Levite. 1 Chron. vi. 27.

ELIADA, E-ly'-a-dah, *the knowledge of God.*—1. The
son of David, by one of his concubines. 2 Sam. v. 16.
2. A general in Jehoshaphat's army. 2 Chron. xvii. 17.

ELIAH, E-ly'-ah, *God the Lord.*—1. A descendant of
Benjamin. 1 Chron. viii. 27.   2. One who returned from
captivity. Ezra x. 26.

ELIAHBA, E-ly'-ah-bah.—One of David's worthies.
2 Sam. xxiii. 32.

ELIAKIM, E-ly'-a-kim, *the resurrection of God, or
God the avenger.*—1. The son of Hilkiah, Hezekiah's
steward. 2 Kings xviii. 18.   2. Jehoiakim, king of Judah.
2 Kings xxiii. 34.

ELIAM, E-ly'-am, *the people of God.*—1. The father of Bathsheba, the wife of Uriah. 2 Sam. xi. 3. 2. A son of Ahithophel, one of David's worthies. 2 Sam. xxiii. 34.

ELIAS, E-ly'-as, *God the Lord, the strong Lord.*— See ELIJAH. John the Baptist. Matt. xvi. 14; Matt. xvii. 12.

ELIASAPH, E-ly'-a-saf, *the Lord increaseth.*—The son of Deuel, a prince of the tribe of Gad. Num. i. 14.

ELIASHIB, E-ly'-a-shib, *the God of conversion.*—A Jewish high-priest. 1 Chron. xxiv. 12.

ELIATHAH, E-ly'-a-thah, *thou art my God, my God comes.*—A son of Heman, and one of the singers in the temple. 1 Chron. xxv. 27.

ELIDAD, E-ly'-dad, *the beloved of God.*—The son of Chislon, a Benjamite, and one of the deputies appointed to divide the land of Canaan. Num. xxxiv. 21.

ELIEL, El'-e-el, *God my God.*—1. A brave man who followed David, and was with him at Ziklag. 1 Chron. xi. 46. 2. Another follower of David. 1 Chron. xii. 11.

ELIENAI, E-le-e'-na-i, *the God of mine eyes.*—One of the posterity of Benjamin. 1 Chron. viii. 20.

ELIEZER, E-le-e'-zer, *the help of God.*—1. A native of Damascus, and the steward of Abraham's house. Gen. xv. 1—3. 2. The son of Moses by Zipporah, born in Midian. Exod. xviii. 4. 3. A Levite of consequence. 1 Chron. xv. 24. 4. The son of Zichri, of the tribe of Reuben, a commander of twenty thousand men, under Solomon. 1 Chron. xxvii. 16. 5. The son of Dodavah, a prophet. 2 Chron. xx. 37. 6. The name of one who returned from Babylon. Ezra x. 23.

ELIHOREPH, El-e-ho'-ref, *the God of winter, of youth.* —A Jewish scribe. 1 Kings iv. 3.

ELIHU, E-ly'-hew, *he is my God himself.*—1. The son of Shemaiah, one of David's worthies. 1 Chron. xii. 20. 2. A porter of the temple. 1 Chron. xxvi. 7. 3. A brother of king David. 1 Chron. xxvii. 18.   4. One of Job's friends, a descendant of Nahor. Job xxxii. 2.   5. Grandfather of Elkanah, the father of Samuel. 1 Sam. i. 1.

ELIJAH, E-ly'-jah, *God the Lord, the strong Lord.*— A Jewish prophet, a native of the town of Tishbe, situated in the land of Gilead, beyond Jordan. See his history. 1 Kings xvii., xviii., xix.

ELIKA, El'-e-kah, *pelican of God.*—The Harodite, one of David's valiant men. 2 Sam. xxiii. 25.

ELIM, E'-lim, *the rams, the strong, the stags, the valleys.* —The sixth encampment of the Israelites. Exod. xv. 27.

ELIMELECH, E-lim'-e-lek, *my God is king.*—A person driven by famine from Bethlehem into Moab. Ruth i. 1—5.

ELIOENAI, El-e-e'-nay-i, *towards him are my eyes, my fountains, towards him is my poverty or misery.*—A descendant of Benjamin. 1 Chron. iii. 23.

ELIPHAL, El'-e-fal, *the God of deliverance.*—The son of Ur, one of David's great warriors. 1 Chron. xi. 35.

ELIPHALET, E-lif'-fa-let, *the God of deliverance.*—A son of David. 2 Sam. v. 16.

ELIPHAZ, El'-e-faz, *the endeavour of God.*—1. A son of Esau and his wife Adah. Gen. xxxvi. 4.   2. One of Job's friends. Job ii. 11.

ELIPHELEH, E-lif'-fe-leh, *the judgment of God.*—A singer and porter in the temple at Jerusalem. 1 Chron. xv. 21.

ELISABETH, or ELIZABETH, E-liz'-a-beth, *God hath sworn, the fulness of God.*—The wife of Zacharias, and mother of John the Baptist. Luke i. 5.

ELISEUS, El-i-see'-us.—The Greek name of Elisha. Luke iv. 27.

ELISHA, E-ly'-shah, *salvation of God.*—The son of Shaphat, Elijah's disciple and successor in the prophetic office. 1 Kings xix., &c.

ELISHAH, E-ly′-shah, *it is God, God that gives help.*— The son of Javan. Gen. x. 4.

ELISHAMA, E-lish′-a-mah, *God hearing.*—1. The son of Ammihud, and prince of the tribe of Ephraim. Num. vii. 48.   2. Two of David's sons bore this name. 1 Chron. iii. 6, 8.   3. The father of Nethaniah. 2 Kings xxv. 25. 4. A Levite, who was sent by Jehoshaphat to turn the Israelites from idolatry. 2 Chron. xvii. 8.

ELISHAPHAT, E-lish′-a-fat, *my God judgeth.*—The son of Zichri, who assisted Jehoiada in raising Joash to the throne. 2 Chron. xxiii. 1.

ELISHEBA, E-lish′-e-bah, *God hath sworn, or fulness of God.*—The daughter of Amminadab, sister of Naashon, and wife of Aaron. Exod. vi. 23.

ELISHUA, El-e-shew′-a, *God is my salvation.*—A son of David. 2 Sam. v. 15.

ELIUD, E-ly′-ud, *God is my praise.*—One in the genealogy of Christ. Matt. i. 14.

ELIZAPHAN, E-liz′-a-fan.—1. The son of Uzziel, uncle to Aaron. Num. iii. 30.   2. One of the deputies appointed to divide the land of promise. Num. xxxiv. 25.

ELIZUR, E-ly′-zur, *God is my strength, my rock.*—The son of Shedeur, and head of the tribe of Reuben in the time of Moses. Num. vii. 30.

ELKANAH, El′-ka-nah, *God the jealous, the reed of God.*—1. The son of Korah, and grandson of Amram. Exod. vi. 24.   2. The husband of Hannah, and father of Samuel. 1 Sam. i. 1.   3. One who went to David at Ziklag. 1 Chron. xii. 6.

ELKOSHITE, El′-ko-shite.—An inhabitant of Elkith, a village in Galilee. Nahum i. 1.

ELLASAR, El′-la-sar, *revolting from God.*—A city of the Canaanites. Gen. xiv. 1.

ELMODAM, El′-mo-dam, *God of measure, of the garment.* —One named in the genealogy of Christ. Luke iii. 28.

ELNAAM, El'-na-am.—One of David's worthies.—1 Chron. xi. 46.

ELNATHAN, El'-na-than, *God has given.*—1. The grandfather of Jehoiada, king of Judah. Jer. xxxvi. 12. 2. A person of consequence mentioned Ezra viii. 16.

ELON, E'-lon, *oak, grove, strong.*—1. A city in the tribe of Dan. Josh. xix. 43. 2. A Hittite, father of Bashemath, the wife of Esau. Gen. xxvi. 34. 3. A man of Zebulun. Num. xxvi. 26. 4. A judge of Israel, who succeeded Ibzan. Judges xii. 11.

ELON-BETH-HANAN, E'-lon-beth'-ha-nan, *the house of great mercy.*—A place in the land of Judah. 1 Kings iv. 9.

ELOTH, E'-loth, *strong.*—A seaport of Edom, on the Red Sea. 2 Chron. viii. 17.

ELPAAL, El'-pa-al.—A descendant of Benjamin. 1 Chron. viii. 12.

EL-PARAN, El-pay'-ran.—A place mentioned Gen. xiv. 6.

ELTEKEH, El'-te-keh.—A city in the tribe of Dan. Josh. xix. 44.

ELTEKON, El'-te-kon.—A town in the tribe of Judah. Josh. xv. 59.

ELTOLAD, El'-to-lad.—A town in the tribe of Judah. Josh. xv. 30.

ELUL, E'-lul, *cry, outcry.*—The sixth month of the Hebrew ecclesiastical year, and the twelfth of the civil year, answering to part of our August and September, containing twenty-nine days.

ELUZAI, E-lew'-za-i, *God is my strength.*—An officer in David's army, who resorted to him at Ziklag. 1 Chron. xii. 5.

ELYMAS, El'-e-mas, *a sorcerer, a magician.*—A sorcerer mentioned Acts xiii. 8.

ELZABAD, El'-za-bad, *the dowry of God.*—1. The son of Shemaiah, a Levite, one of the porters of the temple. 1 Chron. xxvi. 7.   2. The name of one of David's worthies. 1 Chron. xii. 12.

ELZAPHAN, El'-za-fan. — A descendant of Levi. Exod. vi. 22.

EMIMS, E'-mims, *fears of terrors, people.*—Ancient inhabitants of the land of Canaan, beyond Jordan, who were defeated by Chedorlaomer and his allies. Gen. xiv. 5.

EMMANUEL, Em-man'-ew-el, *God with us.*—A name of Jesus Christ. Matt. i. 23.

EMMAUS, Em'-ma-us, *people despised.*—A village seven or eight miles north of Jerusalem, in the tribe of Judah. Luke xxiv. 13.

EMMOR, Em'-mor, *an ass.*—The father of Sychem. Acts vii. 16.

ENAM, E'-nam, *a fountain or well, the eyes of them.*— A town. Josh. xv. 34.

ENAN, E'-nan.—A descendant of Naphtali. Num. i. 15.

EN-DOR, En'-dor, *fountain, or eye of generation.*—A city in the tribe of Manasseh, where the witch resided whom Saul consulted. 1 Sam. xxviii. 7; Josh. xvii. 11.

EN-EGLAIM, En-eg-lay'-im, *the eye of the calves, of chariots, of roundness.*—A town anciently on the east side of Sodom. Ezek. xlvii. 10.

EN-GANNIM, En-gan'-nim, *the eye of protection, or well of gardens.*—1. A city in the tribe of Judah. Josh. xv. 34. 2. A city in the tribe of Issachar. Josh. xix. 21.

EN-GEDI, En'-ge-dy, *fountain of the goat, of happiness.* —1. A city near Sodom.   2. A cave in which Saul was under David's power. 1 Sam. xxiv. 1.

EN-HADDAH, En-had'-dah, *quick sight, or the well of gladness.*—A city belonging to the tribe of Issachar. Josh. xix. 21.

EN-HAKKORE, En-hak′-ko-re, *the fountain of him who prayed.*—A place so named by Samson, where he found water to quench his thirst after slaying the Philistines. Judges xv. 19.

EN-MISHPAT, En-mish′-pat, *fountain of judgment.*—A place sometimes called Kadesh. Gen. xiv. 7.

ENOCH, E′-nok, *dedicated, disciplined, well-regulated.*—1. The son of Cain, in honour of whom the first city built by Cain was called Enoch. Gen. iv. 17. 2. The son of Jared, and father of Methuselah. He pleased God, and was translated to heaven. Heb. xi. 5.

ENON, or ÆNON, E′-non, *a cloud, his fountain.*—A place near Salim, by the river Jordan, where John baptized. John iii. 23.

ENOS, E′-nos, *fallen man, subject to all evil.*—The son of Seth, and father of Cainan. Gen. iv. 26.

EN-ROGEL, En-ro′-gel, *the fuller's fountain.*—A fountain situated to the east of Jerusalem, at the foot of Mount Sion. Josh. xv. 7; xviii. 16.

EN-SHEMESH, En′-she-mesh, *fountain of the sun.*—A place near the frontiers of Judah and Benjamin; but whether a town or fountain is uncertain. Josh. xv. 7.

EN-TAPPUAH, En-tap′-pu-ah, *the well of an apple.*—A place in the tribe of Manasseh. Josh. xvii. 7.

EPAPHRAS, Ep′-a-fras, *covered with foam.*—A native of Colosse, and some affirm, the first bishop of that city. Col. i. 7; iv. 12.

EPAPHRODITUS, E-paf-ro-dy′-tus, *agreeable, handsome.*—An individual sent by the Philippians with money to St. Paul when in prison at Rome. Phil. ii. 25; iv. 18.

EPENETUS, E-pen′-e-tus, *laudable, worthy of praise.*—St. Paul's disciple, whom he calls the first-fruits of Achaia. Rom. xvi. 5.

EPHAH, E′-fah, *weary, to fly as a bird.*—1. The eldest son of Midian, Gen. xxv. 4, who gave his name to a city and a small extent of land in the country of Midian, situated on the eastern shore of the Dead Sea. Isai. lx. 6, &c. 2. Caleb's concubine. 1 Chron. ii. 46. 3. A measure for things dry and liquid among the Jews.

EPHAI, E'-fay.—A Jew, mentioned Jer. xl. 8.

EPHER, E'-fer.—The second son of Midian, and brother of Ephah. Gen. xxv. 4; 1 Chron. i. 33.

EPHES-DAMMIM, E'-fez-dam'-mim, *the effusion or drop of blood.*—A place in Canaan where the Philistines encamped. 1 Sam. xvii. 1.   See also 1 Chron. xi. 13, 14.

EPHESUS, Ef'-fe-sus, *desirable.*—A celebrated city of Ionia, in Asia Minor, situated upon the river Cayster. It was noted for its famous temple of Diana, which for its size and workmanship was accounted one of the seven wonders of the world. Acts xviii. 19.

EPHLAL, Ef'-lal, *judging, or praying.*—A descendant of the patriarch Judah. 1 Chron. ii. 37.

EPHPHATHA, Eff'-fa-thah, *be opened.* Mark vii. 34.

EPHRAIM, E'-fra-im, *that brings forth fruit, or grows.* —1. The second son of the patriarch Joseph, by Asenath, Potiphar's daughter. Gen. xli. 52.   2. A city in the tribe of Ephraim, situated towards Jordan. The wood or forest of Ephraim, in which Absalom's army was routed, and himself killed and buried, lay beyond Jordan. 2. Sam. xviii. 6, &c.

EPHRATAH, Eff'-ra-tah, *abundance, bearing fruit.*— A town in Judea. Psalm cxxxii. 6; Micah v. 2. The same as BETHLEHEM.

EPHRATH, Eff'-rath, *abundance, bearing fruit.*— Caleb's second wife, who was the mother of Hur. 1 Chron. ii. 19.   From her it is thought that the city of Ephratah had its name.   It is sometimes called Ephrath. Gen. xxxv. 19.

EPHRON, E'-fron, *dust.*—The son of Zohar, who sold the cave of Machpelah to Abraham. Gen. xxiii. 8, 10.

EPICUREANS, Ep-e-kew-re'-ans, *who give assistance.* —A sect of philosophers greatly prevailing in Greece and Rome.   Their founder was Epicurus. Acts xvii. 18.

ER, Er, *watch, enemy.*—The eldest son of Judah, and husband of Tamar. Gen. xxxviii. 7.

ERAN, E'-ran.—A descendant of Ephraim. Num. xxvi. 36.

ERASTUS, E-ras'-tus, *lovely, amiable.*—A Corinthian, and disciple of St. Paul : called by this apostle, chamberlain of the city, Rom. xvi. 23 ; that is, of Corinth, where the apostle then was.

ERECH, E'-rek, *length, health.*—A city of Chaldea, built by Nimrod. Gen. x. 10.

ERI, E'-ry.—A son of Gad. Gen. xlvi. 16.

ESAIAS, E-zay'-yas, *the salvation of the Lord.*—The same as ISAIAH. Matt. iii. 3.

ESARHADDON, E'-sar-had'-don, *that binds joy, or closes the point.*—The son of Sennacherib, and his successor in the kingdom of Assyria. 2 Kings xix. 37. He is called Sargon. Isai. xx. 1.

ESAU, E'-saw, *he that does or finishes.*—The son of Isaac by Rebekah, born A.M. 2168. See Gen. xxv. 24, &c.

ESEK, E'-sek, *contention.*—A well of Gerar. Gen. xxvi. 20.

ESH-BAAL, Esh'-ba-al, *the fire of the idol.* The same with Ishbosheth, the fourth son of Saul. 1 Chron. viii. 33. The Hebrews, to avoid pronouncing the word BAAL, *lord,* used BOSHETH, *confusion.* Instead of MEPHIBAAL they said MEPHIBOSHETH; and instead of ISHBAAL, ISH-BOSHETH. 2 Sam. ii. 8.

ESHBAN, Esh'-ban, *fire of the sun.*—A city in the tribe of Judah. Also a descendant from Esau. Gen. xxxvi. 26.

ESHCOL, Esh'-kol, *a bunch of grapes.*—1. One of Abraham's allies, who dwelt with him in Mamre, and accompanied him in the pursuit of Chedorlaomer and other confederate kings, who pillaged Sodom. Gen.

xiv. 24. 2. A valley or brook in which the Hebrew
messengers who went to spy the land of Canaan, cut a
branch of grapes, so large that it was as much as two men
could carry. It was situated in the south part of Judah.
Num. xiii. 24; xxxii. 9.

ESHEAN, E'-she-an.—A mountainous place of Palestine, in the tribe of Judah. Josh. xv. 52.

ESHEK, E'-shek, *contention.*—One of king Saul's
posterity. 1 Chron. viii. 39.

ESHTAOL, Esh'-ta-ol, *stout, strong woman.*—A town
in the tribe of Dan, first belonging to Judah. Josh. xv. 33.

ESHTEMOA, Esh-tem'-o-a, *which is heard, the bosom
of a woman.*—A city in the southern part of Judah. Josh.
xxi. 14.

ESHTEMOH, Esh'-te-moh.—The same as ESHTEMOA.

ESHTON, Esh'-ton.—One of the posterity of Judah.
1 Chron. iv. 11.

ESLI, Es'-ly, *near me, he that separates.*—The son of
Nagge, one of the ancestors of Christ. Luke iii. 25.

ESROM, Es'-rom, *the dart of joy, division of the song.*—
A person mentioned Matt. i. 3.

ESTHER, Es'-ter, *secret, hidden.*—The book of Esther
is so called, because it contains the history of Esther, a
Jewish captive, who by her remarkable accomplishments
gained the affection of king Ahasuerus, and, by marriage
with him, was raised to the throne of Persia. See the
Book.

ETAM, E'-tam, *their bird or covering.*—A city in the
tribe of Judah, lying between Bethlehem and Tekoa.
2 Chron. xi. 6. The rock Etam was that to which Samson
retired when he had burned the harvest of the Philistines.
Judges xv. 8.

ETHAM, E'-tham, *their strength or sign.*—The third
station of the Israelites after they left Egypt. Num.
xxxiii. 6.

87

ETHAN, E'-than, *strong, the gift of the island.*—The Ezrahite, one of the wisest men of his time: nevertheless Solomon was wiser than he. 1 Kings iv. 31.

ETHANIM, Eth'-a-nim, *strong, valiant.*—One of the Hebrew months. 1 Kings viii. 2. In this month Solomon's temple was dedicated.

ETHBAAL, Eth'-ba-al, *towards the idol, he that rules.*—King of the Zidonians, father of Jezebel, wife of Ahab. 1 Kings xvi. 31.

ETHER, E'-ther.—A city of Palestine, in the tribe of Judah. Also of Simeon. Josh. xv. 42 ; xix. 7.

ETHIOPIA, E-the-o'-pe-a, in Hebrew, *Cush, blackness:* in Greek, it signifies *heat.*—A very extensive country of Africa, comprehending Abyssinia, Nubia, and Abex. Gen. ii. 13. See Cush.

ETHNAN, Eth'-nan.—One of the posterity of Asher. 1 Chron. iv. 7.

ETHNI, Eth'-ny.—A descendant of Levi. 1 Chron. vi. 41.

EUBULUS, Yew'-bew-lus, *a prudent counsellor.*—A disciple of St. Paul. 2 Tim. iv. 21.

EUNICE, Yew-ny'-se, *a good victory.*—The mother of Timothy, who was a Jewess by birth, but married to a Greek, Timothy's father. 2 Tim. i. 5.

EUODIAS, Yew-o'-de-as, *sweet scent.*—A person spoken of by St. Paul, Phil. iv. 2.

EUPHRATES, Yew-fra'-tees, *that makes fruitful.*—A large river, the source of which is in the mountains of Armenia. It runs through Cappadocia, Syria, Arabia, Chaldea, and Mesopotamia, and falls into the Persian Gulf. Gen. ii. 14.

EUROCLYDON, Yew-rok'-le-don, *the north-east wind.*—Acts xxvii. 14. A dangerous wind, now called a Levanter.

EUTYCHUS, Yew'-te-kus, *happy, fortunate.* — The name of a young man at Troas, who fell from a window when Paul was preaching. Acts xx. 9.

EVE, *living, enlivening.*—The first woman, and the mother of all that live. Gen. iii. 20.

EVI, E'-vy.—One of the princes of the Midianites. Num. xxxi. 8.

EVIL-MERODACH, E'-vil-mer-o'-dak, *the fool of Merodach, or despising the bitterness of the fool.*—The son and successor of Nebuchadnezzar the Great, king of Babylon. 2 Kings xxv. 27.

EXODUS, Eks'-o-dus, *a going out.*—The second book of Moses, and so called in the Greek version, because it relates the departure of the Israelites out of Egypt.

EZBAI, Ez'-ba-i.—One of David's worthies. 1 Chron. xi. 37.

EZBON, Ez'-bon, *hastening to understand.*—A descendant of Benjamin. Gen. xlvi. 16.

EZEKIAS, Ez-e-ky'-as.—Mentioned Matt. i. 9.

EZEKIEL, E-ze'-ke-el, *the strength of God.*—The son of Buzi, a prophet in the house of Aaron, carried away captive to Babylon by Nebuchadnezzar, with Jehoiachin, king of Judah. Ezek. i. 1, &c. He began to prophesy A.M. 3409, being the fifth year of his captivity.

EZEL, E'-zel, *going abroad, distillation.*—The name of a stone mentioned in the agreement of Jonathan and David. 1 Sam. xx. 19.

EZER, E'-zer.—The son of Ephraim. 1 Chron. vii. 21.

EZION-GABER, E'-ze-on-gay'-ber, *the wood of the man, counsel of the man, of the strong.*—A city of Idumea, on the coast of the Red Sea. Num. xxxiii. 35.

EZRA, Ez'-rah, *helper.*—The author of the book which bears his name : he was of the sacerdotal family, being a direct descendant from Aaron, and successor to Zerubbabel in the government of Judea. See the Book.

EZRAHITE, Ez'-ra-hite.—Mentioned 1 Kings iv. 31.

EZRI, Ez'-ry, *a helper.*—Overseer of tillage in Judea, appointed by Solomon. 1 Chron. xxvii. 26.

F

FELIX, Fe'-liks, *happy, prosperous.*—The successor of Cumanus in the government of Judea. Acts xxiii. 26; xxiv. 3.

FESTUS, Fes'-tus, *festival, joyful.*—The successor of Felix in the government of Judea. Acts xxv. 1.

FORTUNATUS, For-tew-nay'-tus, *happy, prosperous.*—One whom St. Paul mentions 1 Cor. xvi. 17, who came from Corinth to Ephesus to visit the apostle.

G

GAAL, Gay'-al, *contempt, abomination.*—One that fought against Abimelech. Judges ix. 26.

GAASH, Gay'-ash, *tempest, overthrow.*—A hill in the inheritance of Ephraim. Josh. xxiv. 30. The brook mentioned 2 Sam. xxiii. 30 was probably at the foot of this mountain.

GABA, Gay'-bah, *a hill, a cup.*—A city in the tribe of Benjamin. Josh. xviii. 24.

GABBAI, Gab'-bay.—A chief of the tribe of Benjamin. Neh. xi. 8.

GABBATHA, Gab'-ba-thah, *high, elevated :* in Greek, λιθοστροτος, *paved with stones.*—A place in Pilate's palace, from whence he pronounced judgment on Christ. John xix. 13.

GABRIEL, Gay'-bre-el, *God is my strength.*—One of the principal angels in heaven, sent to Daniel to explain to him certain visions. Dan. viii. 16 ; ix. 21. The same angel was sent to Zacharias. Luke i. 19. Also to Mary. Luke i. 26.

GAD, Gad, *a band, happy, armed and prepared.*—
1. The son of Jacob and Zilpah, Leah's servant. Gen.
xxx. 9—11. 2. A prophet, and friend of David, who
followed him during his troubles, when persecuted by Saul.
2 Sam. xxiv. 11.

GADARA, Gad'-a-rah.—The principal town of Perea,
about eight miles eastward of the lake Tiberias. Mark
v. 1.

GADARENES, Gad-a-ree'ns, *surrounded, walled.*—
The inhabitants of Gadara : which see.

GADDI, Gad'-dy, *my happiness, my troop, a kid.*—The
son of Susi, of the tribe of Manasseh. One of the spies.
Num. xiii. 11.

GADDIEL, Gad'-de-el, *the goat of God, the Lord is my
army.*—The son of Sodi, of the tribe of Zebulun. One of
the spies. Num. xiii. 10.

GADI, Gay'-dy.—1. The father of Menahem, who
usurped the kingdom of Israel. 2 Kings xv. 14. 2. The
name of a place, where Bani, one of David's army, was born.
2 Sam. xxiii. 36.

GADITES, Gad'-ites.—Descendants of Gad. Deut.
iii. 12.

GAHAM, Gay'-ham.—A son of Nahor, Abraham's
brother, by his concubine Reumah. Gen. xxii. 24.

GAHAR, Gay'-har.—One whose children were Nethinims. Ezra ii. 47.

GAIUS, Gay'-e-us, *lord, an earthy man.*—St. Paul's
disciple, mentioned Acts xix. 29.

GALAL, Gay'-lal.—A Levite who settled first in Judea,
after the Babylonish captivity. 1 Chron. ix. 15.

GALATIA, Gal-lay'-she-a, *white, of the colour of milk.*
—A province of the Lesser Asia, bounded on the west by
Phrygia, on the east by the river Halys, on the north by
Paphlagonia, and on the south by Lycaonia. It took its
name from the Galatæ, or Gauls, who settled there.

GALATIANS, Gal-lay'-she-ans.—The people of Galatia: to the Christians of this country, St. Paul addressed one of his Epistles.

GALEED, Gal'-e-ed, *the heap of witness.*—A pillar of stones raised by Jacob as witness of the covenant between him and Laban. Gen. xxxi. 47.

GALILÆANS, Gal-le-lee'-ans.—Inhabitants of Galilee. A sect of Jews which sprung up in the time of our Saviour in Judea. One Judas, a native of Gaulan, in Upper Galilee, was the author of it. Luke xiii. 2.

GALILEE, Gal'-le-lee, *wheel, revolution, heap.*—A province of Palestine, which extends principally into the northern parts of it. Matt. iv. 15.

GALLIM, Gal'-lim, *who heap up, cover, roll.*—A city of Benjamin, about four miles north of Jerusalem. 1 Sam. xxv. 44; Isai. x. 30.

GALLIO, Gal'-le-o, *he that sucks, or lives upon milk.*— The brother of the famous Seneca the philosopher. He was at first named Marcus Annæus Novatus; but being adopted by Lucius Junius Gallio, he took the name of his adoptive father. It was to Gallio's tribunal, whilst he was pro-consul of Achaia, that the Jews dragged St. Paul. Acts xviii. 12.

GAMALIEL, Ga-may'-le-el, *recompence, camel, weaned of God.*—1. The son of Pedahzur, who was prince of the tribe of Manasseh, when Moses brought the Israelites out of Egypt. Num. i. 10; ii. 20. 2. A celebrated rabbi, and doctor of the Jewish law, under whose tuition the great apostle of the Gentiles was brought up. Acts xxii. 3.

GAMMADIMS, Gam'-ma-dims.—Soldiers placed in the towers of Tyrus: men who came from Gammade, a town of Phœnicia. Ezek. xxvii. 11.

GAMUL, Gay'-mul, *recompence.*—One of the orders into which the priests were divided. 1 Chron. xxiv. 17.

GAREB, Gay'-reb.—1. A brave officer of David. 2 Sam. xxiii. 38. 2. A hill near Jerusalem. Jer. xxxi. 39.

GATAM, Gay'-tam, *their lowing, their touch.*—The son of Eliphaz, the son of Esau. Gen. xxxvi. 11.

GATH, Gath, *a press.*—A celebrated city of the Philistines, and one of their five principalities. 1 Sam. vi. 17.

GATH-HEPHER, Gath-he'-fer, *the press of the delver.*—A town in Galilee, where the prophet Jonah was born. 2 Kings xiv. 25.

GATH-RIMMON, Gath-rim'-mon, *the press of the granite, exalted press.*—1. A city belonging to Dan. Josh. xix. 45. 2. A city in the half-tribe of Manasseh. Josh. xxi. 25. 3. A city in the half-tribe of Ephraim. 1 Chron. vi. 69.

GAZA, Gay'-zah, *strong, a goat.*—1. A city of the Philistines, made by Joshua part of the tribe of Judah. Josh. xv. 47. 2. A city of Ephraim. 1 Chron. vii. 28.

GAZABAR, Gaz'-a-bar, *treasure.*—A Persian, the father of Mithredath. Ezra i. 8.

GAZER, Gay'-zer, *dividing, or sentence.*—A city of the Philistines, in the tribe of Ephraim. 2 Sam. v. 25.

GAZEZ, Gay'-zez, *a passing over.*—The name of a son and grandson of Caleb. 1 Chron. ii. 46.

GAZZAM, Gaz'-zam.—One who returned from the Babylonish captivity. Ezra ii. 48.

GEBA, Ge'-bah, *a hill, a cup.*—A hill among the cities of Benjamin. 1 Chron. vi. 60.

GEBAL, Ge'-bal, *bound, limit.*—Probably a city in Arabia. Psal. lxxxiii. 7.

GEBER, Ge'-ber.—The son of Uri, and governor of the province of Gilead and Rusan, beyond Jordan, in the reign of Solomon. 1 Kings iv. 19.

GEBIM, Ge'-bim, *grashoppers, height.*—A place, the situation of which is uncertain. Isai. x. 31.

93

GEDALIAH, Ged-a-ly′-ah, *God is my greatness, fringe of the Lord.*—1. The son of Ahikam, who was left by Nebuchadnezzar in Palestine, after the destruction of Jerusalem and the temple, that he might govern the remainder of the people who continued there, and recall those who had fled. Jer. xl., xli. 2. The grandfather of the prophet Zephaniah. Zeph. i. 1. 3. A Levite, the son of Jeduthun. 1 Chron. xxv. 3. 4. The son of Pashur. Jer. xxxviii. 1.

GEDER, Ge′-der.—A place in Judea, the king of which was killed by Joshua. Josh. xii. 13.

GEDERAH, Ge-de′-rah.—A city in the tribe of Judah. Josh. xv. 36.

GEDEROTH, Ge-de′-roth.—A city of Canaan. 2 Chron. xxviii. 18.

GEDEROTHAIM, Ged-e-roth-ay′-im. — A city of Palestine, in the tribe of Judah. Josh. xv. 36.

GEDOR, Ge′-dor.—A city of Palestine, in the tribe of Judah, in the mountains. Josh. xv. 58. 2. The son of Jared. 1 Chron. iv. 18.

GEHAZI, Ge-hay′-zy, *valley of sight, or the breast.*—The servant of Elisha. 2 Kings v. 20 ; viii. 4.

GELILOTH, Gel′-e-loth, *revolution.*—Josh. xviii. 17. The same as GILGAL, as appears from Josh. xv. 7 ; Judges iii. 19.

GEMALLI, Ge-mal′-ly, *wares, or a camel.*—One of the tribe of Dan, whose son was sent to spy out the land of Canaan. Num. xiii. 12.

GEMARIAH, Gem-a-ry′-ah, *accomplishment of the Lord.*—1. The son of Hilkiah, who was sent to Babylon with Elasah, the son of Shaphan, from Zedekiah, king of Judah, to carry tribute-money to Nebuchadnezzar, and a letter from Jeremiah to the captives in Babylon. Jer. xxix. 3. 2. The son of Shaphan, one of Jehoiakim's counsellors. Jer. xxxvi. 12.

GENESIS, Jen′-e-sis, *generation.*—The first book of Moses.

GENNESARET, or **GENNESARETH**, Ge-ness'-a-ret, or Ge-ness'-a-reth, *the garden, or protection of the prince.* —A small district of Galilee, extending about four miles along the north-western shore of the sea of Galilee, or Gennesareth, so called from this same region. It is probable that Gennesareth is a word moulded from Cinneroth, the ancient name of a city and tract of country in this very situation. Matt. xiv. 34.

GENTILES, Jen'-tiles.—The Jews called those who had not received the faith or law of God, by a word meaning *the nations*, in Latin, *gentes*, whence the word Gentiles. In the writings of St. Paul, the Gentiles are generally denoted as Greeks. Rom. i. 14—16; ii. 9; iii.; &c.

GENUBATH, Gen-yew'-bath, *theft, garden, or protection of the daughter.*—The son of Hadad, the Edomite, and Tahpenes, sister to Pharaoh's queen. 1 Kings xi. 20.

GERA, Ge'-ra, *pilgrimage, dispute.*—1. The father of Ehud. Judges iii. 15. 2. The father of Shimei. 2 Sam. xvi. 5.

GERAH, Ge'-rah.—The twentieth part of a shekel. Exod. xxx. 13.

GERAR, Ge'-rar, *a dispute.*—A royal city of the Philistines. Gen. xx. 1.

GERASA, Ger'-a-sah.—A city on the east side of the Dead Sea, by some placed in Arabia, and by others in Cœlo-Syria.

GERGESENES, or **GIRGASHITES**, Ger-ge-see'ns, or Ger'-ga-shites, *those who come from pilgrimage or from fight.*—A people mentioned Matt. viii. 28.

GERIZIM, Ger'-e-zim, *cutters.*—The name of a mountain near Shechem, in the tribe of Ephraim, a province of Samaria. Deut. xi. 29; xxvii. 12.

GERSHOM, Ger'-shom, *a stranger there, a traveller of reputation.*—The son of Moses and Zipporah. Exod. ii. 22.

GERSHON, Ger'-shon, *his banishment, the change of pilgrimage.*—A son of Levi, and prince of one of the great families of the Levites. Num. iii. 21—25.

GESHAM, Ge'-sham, *drawing near*.—A descendant from Hezron. 1 Chron. ii. 47.

GESHEM, Ge'-shem.—An Arabian, who opposed Nehemiah in the building of the temple. Neh. ii. 19.

GESHUR, Ge'-shur, *the sight of the valley.*—A city of Syria, where Talmai was king in the time of David. 2 Sam. xv. 8; xiii. 37.

GESHURI, Gesh'-yew-ry, *the sight of the valley.*—A city of Syria. Deut. iii. 14.

GESHURITES, Gesh'-yew-rites.—The inhabitants of Geshur. Josh. xii. 5.

GETHER, Ge'-ther, *the vale of trial, of searching, the press of iniquity.*—The third son of Aram, the son of Shem. Gen. x. 23.

GETHSEMANE, Geth-sem'-a-ne, *a very fat valley.*—A small village in the mount of Olives, into a garden of which Jesus Christ sometimes retreated; and here he had his bitter agony, and was apprehended by Judas and his band. Matt. xxvi. 36.

GEUEL, Ge-yew'-el, *God's redemption.*—One of the spies, of the tribe of Gad. Num. xiii. 15.

GEZER, Ge'-zer, *dividing, or a sentence.*—A place which Joshua took in Canaan. Josh. xii. 12.

GEZRITES, Gez'-rites.—Inhabitants of Gezer. 1 Sam. xxvii. 8.

GIAH, Gy'-ah, *to draw out, to guide, a sigh.*—A place in Canaan. 2 Sam. ii. 24.

GIBBAR, Gib'-bar, *manly, strong.*—One who returned from the Babylonish captivity. Ezra ii. 20.

GIBBETHON, Gib'-be-thon, *high, elevated.*—A city of the tribe of Dan, given to the Levites. Josh. xxi. 23.

GIBEAH, Gib'-e-ah, *a hill.*—A city in the tribe of Benjamin, lying north of Jerusalem, the birth-place of king Saul. Judges xix., xx., xxi.

GIBEON, Gib'-e-on, *hill, cup, that which is without.*—
A city seated on a hill, about forty furlongs north of
Jerusalem, and the principal city of the Gibeonites. Josh.
ix. 17.

GIBEONITES, Gib'-e-on-ites.—Inhabitants of Gibeon.
See Josh. ix. 3, 4, &c.; 2 Sam. xxi. 1, &c.

GIBLITES, Gib'-lites.—A people of Canaan. Josh. xiii. 5.

GIDDALTI, Gid-dal'-ty.—One of the sons of Heman,
a Levite. 1 Chron. xxv. 4.

GIDDEL, Gid'-del.—One who returned from the
Babylonish captivity. Ezra ii. 47.

GIDEON, Gid'-e-on, *he that bruises, cutting off iniquity.*
—The son of Joash, of the tribe of Manasseh, the same
with Jerubbaal, the seventh judge of Israel. See Judges
vi., vii., viii.

GIHON, Gy'-hon, *valley of grace, impetuous.*—1. The
name of one of the four rivers, the source of which was in
Paradise. Gen. ii. 13. 2. A fountain to the west of Jerusalem, at which Solomon was anointed king, by the high-
priest Zadok, and the prophet Nathan. 1 Kings i. 33.

GILALAI, Gil'-a-lay, *a wheel, or marble.*—A Levite,
who officiated at the dedication of the new walls of
Jerusalem. Neh. xii. 36.

GILBOA, Gil'-bo-ah, *revolution of inquiry.*—A mountain
celebrated for the death of Saul and his son Jonathan.
1 Sam. xxxi. 1, &c. A ridge on the north of Bethshan, or
Scythopolis.

GILEAD, Gil'-le-ad, *the mass of testimony.*—1. The
son of Machir, and grandson of Manasseh. Num. xxvi. 29,
&c. 2. The name of Jephthah's father. Judges xi. 1, 2.
3. Certain mountains which ran from Lebanon southward.
Gen. xxxi. 21; Jer. viii. 22; xlvi. 11.

GILEADITE, Gil'-e-ad-ite.—An inhabitant of Gilead.
Judges x. 3.

GILGAL, Gil'-gal, *wheel, revolution, heap.*—A celebrated
place lying west of Jordan, where the Israelites encamped

some time after their passage over that river, and where Joshua pitched twelve stones taken out of Jordan as a memorial. A considerable city was afterwards built there, which became renowned for many events recorded in the history of the Jews. Josh. v. 10; Judges iii. 19; 1 Sam. xi. 14, 15; 1 Sam. xv. 33.

GILOH, Gy'-loh, *he that rejoices, overturns, or discovers.* —A city of Judah. Josh. xv. 51.

GILONITE, Gy'-lon-ite.—An inhabitant of Giloh. 2 Sam. xv. 12.

GIMZO, Gim'-zo, *that bulrush.*—A city of Judah, which the Philistines took in the reign of Ahaz. 2 Chron xxviii. 18.

GINATH, Gy'-nath.—Father of Tibni. 1 Kings xvi. 21.

GINNETHO, or GINNETHON, Gin'-ne-tho, Gin'-ne-thon.—A priest who sealed the covenant. Neh. x. 6; xii. 4.

GIRGASHITE, Ger'-ga-shite, *one who returns from pilgrimage.*—The inhabitants of Girgashi in Palestine. Deut. vii. 1. Their habitation was beyond the sea of Tiberias.

GISPA, Gis'-pah.—A chief of the Nethinims. Neh. xi. 21.

GITTAH-HEPHER, Git'-tah-he'-fer, *digging a wine-press.*—A place in Palestine, in the tribe of Zebulun. Josh. xix. 13.

GITTAIM, Git'-ta-im, *a wine-press.*—A city in Canaan, in the tribe of Benjamin. 2 Sam. iv. 3.

GITTITE, Git'-tite, *a wine-press.*—An inhabitant of the city of Gath. 2 Sam. vi. 11.

GOATH, Go'-ath, *his touching, or his roaring.*—A place near Jerusalem. Jer. xxxi. 39.

GOB, Gob, *cistern, grashopper, eminence.* — A place where two battles were fought between the Hebrews and Philistines. 2 Sam. xxi. 18, 19.

GOG, Gog, *roof, covering.*—The son of Joel, of the tribe of Reuben. 1 Chron. v. 4.

GOG and MAGOG, May′-gog.—Places mentioned Ezek. xxxviii. 2, 3; xxxix. 1; Rev. xx. 8. Moses speaks of MAGOG, son of Japheth. Gen. x. 2. MAGOG signifies *the country*, and GOG *the prince of it.* It is the general name of the northern nations of Europe and Asia, or the districts north of Caucasus or Mount Taurus.

GOLAN, Go′-lan, *passage, revolution.*—A city of refuge in the half-tribe of Manasseh, given to the Levites. Deut. iv. 43.

GOLGOTHA, Gol′-go-thah, *a heap of skulls.*—Mount Calvary. Matt. xxvii. 33.

GOLIATH, Go-ly′-ath, *revolution, discovery, heap.*—A famous giant of the city of Gath, who was slain by David. 1 Sam. xvii. 4, &c.

GOMER, Go′-mer, *to finish, accomplish, a consumer.*— 1. The eldest son of Japheth, by whom a great part of Asia Minor was first peopled, and especially Phrygia. 2. The daughter of Diblaim, and wife of Hosea. Hosea i. 3.

GOMORRAH, Go-mor′-rah, *a rebellious people.*—One of the five cities consumed by fire. Gen. xix. 24, &c.

GOSHEN, Go′-shen, *approaching, drawing near.*—1. A canton of Egypt, which Joseph procured for his father and brethren to dwell in. Gen. xlvii. 6. 2. A country near Gibeon. Josh. x. 41.

GOZAN, Go′-zan, *fleece, pasture, nourishing the body.* —A river mentioned 2 Kings xvii. 6; xviii. 11; xix. 12. Also a province or kingdom: in all probability the river Gozan ran through the same.

GRECIA, Gre′-she-a.—The country of Greece. Dan. viii. 21; x. 20.

GRECIANS, Gre′-she-ans.—Greeks, the inhabitants of Greece. Joel iii. 6; Acts vi. 1.

GUDGODAH, Gud′-go-dah.—A place in the wilderness through which the Israelites marched. Deut. x. 7.

GUNI, Gew'-ny, *garden, or covering.*—The son of Naphtali, head of the family of the Gunites. Num. xxvi. 48.

GUR, Gur, *the young of a beast, dwelling, fear.*—A narrow pass near Jerusalem. 2 Kings ix. 27.

GUR-BAAL, Gur-bay'-al, *the whelp of the governor.*—A town probably in Arabia. 2 Chron. xxvi. 7.

H

HAAHASHTARI, Hay-a-hash'-ta-ry, *a runner.*—A descendant of Judah. 1 Chron. iv. 6.

HABAIAH, Ha-bay'-yah, *the hiding of the Lord.*—One of the priests of the tribe of Ezra. Ezra ii. 61.

HABAKKUK, Hab'-a-kuk, *he that embraces, a wrestler.* —The author of the book of that name. Of the tribe of Simeon, and native of Bethzacar. Hab. i. 1, &c.

HABAZINIAH, Hab-a-ze-ny'-ah.—One of the descendants of Rechab, the father of Jonadab. Jer. xxxv. 3.

HABERGEON, Ha-ber'-je-on, *a coat of mail.*—Exod. xxviii. 32.

HABOR, Hay'-bor, *a fellow or partaker.*—A city of the Medes in Assyria. 2 Kings xvii. 6.

HACHALIAH, Hak-a-ly'-ah, *who waits for the Lord.* —The father of Nehemiah the governor. Neh. i. 1.

HACHILAH, Hak'-e-lah, *my trust is in her.*—A place in Palestine. 1 Sam. xxvi. 1.

HACHMONI, Hak'-mo-ny, *a wise man.*—The father of Jehiel, the tutor of David's sons. 1 Chron. xxvii. 32.

HACKMONITE, Hak'-mo-nite.—A descendant of Hachmoni. 1 Chron. xi. 11.

HADAD, Hay'-dad, *joy, noise.*—1. The son of Bedad, who succeeded Husham in the kingdom of Moab. Gen. xxxvi. 35. 2. Son to the king of Edom, who was carried into Egypt by the servants of his father, at the time that

Joab, the general of David's troops, extirpated all the males of Edom. 1 Kings xi. 14—17. 3. The son of Baalhanan, king of Edom. 1 Chron. i. 50. 4. One of the twelve sons of Ishmael. 1 Chron. i. 30.

HADADEZER, Had-ad-e′-zer, *the beauty of assistance.*—A king of Zobah, who was defeated by David. 2 Sam. viii. 3, &c.

HADADRIMMON, Hay′-dad-rim′-mon, *the voice of height, the invocation of Rimmon.*—A god of the Syrians. Zech. xii. 11.

HADAR, Hay′-dar.—See HADAD. Gen. xxv. 15.

HADAREZER, Hay-dar-e′-zer, *the beauty of assistance.*—King of Zobah. 1 Chron. xviii. 9.

HADASHAH, Had′-a-shah.—A town of Judah. Josh. xv. 37.

HADASSAH, Ha-das′-sah, *a myrtle, joy.*—The same as ESTHER. Esther ii. 7.

HADATTAH, Ha-dat′-tah.—A town of Judah. Josh. xv. 25.

HADID, Hay′-did.—A city of Benjamin. Ezra ii. 33; Neh. xi. 34.

HADLAI, Had′-lay-i.—A descendant of Ephraim. 2 Chron. xxviii. 12.

HADORAM, Ha-do′-ram, *their beauty, power, praise.*—1. A descendant of Shem. Gen. x. 27. 2. A son of Tou, king of Hamath. 1 Chron. xviii. 10; 2 Sam. viii. 10.

HADRACH, Hay′-drak, *point, joy of tenderness, your chamber.*—A country of Syria, of which Damascus was the bulwark. Zech. ix. 1.

HAGAB, Hay′-gab, *a grashopper.*—A Nethinim. Ezra ii. 46.

HAGABAH, Hag′-ga-bah.—See HAGAB.

HAGAR, Hay′-gar, *a stranger, that fears.*—An Egyptian woman, and servant to Sarah the wife of Abraham. Gen. xvi. 1, &c.

HAGARENES, Hay-gar-ee′ns.—Of the family of Hagar. The descendants of Ishmael. Psalm lxxxiii. 6. They are also called Ishmaelites, and Saracens, and sometimes Arabians.

HAGGAI, Hag′-ga-i, *feast, solemnity.*—1. The tenth of the minor prophets, probably born in Babylon, A.M. 3457, from whence he returned with Zerubbabel. Ezra v. 1. 2. The same as HAGGI, second son of Gad. Gen. xlvi. 16.

HAGGERI, Hag′-ge-ry.—The father of Mibhar, one of David's worthies. 1 Chron. xi. 38.

HAGGI, Hag′-gy, *joy.*—A descendant of Gad, and father of the Haggites. Num. xxvi. 15.

HAGGIAH, Hag-gy′-ah, *the Lord's feast.*—The son of Shimei, one of the descendants of Merari. 1 Chron. vi. 30.

HAGGITH, Hag′-gith, *rejoicing.*—David's fifth wife, and the mother of Adonijah. 2 Sam. iii. 4.

HAKKATAN, Hak′-ka-tan, *little.*—The father of Johanan, who brought one hundred and ten males with him from Babylon. Ezra viii. 12.

HAKKOZ, Hak′-koz, *a thorn.*—A priest in the time of David. 1 Chron. xxiv. 10.

HAKUPHA, Hak-yew′-fah, *a commandment of the mouth.*—A Nethinim. Ezra ii. 51.

HALAH, Hay′-lah.—A country beyond the Euphrates, to which the ten tribes were transported. 2 Kings xvii. 6.

HALAK, Hay′-lak.—A mountain in Palestine. Josh. xii. 7.

HALHUL, Hal′-hul, *praise.*—A city in the tribe of Judah. Josh. xv. 58.

HALLELUJAH, or ALLELUIA, Hal-le-lew′-yah, *praise ye the Lord.*—A note of praise. Rev. xix. 1, 3; Psalm cxlix. 9.

HALOHESH, Hal-lo′-esh.—One who returned from the Babylonish captivity. Neh. iii. 12.

HAM, Ham, *crafty, heat, brown.*—1. The country of the Zuzims, the situation of which is not known. Gen. xiv. 5. 2. The younger son of Noah. Gen. ix. 22, 24.

HAMAN, Hay'-man, *noise, tumult, he that prepares.*— The son of Hammedatha, an Amalekite, of the posterity of Agag. Esther iii. 1; ix. 24.

HAMATH, Hay'-math, *anger, heat, a wall.*—A city of Syria, capital of a province of the same name lying upon the Orontes. Josh. xiii. 5; Judges iii. 3.

HAMMEDATHA, Ham-med'-a-thah, *he that troubles the law.*—The father of Haman. Esther iii. 1.

HAMMELECH, Ham'-me-lek.—One of the court or officers of Jehoiakim. Jer. xxxvi. 26.

HAMMOLEKETH, Ham-mol'-e-keth.—A woman of the tribe of Manasseh. 1 Chron. vii. 18.

HAMMON, Ham'-mon, *people.*—A city of Asher. Josh. xix. 28.

HAMMOTH-DOR, Ham'-moth-dor.—A city belonging to the Levites, in the tribe of Naphtali, granted to the family of Gershom. Josh. xxi. 32.

HAMONAH, Ham'-o-nah, *multitude.*—A city where Ezekiel foretold that Gog and his people should be buried. Ezek. xxxix. 16.

HAMON-GOG, Hay'-mon-gog, *the multitude of Gog.*— A valley in Judea. Ezek. xxxix. 15.

HAMOR, Hay'-mor, *an ass, clay, wine.*—Prince of Shechem, and father of the young man that ravished Dinah. Gen. xxxiii. 19.

HAMUEL, Ha-mew'-el, *godly.*—A descendant of Simeon. 1 Chron. iv. 26.

HAMUL, Hay'-mul, *godly, or merciful.*—The son of Pharez. Gen. xlvi. 12.

HAMUTAL, Ha-mew'-tal, *the shadow of his heat, the heat of the dew.*—The daughter of one Jeremiah of Libnah, the wife of king Joash, and mother to Jehoahaz and Zedekiah, kings of Judah. 2 Kings xxiii. 31.

HANAMEEL, Ha-nam'-e-el, *grace or pity from God.*— The son of Shallum, a kinsman of Jeremiah. Jer. xxxii. 7.

HANAN, Hay'-nan, *full of grace.*—A descendant of Benjamin. 1 Chron. viii. 23.

HANANEEL, Ha-nan'-e-el, *mercy of God.*—A tower at Jerusalem so called. Neh. iii. 1; Zech. xiv. 10.

HANANI, Han'-a-ny, *my grace or mercy.*—1. The father of the prophet Jehu. 1 Kings xvi. 7. 2. A prophet who came to Asa, king of Judah, 2 Chron. xvi. 7, whom Asa ordered to be seized. 3. A Levite and musician appointed to the temple service. 1 Chron. xxv. 4.

HANANIAH, Han-a-ny'-ah, *grace or mercy of the Lord.*—1. One of the three young men of the tribe of Judah, and of the royal family, carried to Babylon, and whose name was changed to that of Shadrach. Dan. i. 7. 2. The son of Zerubbabel. 1 Chron. iii. 19. 3. The son of Azur, who was a false prophet of the city of Gibeon. Jer. xxviii. 1, &c.

HANES, Hay'-nees.—A city near the borders of Egypt. Isai. xxx. 4.

HANIEL, Han'-e-el.—A descendant of Asher. 1 Chron. vii. 39.

HANNAH, Han'-nah, *gracious, merciful, taking rest.*— The wife of Elkanah, of the tribe of Levi, who dwelt at Ramah, and the mother of Samuel. 1 Sam. i. 2.

HANNATHON, Han'-na-thon, *the gift of grace.*—A town in Palestine in the tribe of Zebulun. Josh. xix. 14.

HANNIEL, Han'-ne-el, *the grace or mercy of God.*— The son of Ephod, of the tribe of Manasseh; one of the spies. Num. xxxiv. 23.

HANOCH, Hay'-nok, *dedicated.*—1. The son of Midian, and grandson of Abraham and Keturah. Gen. xxv. 4. 2. The eldest son of Reuben. Gen. xlvi. 9.

HANUN, Hay'-nun, *gracious, merciful, he that rests.*— 1. The son of Naash, king of the Ammonites, who insulted

David's servants by cutting off their beards. 2 Sam. x. 1, &c. 2. The son of Seleph, after the return from Babylon. Neh. iii. 13.

HAPHRAIM, Haf'-ra-im, *searching or digging.* — A city in the tribe of Issachar. Josh. xix. 19.

HARA, Hay'-rah, *mountainous.*—A city or canton of Assyria to which the ten tribes were transported by Tilgath-pilneser. 1 Chron. v. 26.

HARADAH, Har'-a-dah, *the well of great fear.*—The twenty-first encampment of the Israelites in the wilderness. Num. xxxiii. 24.

HARAN, Hay'-ran, *mountainous country which is enclosed.*—1. The son of Caleb and Ephah, his concubine. 1 Chron. ii. 46. 2. The eldest son of Terah, and brother to Abraham and Nahor. Gen. xi. 26. He was the father of Lot. 3. Otherwise Charran, celebrated as the place to which Abraham first removed when he left Hur. Gen. xi. 31, 32.

HARBONA, and HARBONAH, Har-bo'-nah, *his destruction, or dryness.*—Servant of Ahasuerus. Esther i. 10. vii. 9.

HAREPH, Hay'-ref.—A son of Caleb. 1 Chron. ii. 51.

HARETH, Hay'-reth, *liberty.*—A forest in Judah, to which David fled to avoid the persecution of Saul. 1 Sam. xxii. 5.

HARHAIAH, Ha-ra-i'-ah.—A goldsmith who laboured for the new temple at Jerusalem. Neh. iii. 8.

HARHAS, Har'-has.—A keeper of king Josiah's wardrobe. 2 Kings xxii. 14.

HARHUR, Har'-hur, *the heat of liberty.*—One whose sons were of the order of the Nethinims. Ezra ii. 51.

HARIM, Hay'-rim.—1. Persons belonging to the sacerdotal families. Ezra ii. 39. 2. One who returned from the captivity. Ezra ii. 32.

HARIPH, Hay'-rif.—One who returned from the captivity. Neh. vii. 24.

HARNEPHER, Har'-ne-fer.—A descendant of Asher. 1 Chron. vii. 36.

HAROD, Hay'-rod, *astonishment, fear, a well, a fountain.*—1. A well near which Gideon and his troops pitched. Judges vii. 1.   2. The birth-place of Elika and Shammah, two valiant men in David's army. 2 Sam. xxiii. 25.

HARODITE, Hay'-rod-ite.—An inhabitant of Harod. 2 Sam. xxiii. 25.

HAROEH, Har'-o-eh.—A descendant of Judah. 1 Chron. ii. 52.

HAROSHETH, Har'-o-sheth, *agriculture, silence, vessel of earth, forest.*—A city supposed to be near Hazor, in the northern part of Canaan, called afterwards Upper Galilee, or Galilee of the Gentiles. Judges iv. 2.

HARSHA, Har'-shah, *the head of a family.*—Ezra ii. 52.

HARUM, Hay'-rum.—Son of Coz. 1 Chron. iv. 8.

HARUMAPH, Ha-rew'-maf, *destruction.*—One who returned from the captivity. Neh. iii. 10.

HARUPHITE, Ha-rew'-fite.—One of David's brave officers. 1 Chron. xii. 5.

HARUZ, Hay'-ruz.—The grandfather of king Ammon. 2 Kings xxi. 19.

HASADIAH, Has-a-dy'-ah, *the mercy of the Lord.*—The son of Zerubbabel. 1 Chron. iii. 20.

HASENUAH, Has-e-new'-ah.—A descendant of Benjamin. 1 Chron. ix. 7.

HASHABIAH, Hash-a-by'-ah, *the estimation of the Lord.*—1. The son of Amaziah, the Levite. 1 Chron. vi. 45. 2. The son of Jeduthun. 1 Chron. xxv. 3, 19.   3. The name of the proprietor of half the country of Keilah. Neh. iii. 17.

HASHABNAH, Hash-ab'-nah, *the silence of the Lord.*—One of the order of the Levites. Neh. x. 25.

HASHABNIAH, Hash-ab-ny'-ah.—One that builded the wall of Jerusalem. Neh. iii. 10.

HASHBADANA, Hash-bad'-a-nah.—One that was at Ezra's left hand when he read the law. Neh. viii. 4.

HASHEM, Hay'-shem.—A Gizonite of Canaan. 1 Chron. xi. 34.

HASHMONAH, Hash'-mo-nah, *diligence, enumeration, embassy, present.*—The twenty-sixth encampment of the Israelites in the wilderness. Num. xxxiii. 29.

HASHUB, Hay'-shub, *esteemed or numbered.*—One who signed the covenant with Nehemiah. Neh. iii. 11.

HASHUBAH, Ha-shu'-bah, *estimation or thought.*— A descendant of David. 1 Chron. iii. 20.

HASHUM, Hay'-shum.—One whose descendants returned from Babylon to the number of 328. Neh. vii. 22.

HASHUPHA, Ha-shu'-fah.—The son of Zerubbabel. Neh. vii. 46.

HASSENAAH, Has-se-nay'-ah.—After the return from Babylon, he erected the fish-gate at Jerusalem. Neh. iii. 3.

HASUPHA, Ha-su'-fah.—One whose descendants were Nethinims. Ezra ii. 43.

HATACH, Hay'-tak, *smiting.*—Chamberlain to king Ahasuerus. Esther iv. 6.

HATHATH, Hay'-thath.—A descendant of Judah. 1 Chron. iv. 13.

HATIPHA, Hat-ty'-fah.—One whose children were of the order of the Nethinims. Ezra ii. 54.

HATITA, Hat'-te-tah.—One whose descendants were Nethinims. Ezra ii. 42.

HATTIL, Hat'-til.—One whose children were servants to Solomon. Ezra ii. 57.

HATTUSH, Hat'-tush.—A descendant of David. 1 Chron. iii. 22.

HAURAN, Haw'-ran.—A tract of country mentioned only twice in Scripture. Ezek. xlvii. 16, 18. It was situated east of the Holy Land. Some suppose it to be the same as Ituræa. Luke iii. 1.

HAVILAH, Hav'-e-lah, *that suffers pain, brings forth, declares her joy.*—The son of Cush. Gen. x. 7. There were several Havilahs. By one of these it is probable that the western shores of the Persian Gulf were peopled; by another the country of Colchis; and by another, the parts about the southern border of the Dead Sea and the confines of Judea, the country afterwards inhabited by the Amalekites. Also a country spoken of Gen. xxv. 18.

HAVOTH-JAIR, Hay'-voth-jay'-ir, *villages of Jair*, or *that enlighten.*—Villages which Jair, the son of Manasseh, conquered and possessed. They were in the land of Gilead, and belonged to the half-tribe of Manasseh. Num. xxxii. 41.

HAZAEL, Haz'-a-el, *that sees God.*—One who was raised from a private station to be king of Syria, and was guilty of great cruelties. 2 Kings viii. 8—13.

HAZAR-ADDAR, Hay'-zar-ad'-dar.—A boundary of Canaan. Num. xxxiv. 4.

HAZAR-ENAN, Hay'-zar-e'-nan.—A boundary of Canaan. Num. xxxiv. 9.

HAZAR-GADDAH, Hay'-zar-gad'-dah.—A city of Palestine. Josh. xv. 27.

HAZAR-HATTICON, Hay'-zar-hat'-te-kon.—A place in Upper Egypt. Ezek. xlvii. 16.

HAZARMAVETH, Hay'-zar-may'-veth, *court or dwelling of death.*—The third son of Joktan. Gen. x. 26.

HAZAROTH, Ha-zay'-roth.—A place in the country of Moab.

HAZAR-SHUAL, Hay'-zar-shu'-al.—A city in the tribe of Simeon. Josh. xv. 28.

HAZAR-SUSAH, Hay'-zar-su'-sah.—A city in Palestine. Josh. xix. 5.

HAZAR-SUSIM, Hay'-zar-su'-sim.—A city in Simeon. 1 Chron. iv. 31.

HAZELELPONI, Hay'-zel-el-po'-ny, *shade, sorrow of the face.*—A woman of the posterity of Judah. 1 Chron. iv. 3.

HAZERIM, Ha-ze'-rim.—The ancient habitation of the Avim before they were driven away by the Caphtorim. Deut. ii. 23.

HAZEROTH, Ha-ze'-roth, *villages, court.*—One of the encampments of the Israelites in the wilderness. Num. xi. 35.

HAZEZON-TAMAR, Haz'-e-zon Tay'-mar.—The same as ENGEDI, upon the western coast of the Dead Sea. Gen. xiv. 7.

HAZIEL, Hay'-ze-el.—The son of Shimei, a Levite and singer. 1 Chron. xxiii. 9.

HAZO, Hay'-zo.—A son of Nahor. Gen. xxii. 22.

HAZOR, Hay'-zor, *court, hay.*—1. The name of a city in the tribe of Judah. Josh. xv. 23. 2. The name of a city in the tribe of Naphtali. Josh. xix. 36.

HEBER, He'-ber, *one that passes, anger.*—1. The father of Peleg and son of Salah, who was grandson of Shem; born A.M. 1723. Luke iii. 35. From him some have supposed that Abraham and his descendants derived the name of Hebrews. But others have suggested, with greater probability, that Abraham and his family were thus called because they came from the other side of the Euphrates into Canaan, Heber signifying "one that passes," or "a passage," that is, of the Euphrates. 2. The Kenite of Jethro's family, husband to Jael, who killed Sisera. Judges iv. 17, &c.

HEBERITES, He'-ber-ites.—Descendants of Heber. Num. xxvi. 45.

HEBREWS, He'-brews.—Sometimes called Israel, or Jacob, from their progenitor; and in more modern times, *Jews*, from Judah.

109

HEBRON, He'-bron, *society, friendship, enchantment.*—
1. One of the most ancient cities in the world, situated on
an eminence twenty miles southward from Jerusalem, and
twenty northward from Beersheba. Abraham, Isaac, and
Sarah were buried near this place. Gen. xxiii. 2. See
also Josh. xiv. 13; x. 3, 23, 36. 2. The son of Kohath,
chief of the family of the Hebronites. Exod. vi. 18.

HEGAI, or HEGE, Heg'-a-i, He'-ge, *meditation, word,
separation.*—The keeper of the women of king Ahasuerus's
seraglio, and his chamberlain. Esther ii. 3, 8.

HELAH, He'-lah.—The wife of Ashur, the father of
Tekoa. 1 Chron. iv. 5.

HELAM, He'-lam, *their army, trouble, or expectation.*—
A place celebrated for a battle fought between David and
the Syrians. 2 Sam. x. 17.

HELBAH, Hel'-bah.—A city in the tribe of Asher.
Judges i. 31.

HELBON, Hel'-bon, *milk, fatness.*—A place mentioned
Ezek. xxvii. 18.

HELDAI, Hel'-da-i, *the world.*—1. One who furnished
gold and silver to make crowns for Joshua, the son of
Josedech. Zech. vi. 10, 11. 2. One of the twelve captains
appointed by David to do duty in their order at the palace.
1 Chron. xxvii. 15.

HELEB, He'-leb.—The son of Baanah, one of the brave
officers of David's army. 2 Sam. xxiii. 29.

HELED, He'-led.—One of David's worthies. 1 Chron.
xi. 30.

HELEK, He'-lek.—A descendant of Manasseh. Num.
xxvi. 30.

HELEM, He'-lem, *dreaming, or healing.*—A descendant
of Asher. 1 Chron. vii. 35.

HELEPH, He'-lef.—A city in the tribe of Naphtali.
Josh. xix. 33.

HELEZ, He'-lez.—One of the valiant men of David's army. 2 Sam. xxiii. 26.

HELI, He'-ly, *ascending, climbing up*.—The father of Joseph, the Virgin Mary's husband. Luke iii. 23.

HELIOPOLIS, He-le-op'-o-lis, *the city of the sun*.—It is called *On* in the Hebrew text. Gen. xli. 45. It was situated on the Nile, half a day's journey from Babylon, in Egypt.

HELKATH, Hel'-kath, *a field*.—A city in the tribe of Asher. Josh. xxi. 31.

HELKATH-HAZZURIM, Hel'-kath-haz'-zu-rim, *the field of strong men, of the rocks*.—A frontier town of Asher. 2 Sam. ii. 16.

HELON, He'-lon, *a window*.—The father of Eliab. Num. i. 9.

HEMAM, He'-mam.—A descendant of Esau. Gen. xxxvi. 22.

HEMAN, He'-man, *their trouble, their tumult*.—One of the sons of Mahol. 1 Kings iv. 31.

HEMATH, He'-math.—The father of the house of Rechab. 1 Chron. ii. 55.

HEMDAN, Hem'-dan.—One of the posterity of Esau. Gen. xxxvi. 26.

HEN, Hen, *grace, quiet, rest*.—The son of Zephaniah. Zech. vi. 14.

HENA, He'-nah.—A country conquered by the Assyrians. 2 Kings xviii. 34.

HENADAD, Hen'-a-dad.—A Levite who sealed the covenant. Neh. iii. 18.

HENOCH, He'-nok.—The son of Midian. 1 Chron. i. 3.

HEPHER, He'-fer, *a digger, a delver*.—1. The father of the Hepherites. Num. xxvi. 32, 33. 2. A city, the king of which was slain by Joshua. Josh. xii. 17.

HEPHZI-BAH, Hef′-ze-bah, *my pleasure.*—The mother of Manasseh, king of Judah. 2 Kings xxi. 1.

HERAM, He′-ram.—A city in the tribe of Naphtali.

HERES, He′-rees.—A mountain in the tribe of Dan. Judges i. 35.

HERESH, He′-resh.—The name of a Levite. 1 Chron. ix. 15.

HERMAS, Her′-mas, *Mercury, gain.*—An individual mentioned Rom. xvi. 14.

HERMES, Her′-mees, *Mercury, gain.*—A person mentioned Rom. xvi. 14.

HERMOGENES, Her-moj′-e-nees, *begotten of Mercury, of lucre.*—An apostate from the faith of Christ on account of persecution. 2 Tim. i. 15.

HERMON, Her′-mon, *dedicated, anathema, destruction.*—A celebrated mountain in the Holy Land, often spoken of in Scripture. It was in the northern boundary of the country, beyond Jordan, and in the territory which originally belonged to Og, king of Bashan. Josh. xii. 5; xiii. 5.

HERMONITES, Her′-mon-ites. — Dwellers around Hermon. Psalm xlii. 6.

HEROD, Her′-od, *the glory of the skin.*—1. He was surnamed the Great, was the son of Antipater, the Idumean, born B.C. 71. At the age of twenty-five, he was made, by his father, governor of Galilee, and distinguished himself by the suppression of a band of robbers. It was in the latter part of his reign that Jesus Christ was born. 2. Herod, called Philip. See Matt. xiv. 3; Mark vi. 17. The son of Herod the Great, and Mariamne, the daughter of Simon the high-priest. 3. Herod Antipas. See ANTIPAS. 4. Herod Agrippa. See AGRIPPA.

HERODIANS, He-ro′-de-ans.—A sect among the Jews in our Saviour's time. Matt. xxii. 16; Mark xii. 13.

HERODIAS, He-ro′-de-as.—The daughter of Aristobulus and Bernice, sister to king Agrippa, and grandaughter to Herod the Great. Matt. xiv. 3.

112

HERODION, He-ro'-de-on, *song of Juno.*—St. Paul's kinsman. Rom. xvi. 11.

HESED, He'-sed.—An officer of king Solomon. 1 Kings iv. 10.

HESHBON, Hesh'-bon, *invention, industry, thought, he that hastens to understand.*—A celebrated city beyond Jordan, twenty miles eastward of that river, according to Eusebius. It was given to the tribe of Reuben, Josh. xiii. 10; and probably made over to Gad. Josh. xxi. 39.

HESHMON, Hesh'-mon, *hasty message.*—A city in the tribe of Judah. Josh. xv. 27.

HETH, Heth, *trembling, fear.*—The second son of Canaan, and father of the Hittites. Gen. x. 15.

HETHLON, Heth'-lon, *fearful dwelling, his covering.*—A city mentioned by Ezekiel, chap. xlvii. 15; xlviii. 1.

HEZEKI, Hez'-e-ky, *strength.* — A descendant of Benjamin. 1 Chron. viii. 17.

HEZEKIAH, Hez-e-ky'-ah, *strong in the Lord.*—One of the kings of Judah, the son of Ahaz and Abi; born A. M. 3251. At the age of twenty-five, he succeeded his father in the government of the kingdom of Judah, and reigned twenty-nine years in Jerusalem. He acted in a manner well-pleasing to the Lord. 2 Kings xviii.; 2 Chron. xxix.; xxx.; xxxi. 2. The name of a person who returned from the captivity. 1 Chron. iii. 23; Neh. vii. 21.

HEZION, He'-ze-on.—A king of Syria. 1 Kings xv. 18.

HEZIR, He'-zir.—A priest in the reign of David. 1 Chron. xxiv. 15.

HEZRAI, Hez'-ra-i.—A Carmelite. One of David's captains. 2 Sam. xxiii. 35.

HEZRO, Hez'-ro, *the division of song.*—One of David's valiant men. 1 Chron. xi. 37.

HEZRON, Hez'-ron, *dart of joy, division of song.*— 1. The third son of Reuben, head of the family of

Hezronites. Gen. xlvi. 9; Num. xxvi. 6. 2. The son of Pharez. 1 Chron. ii. 5. The same as Esrom. Matt. i. 3.

HIDDAI, Hid'-da-i, *praise, cry.*—One of David's valiant men. 2 Sam. xxiii. 30.

HIDDEKEL, Hid'-de-kel, *a sharp voice.*—One of the four rivers whose course was in Paradise. Gen. ii. 14.

HIEL, Hy'-el, *the life of God.*—The person who rebuilt Jericho, 1 Kings xvi. 34, notwithstanding Joshua's curse, the effects of which he felt. Josh. vi. 26.

HIERAPOLIS, Hy-e-rap'-o-lis, *the holy city.*—It was a city situated in Phrygia, near Colosse. Col. iv. 13.

HIGGAION, Hig-gay'-e-on, *meditation.*—A musical instrument. Psalm ix. 16.

HILEN, Hy'-len.—A city in the tribe of Judah. 1 Chron. vi. 58.

HILKIAH, Hil-ky'-ah, *God is my portion, the Lord's gentleness.*—1. The father of Jeremiah. Jer. i. 1. 2. The father of Eliakim. 2 Kings xxii. 4. 3. Father of the above, and some others. 2 Kings xviii. 18, 26, 37.

HILLEL, Hil'-lel, *praising folly, Lucifer.*—The father of Abdon, judge of Israel. Judges xii. 13.

HINNOM, Hin'-nom, *there they are, their riches.*—A valley south of Jerusalem, where the idolatrous Jews burned their children alive to Moloch, Baal, and the sun. It is also called Tophet. Josh. xv. 8; 2 Kings xxiii. 10; Neh. xi. 30.

HIRAH, Hy'-rah, *exaltation of life.*—A Canaanite of the city of Adullam. Gen. xxxviii. 1.

HIRAM, Hy'-ram, *exaltation of life, their whiteness, he that destroys.*—1. King of Tyre, the son of Abibal. 2 Sam. v. 11. 2. The son of a Tyrian, a skilful artist. 1 Kings vii. 13.

HITTITES, Hit'-tites, *who are broken, or fear.*—The descendants of Heth. Gen. xv. 20.

114

HIVITES, Hy′-vites, *wicked, bad, wickedness.*—A people descended from Canaan. Gen. x. 17.

HIZKIJAH, Hiz-ky′-jah.—A captive mentioned Neh. x. 17.

HOBAB, Ho′-bab, *favoured and beloved.*—The son of Jethro, and brother-in-law of Moses. Num. x. 29.

HOBAH, Ho′-bah, *love, friendship, secrecy.*—A place northward of Damascus. Gen. xiv. 15.

HOD, Hod.—A descendant of Asher. 1 Chron. vii. 37.

HODAIAH, Ho-da-i′-ah.—A descendant of king David. 1 Chron. iii. 24.

HODAVIAH, Hod-a-vy′-ah.—1. Of the tribe of Manasseh. 1 Chron. v. 24. 2. A Levite returned from captivity. Ezra ii. 40.

HODESH, Ho′-desh.—A female descendant of Benjamin. 1 Chron. viii. 9.

HODEVAH, Ho-de′-vah.—A captain who returned from captivity. Neh. vii. 43.

HODIAH, Ho-dy′-ah.—A female descendant of Judah. 1 Chron. iv. 19.

HODIJAH, Ho-dy′-jah.—One who sealed the covenant. Neh. viii. 7.

HOGLAH, Hog′-lah, *his festival, his dance.*—A daughter of Zelophehad. Num. xxvi. 33 ; Josh. xvii. 3.

HOHAM, Ho′-ham.—King of Hebron. Josh. x. 3.

HOLON, Ho′-lon.—A city of refuge in Palestine. Josh. xv. 51.

HOMAM, Ho′-mam.—A descendant of Esau. Gen. xxxvi. 22. See margin.

HOPHNI, Hof′-ny, *he that covers, my fist.*—One of the sons of Eli, the high-priest. 1 Sam. i. 3 ; ii. 22, 23.

HOR, Hor, *who conceives, shows.*—A mountain in Arabia Petræa. Num. xxi. 4.

HORAM, Ho′-ram.—King of Gezer. Josh. x. 33.

HOREB, Ho'-reb, *desert, destruction, dryness.*—A mountain in Arabia Petræa, near to which, or a part of which, was Mount Sinai. Exod. iii. 1. Also a rock, whence Moses drew water. Exod. xvii. 6.

HOREM, Ho'-rem.—A city of Naphtali. Josh. xix. 38.

HOR-HAGIDGAD, Hor-ha-gid'-gad, *hill of felicity.*—The twenty-fifth encampment of the Israelites in the wilderness. Num. xxxiii. 32.

HORI, Ho'-ry.—The son of Lotan, a descendant of Seir. Gen. xxxvi. 22.

HORIMS, Ho'-rims.—An ancient people who dwelt in the mountains beyond Jordan. Deut. ii. 12.

HORITES, Ho'-rites.—The same as HORIMS. Gen. xiv. 6.

HORMAH, Hor'-mah, *devoted to God, destruction.*—The name of a city which was called Zephath, before the Hebrews changed its name. Judges i. 17; Num. xxi. 3.

HORONAIM, Hor-o-nay'-im, *anger, raging.*—A town of Moab. Isai. xv. 5.

HORONITE, Ho'-ron-ite.—An inhabitant of Horon, a city of Arabia. Neh. ii. 10.

HOSANNA, Ho-zan'-nah, *save, I beseech thee.*—A form of benediction. Matt. xxi. 9, 15.

HOSEA and HOSHEA, Ho-zee'-a, Ho-she'-a, *a saviour.*—The son of Beeri, the first of the minor prophets. He is generally supposed to have been a native and inhabitant of the kingdom of Israel, and began to prophesy about 400 B.C. He prophesied sixty years.

HOSHAIAH, Ho-sha-i'-ah.—A person mentioned Neh. xii. 32.

HOTHAM, Ho'-tham.—A descendant of Asher. 1 Chron. vii. 32.

HOTHAN, Ho'-than.—The father of two of David's worthies. 1 Chron. xi. 44.

HOTHIR, Ho'-thir.—A singer in the Jewish temple. 1 Chron. xxv. 4.

HUKOK and HUKKOK, Hew'-kok, Huk'-kok.—A city of Asher. Josh. xix. 34; 1 Chron. vi. 75.

HUL, Hul, *infirmity, bringing forth children* —The son of Aram. Gen. x. 23.

HULDAH, Hul'-dah, *the world, prophetess*.—The wife of Shallum, a prophetess. She was consulted by Josiah. 2 Kings xxii. 14. '

HUMTAH, Hum'-tah.—A city in Palestine. Josh. xv. 54.

HUPHAM, Hew'-fam.—A descendant of Benjamin. Num. xxvi. 39.

HUPPAH, Hup'-pah.—A priest in the time of David. 1 Chron. xxiv. 13.

HUPPIM, Hup'-pim.—A descendant from Benjamin. Gen. xlvi. 21.

HUR, Hur, *liberty, whiteness, cavern*.—1. The son of Caleb. Exod. xvii. 12. 2. The father of Uri. 1 Chron. ii. 19, 20.

HURAI, Hew'-ray.—One of David's worthies. 1 Chron. xi. 32.

HURAM, Hew'-ram.—A descendant of Benjamin. 1 Chron. viii. 5.

HURI, Hew'-ri.—A descendant of Gad. 1 Chron. v. 14.

HUSHAH, Hew'-shah.—The son of Ezer. 1 Chron. iv. 4.

HUSHAI, Hew'-shay, *their haste, sensuality*.—The Archite, David's friend. See 2 Sam. xv. 32; xvi. 17, 18, &c.; xvii. 5.

HUSHAM, Hew'-sham.—The third king of Edom. Gen. xxxvi. 34.

HUSHATHITE, Hew'-sha-thite.—A descendant of Hushah. 2 Sam. xxi. 18.

HUSHIM, Hew'-shim.—A descendant of Dan. Gen. xlvi. 23.

HUZ, Huz.—The son of Nahor. Gen. xxii. 20, 21.

HUZZAB, Huz'-zab, *molten.*—See Nahum ii. 7.

HYMENÆUS, Hy-men-e'-us, *nuptial, marriage.*—A convert of St. Paul, who afterwards apostatized. 2 Tim. ii. 17.

I

IBHAR, Ib'-har, *election, he that is chosen.*—One of David's sons. 2 Sam. v. 15.

IBLEAM, Ib'-le-am.—A city of Palestine. Josh. xvii. 11.

IBNEIAH, Ib-ny'-ah.—A descendant of Benjamin. 1 Chron. ix. 8.

IBNIJAH, Ib-ny'-jah.—A descendant of Benjamin. 1 Chron. ix. 8.

IBRI, Ib'-ry.—A descendant of Levi. 1 Chron. xxiv. 27.

IBZAN, Ib'-zan.—A descendant of Judah, and twelfth judge of Israel. Judges xii. 10.

ICHABOD, Ik'-a-bod, *where is the glory?*—The son of Phinehas, and grandson of Eli. 1 Sam. iv. 19—21.

ICONIUM, I-co'-ne-um, from ικω, "I come."—At present Cogni, formerly the capital of Lycaonia, in Asia Minor. Acts xiii. 51.

IDALAH, Id'-a-lah.—A city of Zebulun. Josh. xix. 15.

IDBASH, Id'-bash.—A descendant of Judah. 1 Chron. iv. 3.

IDDO, Id'-do, *his hand, power, witness.*—1. The son of Levi. 1 Chron. vi. 21. 2. The father of Ahinadab. 1 Kings iv. 14. 3. A prophet of the kingdom of Judah. 2 Chron. xiii. 22. 4. The grandfather of Zechariah. Zech. i. 1. 5. A descendant of Manasseh. 1 Chron. xxvii. 21. 6. The chief of the Nethinims, who were in captivity in the mountains of Casiphia. Ezra viii. 17.

IDUMÆA, I-du-me'-a, *red, earthy.*—The Greek name for the land of Edom, which lay to the south of Judea, and extended from the Dead Sea to the Elanitic Gulf of the Red Sea, where were the ports Elath and Ezion-Geber. But the Idumæa of the New Testament applies only to a small part adjoining Judea on the south, and including even a portion of that country, which was taken possession of by the Edomites, or Idumæans, while the land lay unoccupied, during the Babylonish captivity. Mark iii. 8.

IGAL, I'-gal.—One of the twelve spies. Num. xiii. 7.

IGDALIAH, Ig-da-ly'-ah, *the greatness of the Lord.*— A person mentioned Jer. xxxv. 4.

IGEAL, Ig'-e-al.—A descendant of David. 1 Chron. iii. 22.

IIM, I'-im.—A city of Palestine, in the tribe of Judah. Josh. xv. 29.

IJE-ABARIM, I-je-ab'-a-rim, *heaps of Abarim.*—One of the encampments of the Israelites in the land of Moab. Num. xxi. 11.

IJON, I'-jon, *look, eye, fountain.*—A city of Palestine. 1 Kings xv. 20.

IKKESH, Ik'-kesh.—One of David's officers. 2 Sam. xxiii. 26.

ILAI, I'-lay.—One of David's worthies. 1 Chron. xi. 29.

ILLYRICUM, Il-lir'-e-kum, *joy, rejoicing.*—A province lying north-west of Macedon, along the eastern coast of the Adriatic Gulf. Rom. xv. 19.

IMLAH, Im'-lah, *plenitude, repletion, circumcision.*— The father of Micaiah, the prophet. 1 Kings xxii. 8.

IMMANUEL, Im-man'-u-el, *God with us.*—A name given to our Lord Jesus Christ. Isai. vii. 14.

IMMER, Im'-mer.—Head of a family of priests. 1 Chron. ix. 12; Ezra ii. 37.

IMNAH, Im'-nah.—A son of Asher. 1 Chron. vii. 30.

IMRAH, Im'-rah, *a rebel, changing.*—A descendant of Asher. 1 Chron. vii. 36.

IMRI, Im'-ry.—A descendant of Judah. 1 Chron. ix. 4.

INDIA, In'-de-a, *praise, law.*—An extensive country of Asia.

IPHEDEIAH, If-e-dy'-ah, *the redemption of the Lord.* —A descendant of Benjamin. 1 Chron. viii. 25.

IR, Ir, *watchman.*—A descendant of Benjamin. 1 Chron. vii. 12.

IRA, I'-rah, *city, watch, spoil, heap of vision.*—1. One of David's worthies. 2 Sam. xx. 26.   2. The son of Ikkesh. 1 Chron. xi. 28.

IRAD, I'-rad, *wild ass, heap of descents, of empire.*—The son of Enoch. Gen. iv. 18.

IRAM, I'-ram.—A duke of Edom. Gen. xxxvi. 43.

IRI, I'-ry, *fear, vision.*—A descendant of Benjamin. 1 Chron. vii. 7.

IRIJAH, I-ry'-jah, *the fear, vision, or protection of the Lord.*—The person who arrested Jeremiah when he was put into the dungeon. Jer. xxxvii. 13.

IR-NAHASH, Ir'-na-hash.—A descendant of Judah. 1 Chron. iv. 12.

IRON, I'-ron.—A city of Palestine. Josh. xix. 38.

IRPEEL, Ir'-pe-el.—A city in Palestine. Josh. xviii. 27.

IR-SHEMESH, Ir-she'-mesh.—A city of Palestine. Josh. xix. 41.

IRU, I'-rew.—A son of Caleb. 1 Chron. iv. 15.

ISAAC, I'-zak, *laughter.*—The son of Abraham and Sarah, born A. M. 2107. Gen. xviii. 10, 11; xxi. 6—8.

ISAIAH, I-zay'-yah, *the salvation of the Lord.*—The son of Amos, and the first of the four great prophets. See his prophecy.

ISCAH, Is'-kah, *he that anoints, or covers.*—A daughter of Haran. Gen. xi. 29.

ISCARIOT, Is-kar'-e-ot, *a hireling.*—The name of the disciple who betrayed Christ. Matt. x. 4.

ISHBAH, Ish'-bah, *empty.*—A descendant of Judah. 1 Chron. iv. 17.

ISHBAK, Ish'-bak, *empty, forsaken, abandoned.*—A son of Abraham by Keturah. Gen. xxv. 2.

ISHBI-BENOB, Ish'-by-be'-nob, *he that sits in the prophecy, conversion.*—A descendant of the giants. 2 Sam. xxi. 16.

ISHBOSHETH, Ish'-bo-sheth, *a man of shame.*—A son of king Saul, and acknowledged his successor by part of the tribes of Israel, A.M. 2949, while David reigned at Hebron over Judah. See 2 Sam. ii. 8, 9, &c.

ISHI, I'-shy, *my husband.*—A descendant of Judah. 1 Chron. ii. 31.

ISHIAH, I-shy'-ah.—The grandson of Uzzi. 1 Chron. vii. 3.

ISHIJAH, I-shy'-jah.—One of the captives. Ezra x. 31.

ISHMA, Ish'-mah, *who hears.*—A descendant of Judah. 1 Chron. iv. 3.

ISHMAEL, Ish'-ma-el, *God who hears.*—1. The son of Abraham and Hagar; born A.M.2094. Gen. xvi. 15. 2. The son of Nethaniah, of the royal family of Judah. Jer. xl. 14.

ISHMAELITES, Ish'-ma-el-ites. The descendants of Ishmael, who dwelt in Arabia. Gen. xxxvii. 25 ; Judges viii. 24.

ISHMAIAH, Ish-ma-i'-ah.—The son of Obadiah. 1 Chron. xxvii. 19.

ISHMEELITES, Ish'-me-el-ites.—See ISHMAELITES.

ISHOD, I'-shod.—A descendant of Manasseh. 1 Chron. vii. 18.

ISHPAN, Ish'-pan.—A descendant of Benjamin. 1 Chron. viii. 22.

ISH-TOB, Ish'-tob.—A country situated at the northern extremity of the mountains of Gilead, towards Mount Libanus. 2 Sam. x. 6.

ISHUAH, Ish'-u-ah.—Asher's second son. Gen. xlvi. 17.

ISHUAI, Ish'-u-ay.—A son of Asher. 1 Chron. vii. 30.

ISMACHIAH, Is-ma-ky'-ah.—A priest or Levite in the time of Hezekiah. 2 Chron. xxxi. 13.

ISMAIAH, Is-ma-i'-ah.—A friend of David. 1 Chron. xii. 4.

ISPAH, Is'-pah.—A descendant of Benjamin. 1 Chron. viii. 16.

ISRAEL, Is'-ra-el, *a prince with God, prevailing with God.*—The name which the Angel gave to Jacob at Mahanaim, after having wrestled with him all night. Gen. xxxii. 1, 2, 28—30; Hosea xii. 4.

ISRAELITES, Is'-ra-el-ites.—The descendants or posterity of Jacob. Exod. ix. 7.

ISSACHAR, Is'-sa-kar, *price, reward.*—The fifth son of Jacob and Leah. Gen. xxx. 14—18. Born A.M. 2257.

ISUI, Is'-u-i.—The third son of Asher. Gen. xlvi. 17.

ITALY, It'-ta-le.—A Latin word that has its origin from *vitulus,* or *vitula,* a calf, or from a king called Italus. A celebrated country lying to the south of Europe. Acts xviii. 2. It was during his abode in Italy that St. Paul wrote his Epistle to the Hebrews.

ITHAI, Ith'-a-i.—A Benjamite. 1 Chron. xi. 31.

ITHAMAR, Ith'-a-mar, *island of the palm-tree, woe to the palm or to the change.*—Aaron's fourth son. Exod. vi. 23.

ITHIEL, Ith'-e-el, *God with me, sign.*—The son of Jesaiah. Neh. xi. 7.

ITHMAH, Ith'-mah.—An officer of David. 1 Chron. xi. 46.

ITHNAN, Ith'-nan.—A city of Palestine. Josh. xv. 23.

ITHRAN, Ith'-ran.—A descendant of Asher. Gen. xxxvi. 26.

ITHREAM, Ith'-re-am, *excellence of the people.*—The son of David. 1 Chron. iii. 3; 2 Sam. iii. 5.

ITTAH-KAZIN, It'-tah-kay'-zin.—A city of Palestine. Josh. xix. 13.

ITTAI, It'-ta-i.—The son of Ribbui, surnamed the Gittite, a native of Gibeah. 2 Sam. xv. 19.

ITURÆA, I-tu-re'-a, *which is guarded, a country of mountains.*—A province of Syria, beyond Jordan, to the east of Batanea, and south of Trachonitis. Luke iii. 1.

IVAH, I'-vah, *iniquity*.—A country conquered by the Assyrians, with a city of that name. 2 Kings xviii. 34.

IZHAR, Iz'-har.—The son of Kohath. Exod. vi. 18.

IZRAHIAH, Iz-ra-hy'-ah.—A descendant of Issachar. 1 Chron. vii. 3.

IZRI, Iz'-ry,—A singer in the temple. 1 Chron. xxv. 11.

J

JAAKAN, Jay'-a-kan, *tribulation*.—One whose descendants lived in Beeroth, in the wilderness. Deut. x. 6.

JAAKOBAH, Ja-ak'-o-bah.—A prince of the tribe of Simeon. 1 Chron. iv. 36.

JAALA, Ja-ay'-lah, *hidden*.—One of the Nethinims. Neh. vii. 58.

JAALAH, Ja-ay'-lah.—A person mentioned Ezra ii. 56.

JAALAM, Ja-ay'-lam, *hidden, young man, kids*.—A descendant of Esau. Gen. xxxvi. 5.

JAANAI, Ja-ay'-nay.—One of the posterity of Gad. 1 Chron. v. 12.

JAARE-OREGIM, Ja-ar-e-or'-e-gim.—A Bethlehemite. 2 Sam. xxi. 19.

JAASAU, Jay'-a-sau.—One of the captives. Ezra x. 37.

JAASIEL, Ja-ay'-se-el.—A descendant of Manasseh. 1 Chron. xxvii. 21.

JAAZAH, Ja-ay'-zah.—A city of the Levites.

JAAZANIAH, Ja-az-a-ny'-ah, *whom the Lord will hear, the balances, the arms*.—The son of Shaphan. 2 Kings xxv. 23.

JAAZER, Ja-ay'-zer.—A city of the Amorites. Num. xxi. 32.

JAAZIAH, Jay-a-zy'-ah.—A descendant of Levi. 1 Chron. xxiv. 26.

JAAZIEL, Ja-ay'-ze-el.—A porter of the temple. 1 Chron. xv. 18.

JABAL, Jay'-bal, *which glides away.*—A son of Lamech. Gen. iv. 20.

JABBOK, Jab'-bok, *evacuation, dissipation.*—A brook on the other side Jordan, the spring of which is in the mountains of Gilead. It falls into Jordan, near the sea of Tiberias. Gen. xxxii. 22.

JABESH, Jay'-besh, *dryness, confusion, shame.*—The name of a city in the half-tribe of Manasseh, beyond Jordan. Judges xxi. 8; 1 Sam. xi. 1.

JABESH-GILEAD, Jay'-besh-gil'-le-ad.—The same as JABESH.

JABEZ, Jay'-bez, *sorrow, trouble.*—1. The name of a city. 1 Chron. ii. 55. 2. The name of a person. 1 Chron. iv. 9.

JABIN, Jay'-bin, *he that understands, he that builds.*—1. The king of Hazor, situated in the northern parts of Canaan. Josh. xi. 1. 2. The name of another king of Hazor, who oppressed the Israelites for twenty years. Judges iv. 2.

JABNEEL, Jab'-ne-el, *building, or understanding of God.*—1. A town in the frontiers of Naphtali. Josh. xix. 33. 2. A town in the tribe of Judah. Josh. xv. 11.

JACHAN, Jay'-kan, *that strengthens.*—A descendant of Gad. 1 Chron. v. 13.

JACHIN, Jay'-kin, *that strengthens.*—1. The fourth son of Simeon. Gen xlvi. 10. 2. The head of a family of priests. 1 Chron. xxiv. 17. 3. The name of a pillar in the temple. 1 Kings vii. 21.

JACHINITES, Jay'-kin-ites.—Descendants of Jachin. Num. xxvi. 12.

JACOB, Jay'-kob, *he that supplants, the heel.*—1. The son of Isaac and Rebecca, born A.M. 2167. Gen. xxv. 26. See his history in the book of Genesis. 2. The son of Matthan, the father of Joseph, the reputed father of Christ. Matt. i. 16.

JADA, Jay'-dah, *knowing.*—A descendant of Judah. 1 Chron. ii. 32.

JADDUA, Jad-dew'-ah.—1. A high-priest of the Jews in the time of Alexander the Great. 2. One who returned from captivity. Neh. x. 21.

JAEL, Jay'-el, *he that ascends, a kid.*—The wife of Heber, the Kenite: she slew Sisera, the Canaanitish general. Judges iv. 17.

JAGUR, Jay'-gur.—A city of Judah. Josh. xv. 21.

JAH, Jah.—One of the names of God, found in the composition of many Hebrew words. It signifies *my Lord, praise the Lord, the Lord is my king, the everlasting God.* Psalm lxviii. 4.

JAHALEEL, Ja-hay'-le-el.—A descendant of Judah.

JAHALELEL, Ja-hal'-e-lel.—A descendant of Levi.

JAHATH, Jay'-hath.—1. A descendant of Judah. 1 Chron. iv. 2. 2. A surveyor of the workmen employed by Josiah in repairing the temple. 2 Chron. xxxiv. 12.

JAHAZ, Jay'-haz, *dispute, going out of the Lord.*—A city beyond Jordan, near where Sihon was defeated by Moses. Num. xxi. 23.

JAHAZA, Ja-hay'-zah.—The same as JAHAZ. Josh. xiii. 18.

JAHAZIAH, Ja-ha-zy'-ah.—The son of Tikvah. Ezra x. 15.

JAHAZIEL, Ja-hay'-ze-el.—One who deserted Saul's party to join David. 1 Chron. xii. 4.

JAHDAI, Jah'-da-i.—A descendant of Judah. 1 Chron. ii. 47.

JAHDIEL, Jah'-de-el.—One of the posterity of Manasseh. 1 Chron. v. 24.

JAHDO, Jah'-do.—A descendant of Gad. 1 Chron. v. 14.

JAHLEEL, Jah'-le-el.—The third son of Zebulun, head of the family of Jahleelites. Gen. xlvi. 14.

JAHMAI, Jah'-ma-i.—The son of Tola. 1 Chron. vii. 2.

JAHZAH, Jah'-zah.—A city of Palestine. 1 Chron. vi. 78.

JAHZEEL, Jah'-ze-el.—A descendant of Naphtali Gen. xlvi. 24.

JAHZERAH, Jah'-ze-rah.—A descendant of Levi. 1 Chron. ix. 12.

JAIR, Jay'-er, *my light, that diffuses light.*—1. One of the judges of the family of Manasseh. Judges x. 3. 2. The son of Shimei, father of Mordecai. Esther ii. 5.

JAIRUS, Ja-i'-rus, *is enlightened.*—Chief of the synagogue at Capernaum. Mark v. 22.

JAKAN, Jay'-kan.—A descendant of Abraham. 1 Chron. i. 42.

JAKEH, Jay'-keh.—Father of Agar. Prov. xxx. 1.

JAKIM, Jay'-kim.—1. A descendant of Benjamin. 1 Chron. viii. 19. 2. A priest of David's appointing. 1 Chron. xxiv. 12.

JALON, Jay'-lon.—A descendant of Judah. 1 Chron. iv. 17.

JAMBRES, Jam'-brees, *the sea with poverty.*—A magician in Egypt, who withstood Moses. 2 Tim. iii. 8.

JAMES, James.—The same in signification as JACOB. 1. Surnamed the Greater or Elder, to distinguish him from James the Younger: was brother to St. John the Evangelist, and son to Zebedee and Salome. Matt. iv. 21. 2. James the Less, called the brother (kinsman) of our Lord. Gal. i. 19. He was the son of Cleopas, and Mary, sister to the Virgin; consequently cousin-german to Jesus Christ, according to the flesh. 1 Cor. xv. 7.

JAMIN, Jay'-min.—A son of Simeon, Gen. xlvi. 10; and father of the Jaminites. Num. xxvi. 12.

JANNA, Jan'-nah, *who speaks, who answers.*—The father of Melchi. Luke iii. 24.

JANNES, Jan'-nees, *who speaks, who answers, affliction.*—An Egyptian magician, who withstood Moses. 2 Tim. iii. 8.

JANOAH, Ja-no'-ah.—A city in the tribe of Ephraim. 2 Kings xv. 29.

JANUM, Jay'-num.—A city in Judah. Josh. xv. 53.

JAPHETH, Jay'-feth, *persuades, handsome.*—The son of Noah, commonly named third in order of Noah's sons, and was born in the five hundredth year of that patriarch. Gen. v. 32. He was the oldest of Noah's sons. Gen. x. 21.

JAPHIA, Ja-fy'-ah, *which enlightens, groans.*—A city of Zebulun. Josh. xix. 12.

JAPHLET, Jaf'-let.—A descendant of Asher. 1 Chron. vii. 32.

JAPHLETI, Jaf'-le-ty.—A town of Palestine. Josh. xvi. 3.

JAPHO, Jay'-fo.—A city of Dan. Josh. xix. 46. The same as JOPPA. Acts ix. 36.

JAR, Jar.—A Hebrew month, answering to our April. It consisted of twenty-nine days. Num. ix. 10, 11.

JARAH, Jay'-rah.—One of the posterity of king Saul. 1 Chron. ix. 42.

JAREB, Jay'-reb, *a revenger.*—A king of Assyria. Hosea v. 13.

JARED, Jay'-red, *he that descends or commands.*—The father of Enoch. Gen. v. 15.

JARESIAH, Jar-e-sy'-ah.—A descendant of Benjamin. 1 Chron. viii. 27.

JARHA, Jar'-hah.—An Egyptian servant. 1 Chron. ii. 34.

JARIB, Jay'-rib.—A descendant of Simeon. Ezra viii. 16.

JARMUTH, Jar'-muth.—A city of Judah. Josh. x. 5.

JAROAH, Ja-ro'-ah.—A descendant of Gad. 1 Chron. v. 14.

JASHEN, Jay'-shen.—One of David's worthies. 2 Sam. xxiii. 32.

JASHER, Jay'-sher, *righteous*.—A person who wrote a book extant in the time of Joshua and Samuel, and to which they referred. Josh. x. 13; 2 Sam. i. 18.

JASHOBEAM, Ja-sho'-be-am.—1. The Hachmonite, a captain over thirty men in David's army. 1 Chron. xi. 11. 2. A descendant of Korah. 1 Chron. xii. 6.

JASHUB, Jash'-ub.—Of the tribe of Issachar. Num. xxvi. 24.

JASHUBI-LEHEM, Jash'-ew-by-le'-hem.— A place mentioned 1 Chron. iv. 22: uncertain where.

JASIEL, Jay'-se-el.—One of David's warriors. 1 Chron. xi. 47.

JASON, Jay'-son, *he that cures, that gives medicine*.—A kinsman of St. Paul. Rom. xvi. 21; Acts xvii. 7.

JATHNIEL, Jath'-ne-el.—A porter of the temple. 1 Chron. xxvi. 2.

JATTIR, Jat'-tir.—A city of Palestine. Josh. xv. 48.

JAVAN, Jay'-van, *that deceives, clay*.—The fourth son of Japheth. Gen. x. 2.

JAZER, Jay'-zer, *assistance, he that helps*.—A city in Gad. Num. xxxii. 1; Isai. xvi. 8.

JAZIEL, Jay'-ze-el.—A porter in the temple.

JAZIZ, Jay'-ziz.—David's chief shepherd. 1 Chron. xxvii. 31.

JEARIM, Je'-a-rim.—A mountain of Palestine. Josh. xv. 10.

JEATERAI, Je-at'-e-ray.—A descendant of Levi. 1 Chron. vi. 21.

JEBERECHIAH, Jeb-er-e-ky'-ah.—Father of Zechariah, the priest. Isai. viii. 2.

JEBUS, Je'-bus, *treads under foot, contemns.* — The ancient name of Jerusalem. Judges xix. 10.

JEBUSITES, Jeb'-ew-sites.—Inhabitants of Jebus. Gen. x. 16.

JECAMIAH, Jek-a-my'-ah, *the resurrection.* — The son of Jeconiah, of the royal family of Judah. 1 Chron. iii. 18.

JECHOLIAH, Jek-o-ly'-ah, *perfection of the Lord.*— The wife of Amaziah, king of Judah, and mother of Azariah. 2 Kings xv. 2.

JECONIAH, Jek-o-ny'-ah, *preparation or steadfastness of the Lord.*—The son of Jehoiakim, king of Judah : he succeeded his father, A.M. 3406. 1 Chron. iii. 16

JEDAIAH, Je-day'-yah.—1. A priest who returned from captivity. Ezra ii. 36. 2. Another priest mentioned Neh. iii. 10. 3. A descendant of Levi. 1 Chron. xxiv. 7.

JEDIAEL, Je-dy'-a-el, *the knowledge or joy of the Lord.* —One of David's worthies. 1 Chron. xi. 45.

JEDIAH, Je-dy'-ah, *well beloved.* — One of David's servants.

JEDIDAH, Je-dy'-dah, *well beloved, amiable.* — The mother of king Josiah. 2 Kings xxii. 1.

JEDIDIAH, Jed-e-dy'-ah, *beloved of the Lord.*—A son of king David. 2 Sam. xii. 25.

JEDUTHUN, Jed'-u-thun, *his law, who gives praise.*— A Levite of Merari's family, and one of the four great masters of music belonging to the temple. 1 Chron. xvi. 38, 41, 42; Psalm xxxix., title.

JEEZER, Je-e'-zer.—A son of Gilead. Num. xxvi. 30.

JEGAR-SAHADUTHA, Je'-gar-sa-ha-dew'-thah, *the heap of witness.*—The place where Jacob and Laban covenanted. Gen. xxxi. 47.

JEHALELEEL, Je-hal-le′-le-el. — A descendant of Merari. 1 Chron. iv. 16.

JEHALELEL, Je-hay′-le-lel.—One of the porters of the temple. 2 Chron. xxix. 12.

JEHAZIEL, Je-hay′-ze-el.—One of the twenty-four families of priests. 1 Chron. xii. 4.

JEHDEIAH, Jeh-dy′-ah.—A Meronothite, and keeper of the asses in king David's time. 1 Chron. xxiv. 20.

JEHEZEKEL, Je-hez′-e-kel. — An order of priests. 1 Chron. xxiv. 16.

JEHIAH, Je-hy′-ah. — A doorkeeper for the ark. 1 Chron. xv. 24.

JEHIEL, Je-hy′-el.—1. One who returned from captivity. Ezra x. 26. 2. One of David's valiant men. 1 Chron. ix. 35.

JEHIELI, Je-hy′-e-ly.—A descendant of Levi. 1 Chron. xxvi. 22.

JEHIZKIAH, Je-hiz-ky′-ah.—A descendant of Ephraim. 2 Chron. xxviii. 12.

JEHOADAH, Je-ho′-a-dah.—The son of Ahaz. 1 Chron. viii. 36.

JEHOADDAN, Je-ho-ad′-dan.—Mother of Amaziah. 2 Kings xiv. 2.

JEHOAHAZ, Je-ho′-a-haz, *the prize of the Lord.*— 1. The son of Jehu, king of Israel, who succeeded his father, A.M. 3146. 2 Kings x. 35. 2. Otherwise Shallum, the son of Josiah, king of Judah. Jer. xxii. 11.

JEHOASH, Je-ho′-ash, *the fire or victim of the Lord.*— Son of Ahaziah, king of Judah. 2 Kings xi. 21. The same as JOASH.

JEHOHANAN, Je-ho′-ha-nan.—A porter of the temple. 1 Chron. xxvi. 3.

JEHOIACHIN, Je-hoy′-a-kin, *preparation or strength of the Lord.*—Sometimes called CONIAH, Jer. xxii. 24; and JECONIAH, 1 Chron. iii. 16. He was the son of Jehoiakim, king of Judah, and grandson of Josiah. He ascended the throne, and reigned only three months. 2 Kings xxiv. 8. He was born about the time of the first Babylonish captivity, A.M. 3398.

JEHOIADA, Je-hoy′-a-dah, *knowledge of the Lord.*—The successor of Azariah in the priesthood, and was himself succeeded by Zechariah. 2 Kings xi., xii.

JEHOIAKIM, Je-hoy′-a-kim, *the resurrection of the Lord.*—Sometimes called ELIAKIM, the brother and successor of Jehoahaz, king of Judah, who was advanced to the throne by Pharaoh Necho, king of Egypt, A.M. 3394. 2 Kings xxiii. 34. He reigned eleven years in Jerusalem, and was a wicked king.

JEHOIARIB, Je-hoy′-a-rib.—The head of a family of priests. 1 Chron. xxiv. 7. The Maccabees descended from this family.

JEHONADAB, Je-hon′-a-dab, *who acts in good earnest.*—A father of the Rechabites. 2 Kings x. 15.

JEHONATHAN, Je-hon′-a-than, *given of God.*—A Levite in the reign of Jehoshaphat. 2 Chron. xvii. 8.

JEHORAM, Je-ho′-ram, *exaltation, rejected of God.*—The son of Jehoshaphat. 1 Kings xxii. 50.

JEHOSHAPHAT, Je-hosh′-a-fat, *God judges.*—1. King of Judah, the son of Asa. He ascended the throne A.M. 3090, at the age of thirty-five, and reigned twenty-five years. 1 Kings xv. 24; 2 Chron. xvii. 1, 2, &c. 2. A secretary of state. 1 Kings iv. 3. 3. Solomon's steward. 1 Kings iv. 17. 4. A noted valley in Judea, called the valley of Kidron, from the brook Kidron running through it. It lies east of Jerusalem, between the city and the Mount of Olives. Joel iii. 2.

JEHOSHEBA, Je-hosh′-e-bah.—Wife of Jehoiada, the high-priest. 2 Kings xi. 2.

JEHOSHUA, Je-hosh'-u-ah, *the saviour.* — Nun Jehoshua was the father of Oshea, one of the spies. Num. xiii. 16.

JEHOVAH, Je-ho'-vah, *self-existing.*—The proper and incommunicable name of God. Exod. vi. 3.

JEHOVAH-JIREH, Je-ho'-vah-jy'-reh, *the Lord will see or provide, will be manifested.* — The place where Abraham offered his son. Gen. xxii. 14.

JEHOVAH-NISSI, Je-ho'-vah-nis'-sy, *the Lord my banner.*—The name of an altar built by Moses, on the defeat of Amalek. Exod. xvii. 15.

JEHOVAH-SHALOM, Je-ho'-vah-shay'-lom, *the Lord send peace.*—An altar built by Gideon. Judges vi. 24.

JEHOVAH-SHAMMAH, Je-ho'-vah-sham'-mah, *the Lord is there.*—Ezek. xlviii. 35.

JEHOVAH-TSIDKENU, Je-ho'-vah-tsid'-ke-new, *the Lord our righteousness.*—Jer. xxiii. 6.

JEHOZABAD, Je-hoz'-a-bad.—One of the assassins of king Joash. 2 Kings xii. 21.

JEHU, Je'-hew, *he that is or exists.*—1. The son of Jehoshaphat, and grandson of Nimshi, captain of the troops of Joram, the king of Israel: was appointed by God to reign over Israel, and to avenge the sins committed by the house of Ahab. 1 Kings xix. 16. 2. A prophet, the son of Hanani, who was sent to Baasha, king of Israel, to prophesy against that prince, and was slain by his orders. 1 Kings xvi. 7.

JEHUBBAH, Je-hub'-bah.—A descendant of Asher. 1 Chron. vii. 34.

JEHUCAL, Je'-hu-kal, *mighty.*—Son of Shelemiah. Jer. xxxvii. 3.

JEHUD, Je'-hud, *praising.*—A city in Palestine, in Dan. Josh. xix. 45.

132

JEHUDI, Je-hew'-dy, *praise.*— A grandson of Shelemiah. Jer. xxxvi. 21.

JEHUDIJAH, Je-hew-dy'-jah, *praise of the Lord.*— The mother of Jered. 1 Chron. iv. 18.

JEHUSH, Je'-hush.—A descendant of king Saul. 1 Chron. viii. 39.

JEIEL, Je-i'-el.—One of David's valiant men. 1 Chron. v. 7.

JEKABZEEL, Je-kab'-ze-el.—A village in Canaan. Neh. xi. 25.

JEKAMEAM, Jek-a-me'-am.—A descendant of Levi. 1 Chron. xxiii. 19.

JEKAMIAH, Je-ka-my'-ah.—Son of Shallum. 1 Chron. ii. 41.

JEKUTHIEL, Je-kew'-the-el.—A descendant of Judah. 1 Chron. iv. 18.

JEMIMA, Je-my'-mah, *handsome as the day.*—A daughter of Job. Job xlii. 14.

JEMUEL, Jem-yew'-el.—A descendant of Simeon. Gen. xlvi. 10.

JEPHTHAH, Jef'-thah, *he that opens.*—Judge of Israel, and successor to Jair. He was a native of Mizpeh, son of a harlot and one Gilead. Judges xi. 1, 2, &c.

JEPHUNNEH, Je-fun'-nee, *he that beholds.*—Caleb's father. Num. xiii. 6.

JERAH, Je'-rah, *the moon, to scent or smell.*—A descendant of Shem. Gen. x. 26.

JERAHMEEL, Je-ram'-me-el, *mercy or love of God.*— 1. One that was sent to apprehend Jeremiah the prophet. Jer. xxxvi. 26. 2. A son of Hezron. 1 Chron. ii. 9. 3. The son of Kish. 1 Chron. xxiv. 29.

JERED, Je'-red.—The son of Ezra. 1 Chron. i. 2.

JEREMAI, Jer'-e-may.—One of the captives. Ezra x. 33.

133

JEREMIAH, Jer-e-my'-ah, *the grandeur of the Lord.* —1. The son of Hilkiah, of the race of the priests, a native of Anathoth, in the tribe of Benjamin. Jer. i. 1. He was set apart for the office from his birth. He began to prophesy in the reign of Josiah, A.M. 3375. 2. The name of the father of Hamutal, who was the wife of Josiah. 2 Kings xxiv. 18. 3. A descendant of Manasseh. 1 Chron. v. 24. 4. A soldier who joined David at Ziklag. 1 Chron. xii. 4, 10. 5. The name of another who joined David at Ziklag. 1 Chron. xii. 13.

JEREMOTH, Jer'-e-moth, *eminences.*—A descendant of Benjamin. 1 Chron. viii. 14.

JERIAH, Je-ry'-ah.—One of the tribe of Levi. 1 Chron. xxiii. 19.

JERIBAI, Jer'-e-bay.—One of David's valiant men. 1 Chron. xi. 46.

JERICHO, Jer'-re-ko, *his moon, sweet smell.*—1. A city in the tribe of Benjamin, about seven leagues from Jerusalem, and two from Jordan. Josh. ii. 1. 2. A person who returned from captivity. Ezra ii. 34.

JERIEL, Jee'-re-el.—A son of Tola. 1 Chron. vii. 2.

JERIJAH, Je-ry'-jah.—An Hebronite, an officer of David. 1 Chron. xxvi. 31.

JERIMOTH, and **JEREMOTH,** Jer'-e-moth, *eminences, he that fears or regrets death.*—1. A descendant of Benjamin. 1 Chron. vii. 7. 2. A son of Becher. 1 Chron. vii. 8. 3. A son of Beriah. 1 Chron. viii. 14. 4. A son of Merari. 1 Chron. xxiii. 23. 5. A son of Mushi. 1 Chron. xxiv. 30. 6. A descendant of Levi. 1 Chron. xxv. 4.

JERIOTH, Jee'-re-oth.—A wife of Caleb. 1 Chron. ii. 18.

JEROBOAM, Jer-o-bo'-am, *fighting against, increasing the people.*—The son of Nebat and a widow called Zeruah. 1 Kings xi. 26. He was born at Zareda, in the tribe of Ephraim: appointed king of the ten tribes when they revolted from Rehoboam. His name is often mentioned in Scripture as making Israel to sin; being the author of the idolatry as well as the schism of the ten tribes. 2. The son of Joash, king of Israel. He ascended the throne A.M. 3179, and reigned forty years. 2 Kings xiii. 13.

JEROHAM, Jer′-o-ham.— A descendant of Levi. 1 Sam. i. 1.

JERUBBAAL, Je-rub′-ba-al, or Jer-ub-bay′-al, *he that revenges the idol, let Baal defend his cause.*—The name of Gideon. Judges vi. 32.

JERUBBESHETH, Je-rub′-be-sheth, *let the idol of confusion defend itself.*—A person mentioned 2 Sam. xi. 21.

JERUEL, Jer′-u-el, *a vision.*—The name of a wilderness to the west of the Dead Sea. 2 Chron. xx. 16.

JERUSALEM, Je-rew′-sa-lem, *the vision or possession of peace.* — Formerly called Jebus and Salem. Josh. xviii. 28; Heb. vii. 2. The capital of Judea, situated partly in the tribe of Benjamin, and partly in the tribe of Judah. It was not completely reduced by the Israelites till the time of David. 2 Sam. v. 6—9. Here was the centre of true worship, and the place where God did in a peculiar manner dwell, first in the tabernacle, afterwards in the temple. It was taken and burnt by Titus, A. D. 70, in accordance with the prophecies of Jesus Christ.

JERUSHA, Je-rew′-shah, *he that possesses the inheritance, exiled.*—The mother of Jotham. 2 Kings xv. 33.

JESAIAH, Je-say′-yah.—One who joined David at Ziklag. 1 Chron. iii. 21.

JESHAIAH, Jesh-a-i′-ah.—A son of Jeduthun. 1 Chron. xxv. 15.

JESHANAH, Jesh′-a-nah. — A city in the tribe of Ephraim. 2 Chron. xiii. 19.

JESHARELAH, Jesh-ar′-e-lah.—A Levite. 1 Chron. xxv. 14.

JESHEBEAB, Jesh-eb′-e-ab.—A porter of the temple. 1 Chron. xxiv. 13.

JESHER, Jee'-sher.—A son of Caleb. 1 Chron. ii. 18.

JESHIMON, Jesh'-e-mon, *solitude, desolation.*—A city in the wilderness of Maon, belonging to the tribe of Simeon. 1 Sam. xxiii. 24.

JESHISHAI, Je-shish'-a-i. — A descendant of Gad. 1 Chron. v. 14.

JESHOHAIAH, Jesh-ho-ha-i'-ah.—A descendant of Simeon. 1 Chron. iv. 36.

JESHUAH, Jesh'-u-ah, *a saviour.*—A high-priest of the Jews. 1 Chron. xxiv. 11.

JESHURUN, Jesh'-u-run, *upright.* — The people of Israel. Deut. xxxiii. 5.

JESIMIEL, Je-sim'-e-el.—A descendant of Simeon. 1 Chron. iv. 36.

JESSE, Jes'-se, *to be, my present.*—The father of David. Ruth iv. 17, 22; 1 Chron. ii. 13.

JESUI, Jes'-u-i, *who is equal, flat country.*—A son of Asher. Num. xxvi. 44.

JESUITES, Jes'-u-ites.—The posterity of Jesui. Num. xxvi. 44.

JESUS, Jee'-sus, *a saviour, who saveth his people from their sins.*—The Son of God, the Saviour of the world. See the New Testament, *passim.*

JETHER, Jee'-ther, *he that remains, excels, searches.*— 1. The son of Gideon. Judges viii. 20. 2. The husband of Abigail. 1 Chron. ii. 17.

JETHETH, Jee'-theth.—A descendant of Esau. Gen. xxxvi. 40.

JETHLAH, Jeth'-lah.—A city in the tribe of Dan. Josh. xix. 42.

JETHRO, Jee'-thro, *his excellence or posterity.*—Priest or prince of Midian, the father-in-law of Moses. Exod. xviii. 12.

JETUR, Jee'-tur, *he that keeps, succession, mountainous.* —A son of Esau. Gen. xxv. 15.

JEUEL, Jee'-u-el.—A descendant of Terah. 1 Chron. ix. 6.

JEUSH, Jee'-ush, *devoured, gnawed by the moth.*—A son of Esau. Gen. xxxvi. 5.

JEUZ, Jee'-uz.—A descendant of Benjamin. 1 Chron. viii. 10.

JEWRY, Jew'-re.—The land of Canaan. Dan. v. 13.

JEWS, Jews.—A name given to the descendants of Abraham, by his son Isaac, and derived from the patriarch Judah.

JEZANIAH, Jez-a-ny'-ah.—A person mentioned Jer. xlii. 1, and thought to be the same as Azariah, mentioned Jer. xliii. 2.

JEZEBEL, Jez'-e-bel, *island of the habitation, woe to the habitation, isle of the dunghill.*—1. The daughter of Ethbaal, king of the Zidonians, and wife to Ahab, king of Israel. 1 Kings xvi. 31. 2. A name used proverbially, Rev. ii. 20.

JEZER, Jee'-zer.—The son of Naphtali. Gen. xlvi. 24.

JEZERITES, Jee'-zer-ites. — Descendants of Jezer. Num. xxvi. 49.

JEZIEL, Jee'-ze-el.—One who joined David at Ziklag. 1 Chron. xii. 3.

JEZLIAH, Jez-ly'-ah. — A descendant of Benjamin. 1 Chron. viii 18.

JEZOAR, Jez'-o-ar.—A descendant of Judah. 1 Chron. iv. 7.

JEZRAHIAH, Jez-ra-hy'-ah, *the Lord is the east, the Lord arises.*—A singer in the temple. Neh. xii. 42.

JEZREEL, Jez'-re-el, *seed of God, dropping of the friendship of God.*—1. A city of Palestine. Josh. xv. 56. 2. A son of Etam, of the tribe of Judah. 1 Chron. iv. 3.

3. A son of the prophet Hosea. Hosea i. 4. 4. The name also of a city in the tribe of Manasseh. Josh. xix. 18.

JEZREELITE, Jez'-re-el-ite.—An inhabitant of Jezreel. 1 Kings xxi. 1.

JEZREELITESS, Jez'-re-el-i-tess.—A woman of Jezreel. 2 Sam. iii. 2.

JIBSAM, Jib'-sam.—A son of Tola. 1 Chron. vii. 2.

JIDLAPH, Jid'-laf, *he that distils, joins hands.*—A son of Nahor. Gen. xxii. 22.

JIMNAH, Jim-'nah.—A son of Asher. Gen. xlvi. 17.

JIPHTAH, Jif'-tah.—A city of Palestine. Josh. xv. 43.

JIPHTHAH-EL, Jif'-thah-el.—A valley in Palestine. Josh. xix. 14.

JOAB, Jo'-ab, *paternity, having a father, voluntary.*—The son of Zeruiah, David's sister, and brother to Abishai and Asahel. 1 Chron. ii. 16. He was one of the most valiant men, and the greatest general in David's time, but one of the most cruel and imperious. 2 Sam. ii. 13, 14, &c.; iii. 27—39; xi. 6, 16; xviii., xix., xx.

JOAH, Jo'-ah, *who has a brother, brother of the Lord.*—1. A descendant of Levi. 2 Kings xviii. 18. 2. Secretary to king Josiah. 2 Chron. xxxiv. 8.

JOAHAZ, Jo'-a-haz.—The recorder to king Josiah. 2 Chron. xxxiv. 8.

JOANNA, Jo-an'-nah, *the grace or mercy of God.*—1. The wife of Chuza, Herod's steward; one of those women that followed Jesus. Luke viii. 3. 2. The son of Rhesa. Luke iii. 27.

JOASH, Jo'-ash, *who despairs, burns, is on fire.*—1. The father of Gideon. Judges vi. 11. 2. A servant of Ahab. 1 Kings xxii. 26. 3. A descendant of Shelah. 1 Chron. iv. 22. 4. The son of Ahaziah, king of Judah. He was secretly conveyed away when a child, and lodged with his nurse, in the temple, so privately, that he remained undiscovered by his enemies. He was here six years, and was seven years of age when he began to reign. 2 Chron. xxii. 11; 2 Kings xi. 5. King of Israel, son and successor of Jehoahaz. 2 Kings xiii.

JOATHAM, Jo'-a-tham.—The son of Ozias. Matt. i. 9.

JOB, Jobe, *he that weeps, speaks, or cries out of a hollow place.*—1. The third son of Issachar. Gen. xlvi. 13. 2. A patriarch celebrated for his patience, and the constancy of his piety and virtue. See the book of Job.

JOBAB, Jo'-bab.—1. The son of Joktan. Gen. x. 29. 2. A king of Edom. Gen. xxxvi. 33, 34.

JOCHEBED, Jok'-e-bed, *glorious, honourable, a person of merit, the glory of the Lord.*—The wife of Amram, and mother of Miriam, Moses, and Aaron. Exod. vi. 20.

JOED, Jo'-ed.—One who returned from captivity. Neh. xi. 7.

JOEL, Jo'-el, *that wills, commands, or swears.*—1. The oldest son of Samuel the prophet. 1 Sam. viii. 1, &c. 2. The son of Pethuel, the second of the twelve minor prophets. Also the name of five other persons, concerning whom nothing is related.

JOELAH, Jo-e'-lah.—A friend of king David. 1 Chron. xii. 7.

JOEZER, Jo-e'-zer, *he that aids.*—One of David's officers. 1 Chron. xii. 6.

JOGBEHAH, Jog'-be-hah.—A city of the Amorites. Num. xxxii. 35.

JOGLI, Jog'-ly.—A descendant of Dan. Num. xxxiv. 22.

JOHA, Jo'-hah.—A descendant of Benjamin. 1 Chron. viii. 16.

JOHANAN, Jo-hay'-nan, *who enlivens or gives life.*—1. See 2 Kings xxv. 23; Jer. xl. 15, 16. 2. The son of Josiah. 1 Chron. iii. 15. 3. A high-priest of the Jews. 1 Chron. vi. 9, 10. 4. The son of Elioenai. 1 Chron. iii. 24.

JOHN, Jon, *the gift or mercy of the Lord.*—1. The Baptist, the forerunner of Christ, the son of Zacharias and Elisabeth. Luke i. 7, 13, 15. 2. The Evangelist. He was

139

a native of Bethsaida, in Galilee, and the son of Zebedee and Salome, and by trade a fisherman. Matt. iv. 21. He was "the disciple whom Jesus loved." 3. John, surnamed Mark. The son of a woman called Mary, at whose house the apostles and other Christians frequently met at Jerusalem. Acts xii. 12.

JOIADA, Joy'-a-dah.—A Jewish priest. Neh. xii. 11.

JOIARIB, Joy'-a-rib.—One of the captives. Ezra viii. 16.

JOKDEAM, Jok'-de-am.—A city of Palestine. Josh. xv. 56.

JOKIM, Jo'-kim.—A descendant of Judah. 1 Chron. iv. 22.

JOKNEAM, Jok'-ne-am.—A city of Palestine. Josh. xii. 22.

JOKSHAN, Jok'-shan, *hard, difficult, scandalous.*—The second son of Abraham by Keturah. Gen. xxv. 2.

JOKTAN, Jok'-tan, *small, disgust, weariness, dispute.*—The eldest son of Eber. Gen. x. 25.

JOKTHEEL, Jok'-the-el.—The name of a city. Josh. xv. 38.

JONA, or JONAS, Jo'-nah, Jo'-nas, *a dove, he that oppresses.*—The name of Peter's father. Matt. xvi. 17.

JONADAB, Jon'-a-dab, *who acts in good earnest.*—A relative of David. 2 Sam. xiii. 3.

JONAH, Jo'-nah, *a dove, he that oppresses.*—The son of Amittai, and the fifth of the minor prophets. He was a Galilean, and a native of Gath-hepher. 2 Kings xiv. 25.

JONAN, Jo'-nan.—An ancestor of Joseph, husband of the Virgin Mary. Luke iii. 30.

JONATHAN, Jon'-a-than, *given of God.*—1. A Levite, and son of Gershom, and grandson of Moses. Judges xviii. 30. 2. The son of Saul, and sincere and steady friend of David. 1 Sam. xiii. 16, &c. 3. The son of Shage, the Hararite, one distinguished for bravery in David's army. 1 Chron. xi. 34. 4. The son of Shimea.

1 Chron. xx. 7. 5. The son of Asahel. Ezra x. 15. 6. The high-priest of the Jews. Neh. xii. 11. 7. A scribe, and keeper of the prisons in Jerusalem, under king Zedekiah. Jer. xxxvii. 15.

JOPPA, Jop'-pah, *beauty, comeliness.*—A seaport town in Palestine, lying south of Cæsarea, and formerly the only port to Jerusalem. 2 Chron. ii. 16; Acts ix. 36; Acts x. 8.

JORAH, Jo'-rah, *cast.*—One of the captives. Ezra ii. 18.

JORAI, Jo'-ra-i.—A descendant of Gad. 1 Chron. v. 13.

JORAM, Jo-ram, *to cast, elevated.*—The son of Toi, king of Hamath, in Syria. 2 Sam. viii. 10. 2. The son and successor of Ahab, king of Israel. 2 Kings viii. 16.

JORDAN, Jor'-dan, *the river of judgment, that rejects judgment, descent.*—A river of Judea, rising in Mount Libanus. It runs 150 miles through Palestine, and empties itself into the Dead Sea: its common breadth is not more than sixty feet.

JORIM, Jo'-rim, *he that exalts the Lord.*—The son of Matthat. Luke iii. 29.

JORKOAM, Jor'-ko-am.—A descendant of Judah. 1 Chron. ii. 44.

JOSABAD, Jos'-a-bad.—An officer in David's army. 1 Chron. xii. 4.

JOSAPHAT, Jos'-a-fat.—One in Christ's genealogy. Matt. i. 8.

JOSE, Jo'-se, *raised, who exists or pardons, saviour.*—The son of Eliezer. Luke iii. 29.

JOSEDECH, Jos'-e-dech.—A high-priest. Haggai i. 1.

JOSEPH, Jo'-zef, *increase, addition.*—1. The son of Jacob and Rachel, and brother to Benjamin. Gen. xxx. 22—24. He was born in Mesopotamia, A.M. 2259. See his history in the latter part of the book of Genesis. 2. Grandson of Matthan, husband to the blessed Virgin, and reputed father of Jesus Christ. Matt. i. 15, 16. 3. A person of Arimathea, and privately a disciple of Jesus Christ. John xix. 38; Luke xxiii. 50, 51.

JOSES, Jo′-sees, *raised, who exists or pardons, saviour.* —The son of Mary Cleophas, brother to James the Less, and a near relative of our Lord. Matt. xiii. 55; xxvii. 56; Mark xv. 40. He was the son of Mary, sister to the Virgin, and of Cleophas, Joseph's brother.

JOSHAH, Jo′-shah. — A descendant of Simeon. 1 Chron. iv. 34.

JOSHAVIAH, Josh-a-vy′-ah.—One of David's worthies. 1 Chron. xi. 46.

JOSHBEKASHAH, Josh-bek′-a-shah.—A singer in the temple. 1 Chron. xxv. 4.

JOSHUA, Josh′-u-ah, *the lord, the saviour.*—The son of Nun, of the tribe of Ephraim, and born A.M. 2460. He devoted himself to the service of Moses, and in Scripture is frequently called his servant. Exod. xxiv. 13. He led the people of Israel into Canaan, having succeeded Moses.

JOSIAH, Jo-sy′-ah, *the fire of the Lord.*—The son of Amon, king of Judah, and Jedidah, the daughter of Adaiah of Boscath. 2 Kings xxii. 1. He began to reign when only eight years of age, A.M. 3363. 2 Chron. xxxiv. 1, &c.

JOSIBIAH, Jo-se-by′-ah.—A descendant of Simeon. 1 Chron. iv. 35.

JOSIPHIAH, Jo-se-fy′-ah.—One of the captives. Ezra viii. 10.

JOTBAH, Jot′-bah.—A city in the tribe of Judah. 2 Kings xxi. 19.

JOTBATHAH, Jot′-ba-thah.—An encampment of the Hebrews in the wilderness. Num. xxxiii. 34.

JOTHAM, Jo′-tham, *perfection of the Lord.*—1. Gideon's youngest son, who escaped the massacre of his brethren. Judges ix. 5. 2. The son and successor of Uzziah, otherwise called Azariah, king of Judah, who having been smitten with leprosy, the government was committed to Jotham, A.M. 3221. He governed twenty-five years before his father's death; and then assumed the title of king, and reigned sixteen years alone. 2 Kings xv. 32.

JOZACHAR, Joz'-a-kar.—One who slew king Joash. 2 Kings xii. 21.

JOZADAK, Joz'-a-dak.—One of the captives. Ezra iii. 2.

JUBAL, Jew'-bal, *he that runs, he that produces, a trumpet.*—A son of Lamech, and inventor of musical instruments. Gen. iv. 21.

JUBILE, Jew'-be-lee.—The fiftieth year among the Jews, which immediately followed the seven weeks of years, or seven times seven years, mentioned Lev. xxv. 10.

JUCAL, Jew'-kal.—The son of Shelemiah. Jer. xxxviii. 1.

JUDAH, Jew'-dah, *the praise of the Lord.*—The son of Jacob and Leah, who was born in Mesopotamia, A.M. 2255. Gen. xxix. 35.

JUDAS, Jew'-das, *the praise of the Lord.*—1. Iscariot, the traitor. The disciple who was entrusted with the donations presented to our Lord, and at length became so wicked as to betray his Master. 2. Thaddeus, or Lebbeus, and Zelotes. Matt. xiii. 55. He was the author of the Epistle which has his name. 3. St. Paul's host at Damascus. Acts ix. 9—11.

JUDE, Jude.—See JUDAS.

JUDEA, Ju-de'-a, *confessing, or praise.*—A province of Asia, anciently called the land of Canaan, or Palestine, and afterwards the land of Promise, the land of Israel, and then Judea.

JULIA, Jew'-le-a, *downy.*—One whom Paul salutes, Rom. xvi. 15.

JULIUS, Jew'-le-us, *downy.*—The centurion into whose hands St. Paul was committed, to be conveyed to Rome. Acts xxvii. 1, &c.

JUNIA, Jew'-ne-a, *from Juno, or juventus, youth.*—A kinswoman of St. Paul. Rom. xvi. 7.

JUPITER, Jew'-pit-ter, *the father that helpeth.*—The most powerful of the heathen deities. Acts xiv. 12.

JUSHAB-HESED, Jew-shab′-he-sed. — A descendant of David. 1 Chron. iii. 20.

JUSTUS, Jus′-tus, *just, upright.*—1. A Jew called Jesus. Col. iv. 11.   2. One chosen in the place of Judas. Acts i. 23.

JUTTAH, Jut′-tah.—A city of Palestine. Josh. xv. 55.

K

KABZEEL, Kab′-ze-el, *the congregation of God.*—A city of Palestine, in the tribe of Judah. Josh. xv. 21.

KADESH, Kay′-desh, *holiness.*—A town in Judea. The same as En-mishpat. Gen. xiv. 7.

KADESH-BARNEA, Kay′-desh-bar′-ne-a, *holiness, of an inconstant son, of the corn, of purity.*—A city celebrated for several remarkable events. Miriam's death. Num. xx. 1.   The smiting the rock. Num. xxvii. 14.   The place from which the spies were sent to see the land of Canaan. Num. xxxii. 8.

KADMIEL, Kad′-me-el, *God of rising.*—One of the captives. Ezra ii. 40.

KADMONITES, Kad′-mon-ites, *ancients, easterns.*— Ancient inhabitants of Canaan, dwelling beyond Jordan, to the east of Phœnicia. Gen. xv. 19.

KALLAI, Kal′-la-i.—One who returned from captivity. Neh. xii. 20.

KANAH, Kay′-nah.—The name of a river. Josh. xvi. 8.

KAREAH, Ka-re′-ah.—The father of Johanan. Jer. xl. 8.

KARKAA, Kar′-ka-ah.—A town on the confines of Judah, lying southward. Josh. xv. 3.

KARKOR, Kar′kor.—A place mentioned Judges viii. 10.

KARNAIM, Kar′-na-im.—A city of Gilead. Gen. xiv. 5.

KARTAH, Kar'-tah.—A city of Palestine. Josh. xxi. 34.

KARTAN, Kar'-tan.—A city of the Levites. Josh. xxi. 32.

KATTATH, Kat'-tath.—A city of Palestine. Josh. xix. 15.

KEDAR, Ke'-dar, *blackness, sorrow.*—The son of Ishmael. The father of an Arabian tribe. Gen. xxv. 13.

KEDEMAH, Ked'-de-mah, *oriental.*—Ishmael's youngest son, Gen. xxv. 15, who dwelt, as did his brethren, eastward of the mountains of Gilead.

KEDEMOTH, Ked'-de-moth, *old age, orientals.*—A town in the tribe of Reuben, eastward of the brook Arnon. Josh. xiii. 18.

KEDESH, Ke'-desh, *holy.*—A town in Upper Galilee. Josh. xix. 37.

KEHELATHAH, Ke-hel'-a-thah.— An encampment in the wilderness. Num. xxxiii. 22.

KEILAH, Ky'-lah, *she that divides or cuts.*—A town in the tribe of Judah. Josh. xv. 44.

KELITA, Kel'-e-tah.—The name of a Levite. Ezra x. 23.

KEMUEL, Kem-yew'-el, *God is risen.*—1. The third son of Nahor, the father of Aram, and of the Syrians. Gen. xxii. 21. 2. The son of Shiphtan, of the tribe of Ephraim. Num. xxxiv. 24.

KENAN, Ke'-nan.—1 Chron. i. 2. Otherwise CAINAN. Gen. v. 9.

KENATH, Ke'-nath.—A town in the tribe of Manasseh, beyond Jordan. Num. xxxii. 42.

KENAZ, Ke'-naz, *this nest, lamentation, possession.*— 1. The fourth son of Eliphaz, the son of Esau. Gen. xxxvi. 15. 2. The father of Othniel and Caleb. Josh. xv. 17; Judges i. 13.

KENITES, Ken'-ites, *possession, lamentation, nest.*—A people who dwelt eastward of the Dead Sea, and extended into Arabia Petræa; for Jethro, the priest of Midian, and father-in-law to Moses, was a Kenite. Judges i. 16.

KENIZZITES, Ken'-niz-zites.—An ancient people of Canaan, whose land God promised to the descendants of Abraham. Gen. xv. 19.

KEREN-HAPPUCH, Ker-en-hap'-puk, *the horn or child of beauty.*—One of Job's daughters. Job xlii. 14.

KERIOTH, Ke'-re-oth, *the cities, the callings.*—A city of Palestine, and one of the boundaries of the tribe of Judah. Josh. xv. 25.

KEROS, Ke'-ros, *crooked.*—One who returned from the captivity of Babylon. Ezra ii. 44.

KETURAH, Ke-tew'-rah, *he that burns or makes the incense to fume, odoriferous.*—Abraham's second wife. Gen. xxv. 1.

KEZIA, Ke-zy'-ah, *superficies, angle, pleasant as Cassia.*—The name of Job's second daughter. Job xlii. 14.

KEZIZ, Ke'-ziz, *end, extremity.*—A valley in the tribe of Benjamin. Josh. xviii. 21.

KIBROTH-HATTAAVAH, Kib'-roth-hat-tay'-a-vah, *the graves of lust.*—One of the encampments of the Israelites in the wilderness. Num. xi. 34, 35.

KIBZAIM, Kib'-za-im, *congregation.*—A city in the tribe of Ephraim. Josh. xxi. 22.

KIDRON, Ky'-dron, *obscurity, obscure.*—A brook, running through the valley of Jehoshaphat on the east side of Jerusalem, between the city and the Mount of Olives. 1 Kings xv. 13; 2 Kings xxiii. 4.

KINAH, Ky'-nah.—A town in the tribe of Judah. Josh. xv. 22.

KIR, Ker, *a wall, black, coldness.*—A place in Media in Asia. 2 Kings xvi. 9.

KIR-HARASETH, Ker-har'-a-seth, *the city of the sun.*—A royal city of the Moabites. 2 Kings iii. 25.

KIR-HARESH, Ker-hay'-resh.—A town, the same as Rabbath-Moab. Isai. xvi. 11.

KIRIOTH, Kir'-e-oth, *a city.*—A city of the Moabites. Amos ii. 2.

KIRJATH, Kir'-jath, *city, vocation, lesson, meeting.*—A town near Gibeon, in the tribe of Benjamin. Josh. xviii. 28.

KIRJATHAIM, Kir'-jath-ay'-im, *the two cities.*—A town beyond Jordan. Josh. xiii. 19. Also, the name of a city in the tribe of Naphtali. 1 Chron. vi. 76.

KIRJATH-ARBA, Kir'-jath-ar'-bah, *the city of four.*—A place built by Arba, the ancient name of Hebron. Judges i. 10.

KIRJATH-ARIM, Kir'-jath-ay'-rim, *the city of cities, the city of those that watch.*—A city in the tribe of Benjamin. Ezra ii. 25.

KIRJATH-BAAL, Kir'-jath-bay'-al, *the city of Baal, of those that command, of those that possess.*—The same as Kirjath-jearim. A city of Judah, on the confines of Benjamin, where the ark was lodged for many years in the house of Abinadab. Josh. xv. 9; 1 Chron. xiii. 6.

KIRJATH-HUZOTH, Kir'-jath-hew'-zoth, *a city of streets, or populous.*—A place in the land of Moab. Num. xxii. 39.

KIRJATH-JEARIM, Kir'-jath-je'-a-rim, *the city of woods.*—See KIRJATH-BAAL.

KIRJATH-SANNAH, Kir'-jath-san'-nah, *the city of the bush, of enmity.*—A city of Palestine, in the tribe of Judah, in the mountains; also called Debir. Josh. xv. 49.

KIRJATH-SEPHER, Kir'-jath-se'-fer, *the city of letters, of the book.*—A city sometimes called Debir, in the tribe of Judah, which was given to Caleb. Josh. xv. 16, 17.

KISH, Kish, *hard, difficult, straw.*—The son of Abiel, and father of Saul. 1 Sam. ix. 1, &c.

KISHI, Kish'-i.—The son of Abdi, and father of Ethan. 1 Chron. vi. 44.

KISHION, Kish'-e-on.—A place in Palestine, in the tribe of Issachar. Josh. xix. 20.

KISHON, Ky'-shon.—A brook which has its source in the valley of Jezreel. Judges iv. 7.

KISON, Ky'-son.—The same as KISHON. Psalm lxxxiii. 9.

KITHLISH, Kith'-lish.—A town belonging to the tribe of Judah. Josh. xv. 40.

KITRON, Kit'-ron, *making sweet, perfuming.*—A city assigned to Zebulun, but which they could not conquer. Judges i. 30.

KITTIM, Kit'-tim, *they that bruise, gold, colouring.*— The son of Javan, and great-grandson of Noah. Gen. x. 4. See CHITTIM.

KOA, Ko'-ah, *hope, a line.*—The name of a province of the Babylonish empire; or, as St. Jerome understands the word, a title or degree of honour among the Babylonians. Ezek. xxiii. 23.

KOHATH, Ko'-hath, *congregation, obedience, to make blunt.*—The second son of the patriarch Levi, and father of Amram, Izhar, Hebron, and Uzziel. Gen. xlvi. 11; Exod. vi. 18.

KOHATHITES, Ko'-hath-ites. — The posterity of Kohath. Num. iv. 18.

KOLAIAH, Ko-la-i'-ah, *the voice of the Lord.*—One who returned from the Babylonish captivity. Neh. xi. 7.

KORAH, Ko'-rah, *bald, frozen.*—1. The son of Esau and Aholibamah. Gen. xxxvi. 14—16. 2. The son of Izhar, and grandson of Levi, and father of Asher, Elkanah, Aliasaph, and head of the Korites, a celebrated family among the Levites. Num. xvi. 1, &c.

KORE, Ko'-re.—A grandson of Korah. 1 Chron. ix. 19.

KOZ, Koz.—One who returned from captivity. Ezra ii. 61.

KUSHAIAH, Kush-ay'-yah. — Or Kishi, the son of Obdi, a Levite. 1 Chron. xv. 17. He was a singer before the ark. 1 Chron. vi. 44.

L

LAADAH, Lay'-a-dah, *to praise, or assemble.* — A descendant of Judah, son of Shelah. 1 Chron. iv. 21.

LAADAN, Lay'-a-dan.—The son of Gershon. 1 Chron. xxiii. 7, 8.

LABAN, Lay'-ban, *white, shining, gentle.*—1. The son of Bethuel, grandson of Nahor, and brother of Rebekah, and father of Rachel and Leah. Gen. xxviii. 2, &c. 2. The name of a place beyond Jordan in the plains of Moab. Deut. i. 1.

LACHISH, Lay'-kish, *she walks, who exists of himself.* —A city of Palestine, south of Judah, in the tribe of Dan. Josh. x. 23.

LAEL, Lay'-el, *to God, or to the mighty.*—One of the family of the Levites. Num. iii. 24.

LAHAD, Lay'-had.—A descendant of Judah. 1 Chron. iv. 2.

LAHAI-ROI, La-hay'-roy, *the well of him that liveth and seeth me.*—A well near to which the patriarch Isaac dwelt. Gen. xvi. 14.

LAHMAM, or **LAHMAS**, Lah'-mam, Lah'-mas, *the bread of them.*—A town in the tribe of Judah. Josh. xv. 40.

LAHMI, Lah'-my, *my bread, my war.*—The brother of Goliath the giant. 1 Chron. xx. 5.

LAISH, Lay'-ish, *a lion.*—1. A city of Palestine, near the river Jordan, afterwards Leshem, in the tribe of Reuben. Judges xviii. 29. 2. The father of Phaltiel. 1 Sam. xxv. 44.

LAKUM, Lay'-kum.—A city of Palestine, in the tribe of Naphtali. Josh. xix. 33.

LAMECH, Lay'-mek, *poor, made low, smitten.*—1. A descendant of Cain, the son of Methusael, and father of Jabal, Jubal, Tubal-Cain, and Naamah. Gen. iv. 18—22. 2. The father of Noah, and son of Methuselah. Gen. v. 25, 31.

LAODICEA, Lay-o-de-see'-a, *just people.*—There were several cities of this name; but the Scriptures speak only of that in Phrygia, upon the river Lycus, near Colosse. Its ancient name was Diospolis. Col. ii. 1.

LAODICEANS, Lay-o-de-see'-ans. — Inhabitants of Laodicea.

LAPIDOTH, Lap'-pe-doth, *enlightened, lamps.*—The husband of Deborah, the prophetess. Judges iv. 4.

LASEA, Lay-see'-a.—A city near the Fair Havens, in the island of Crete. Acts xxvii. 8.

LASHA, Lay'-shah, *to call, to anoint.*—A city nearly equi-distant from the Dead Sea and the Red Sea. Gen. x. 19.

LASHARON, La-shay'-ron.—A city of Canaan, on the west side of Jordan. Josh. xii. 18.

LAZARUS, Laz'-za-rus, *the help of God.*—1. The brother of Martha and Mary, who dwelt at Bethlehem. John xi. 2. The name of a beggar. Luke xvi. 20.

LEAH, Le'-ah, *painful, wearied.*—The wife of Jacob, and eldest daughter of Laban. See Gen. xxix. 23—26.

LEBANAH, Leb'-a-nah.—One whose children were of the order of the Nethinims. Ezra ii. 45.

LEBANON, Leb'-a-non, *white, incense.*—A famous chain of mountains which separate Syria from Palestine. The western part of this mountain is sometimes called Libanus; the opposite, Anti-Libanus. Josh. xi. 17.

LEBAOTH, Leb'-a-oth.—A town in the tribe of Judah. Josh. xv. 32.

LEBBÆUS, Leb-be'-us, *a man of heart.*—Called also Judas, and Thaddeus. He was brother of James the Less, son of Mary sister to the Virgin Mary, and to Cleophas, brother to Joseph. Matt. x. 3.

LEBONAH, Le-bo'-nah.—A place about four leagues from Shechem southward, and two leagues from Bethel. Judges xxi. 19.

LECAH, Le'-kah.—The son of Er, and grandson of Judah. 1 Chron. iv. 21.

LEHABIM, Le'-ha-bim, *flames, the points of a sword.*—The third son of Misraim. Gen. x. 13.

LEHI, Le'-hy, *jaw-bone.*—A place where Samson slew a thousand Philistines with the jaw-bone of an ass. It was in the tribe of Dan. Judges xv. 19.

LEMUEL, Lem'-u-el, *God with them.*—Supposed to be king Solomon. Prov. xxxi. 1.

LESHEM, Le'-shem.—Formerly LAISH, for which see Josh. xix. 47.

LETUSHIM, Le-tew'-shim.—The second son of Dedan, the son of Abraham and Keturah. Gen. xxv. 3.

LEUMMIM, Le-um'-min.—A great-grandson of the patriarch Abraham. Gen. xxv. 3.

LEVI, Le'-vy, *held, associated.*—1. The third son of Jacob and Leah, born in Mesopotamia, A.M. 2254. Gen. xxix. 34. The tribe descending from him was chosen by God for the temple service. 2. The name of St. Matthew. Mark ii. 14.

LEVIATHAN, Le-vy'-a-than, from two Hebrew words, which signify *joined* and *dragon.*—A monstrous animal of some kind, but what is not determined. See Job xli.

LEVITES, Le'-vites.—The posterity of Levi, dedicated to the service of the temple.

LEVITICUS, Le-vit'-e-kus.—A canonical book of Scripture, being the third book of the Pentateuch; so called because it contains principally the laws and regulations of the Levites, priests, and sacrifices.

LIBNAH, Lib'-nah, *white, whiteness.*—A city in the southern part of the tribe of Judah. Josh. xv. 42.

LIBNI, Lib'-ny, *white, whiteness.*—A son of Gershon, and grandson to the patriarch Levi. Exod. vi. 17.

LIBNITES, Lib'-nites.—The descendants of Libni. Num. iii. 21.

LIBYA, Lib'-e-a, *the heart of the sea.*—A province in Africa, supposed to have been peopled by Lehabim, the son of Mizraim. Acts ii. 10.

LIBYANS, Lib'-e-ans.—The people of Libya.

LIGURE, Ly'-gure.—The first precious stone in the third row of the Jewish high-priest's breast-plate, and on it was engraven the name of Gad. Exod. xxviii. 19.

LIKHI, Lik'-hy.—One of the posterity of the patriarch Manasseh. 1 Chron. vii. 19.

LINUS, Ly'-nus, *nets.*—A person mentioned by St. Paul, 2 Tim. iv. 21.

LO-AMMI, Lo-am'-my, *not my son.*—The metaphorical son of the prophet Hosea. Hosea i. 9.

LOD, Lod.—Otherwise Lydda, or Diospolis. See 1 Chron. viii. 12.

LODEBAR, Lod'-e-bar.—A place, the situation of which is uncertain; it was probably beyond Jordan. 2 Sam. ix. 4.

LOIS, Lo'-is.—Timothy's grandmother. 2 Tim. i. 5.

LO-RUHAMAH, Lo-roo'-ha-mah, *not having obtained mercy, not pitied.*—The metaphorical daughter of the prophet Hosea. Hosea i. 8.

LOT, Lot, *wrapt up, myrrh, resin.*—The son of Haran, and nephew of Abraham. He accompanied his uncle from Ur to Haran, and thence to Canaan. Gen. xiii. 8, 9.

LOTAN, Lo'-tan.—A duke of the Horites, a descendant of Esau. and son of Seir. Gen. xxxvi. 20.

LUBIM, Lew'-bim.—The name of Libya in Africa, supposed to have been peopled by Lehabim. Nahum iii. 9.

LUBIMS, Lew'-bims.—The people of Libya.

LUCAS, Lew'-kas, *luminous.*—A fellow-labourer with St. Paul. Philem. 24.

LUCIFER, Lew'-se-fer, *bringing light.*—Taken metaphorically for the king of Babylon, who exceeded all other kings in splendour; or for Satan, who in the writings of the Fathers is often denominated Lucifer. See Isai. xiv. 12.

LUCIUS, Lew'-she-us, *luminous.*—1. One of the prophets in the church of Antioch. Acts xiii. 1. 2. And St. Paul's kinsman. Rom. xvi. 21. Supposed by some to be the same.

LUD, Lud, *nativity or generation.*—The fourth son of Shem. Gen. x. 22.

LUDIM, Lew'-dim.—The son of Mizraim. Gen. x. 13.

LUHITH, Lew'-hith.—A place in the Moabite country, probably between the cities of Ar and Zoar. Isai. xv. 5; Jer. xlviii. 5.

LUKE, Luke, *luminous.*—One of the Evangelists, a Syrian, a native of Antioch, and a physician. He was St. Paul's companion in most of his travels. 2 Tim. iv. 11; Philem. 23, 24.

LUZ, Luz, *separation, departure.*—1. The ancient name of Bethel. Gen. xxviii. 19. 2. A city of Arabia Petræa, built by a man of Bethel. Judges i. 23.

LYBIA, Lib'-e-a.—See LIBYA.

LYCAONIA, Ly-ka-o'-ne-a, *she-wolf.*—A province of Asia Minor, having Galatia on the north, Pisidia to the south, Cappadocia to the east, and Phrygia to the west. Acts xiv. 6.

LYCIA, Lish'-e-a.—A province of Asia Minor. At the port of Myra, in Lycia, St. Paul embarked, when he sailed for Rome. Acts xxvii. 5.

LYDDA, Lid'-da, *nativity.*—The same as DIOSPOLIS. It lay on the road from Jerusalem to Cesarea, four or five leagues to the east of Joppa. Acts ix. 32, 35.

LYDIA, Lid'-e-a.—1. A woman of Thyatira, a seller of purple, who dwelt in the city of Philippi, in Macedonia.

Acts xvi. 14, 40. 2. A province of Asia Minor. 3. A part of Egypt, peopled by Ludim, the son of Mizraim. Jer. xlvi. 9.

LYSANIAS, Ly-say′-ne-as, *that drives away sorrow.*—Tetrarch of Abilene, which country he possessed when John the Baptist began his mission. Luke iii. 1.

LYSTRA, Lis′-tra, *that dissolves or disperses.*—A city of Lycania, the native place of Timothy. Here the apostles, having healed a cripple, were taken for gods. Acts xiv. 6—18.

M

MAACAH, May′-a-kah, *to squeeze.*—The same as BETH-MAACAH. A small province of Syria, to the east and north of the sources of the river Jordan, upon the road to Damascus. 2 Sam. x. 8.

MAACHAH, May′-a-kah, *to squeeze or bruise.*—1. The son of Nahor and his concubine Reumah. Gen. xxii. 24. 2. Daughter of Talmai, king of Geshur, wife of David, and mother of Absalom. 2 Sam. iii. 3. 3. Daughter of Abishalom, wife of Rehoboam, and mother of Abijam. 1 Kings xv. 2. 4. Wife of Abijam, and mother of Asa. 1 Kings xv. 10. 5. Concubine of Caleb. 1 Chron. ii. 48. 6. Father of Achish, king of Gath. 1 Kings ii. 39. 7. Father of Shephatiah, head of the tribe of Simeon in the time of David. 1 Chron. xxvii. 16.

MAACHATHI, Ma-ak′-a-thy.—A place in Syria, in the half-tribe of Manasseh. Deut. iii. 14.

MAACHATHITES, Ma-ak′-a-thites.—The people of Maachathi. Josh. xiii. 13.

MAADAI, Ma-ad′-ay.—Son of Bani, who returned from captivity, and was one of those who dismissed his wife. Ezra x. 34.

MAADIAH, Ma-a-dy′-ah.—A priest in Zerubbabel's time. Neh. xii. 5.

MAAI, Ma-ay′-i.—The name of a Jewish priest. Neh. xii. 36.

MAALEH-ACRABBIM, Ma-al'-eh a-krab'-bim, *the going up to Acrabbim.*—One of the borders of the tribe of Judah, in Palestine. Josh. xv. 3.

MAARATH, May'-a-rath.—A city belonging to the tribe of Judah. Josh. xv. 59.

MAASEIAH, Ma-a-sy'-ah, *the work of the Lord.*— 1. The son of Ahaz, king of Israel, who was assassinated by Zichri. 2 Chron. xxviii. 7. 2. The son of Adaiah, who was one of those to whom the high-priest Jehoiada discovered his design of dethroning Athaliah, and setting Joash on the throne. 1 Chron. xv. 18.

MAASIAI, Ma-a-sy'-ay, *the work of the Lord.*— The chief of the last of the twenty-four families of the priests. 1 Chron. ix. 12.

MAATH, May'-ath.—One of the ancestors of Joseph. Luke iii. 26.

MAAZ, May'-az.—The grandson of Jerahmeel, of the tribe of Judah. 1 Chron. ii. 27.

MACEDONIA, Mas-se-do'-ne-a, *adoration, prostration.* —A large province of Greece, now under the dominion of the Turks, bounded on the north by the mountains of Hæmus, on the south by Epirus and Achaia, on the east by the Ægean Sea, and on the west by the Ionian and Adriatic Seas. Acts xvi. 9.

MACHBANAI, Mak'-ba-nay.—One of the valiant men in David's army. 1 Chron. xii. 13.

MACHBENAH, Mak'-be-nah. — A son of Caleb. 1 Chron. ii. 49.

MACHI, May'-ky.—One of the tribe of Gad. Num. xiii. 15.

MACHIR, May'-kir, *he that sells or knows.*—1. Son of Manasseh, and grandson of the patriarch Joseph, chief and prince of the Machirites. Num. xxvi. 29. 2. Son of Ammiel, of the city of Lodebar, in whose family Mephibosheth was brought up. 2 Sam. ix. 5.

MACHNADEBAI, Mak-na-de′-bay.—One who returned from the Babylonish captivity. Ezra x. 40.

MACHPELAH, Mak-pe′-lah, *double*.—The name of the plain wherein the cave was situated which Abraham bought for a burying-place. Gen. xxiii. 9.

MADAI, Mad′-a-i.—The third son of Japheth. Gen. x. 2. It is commonly thought that he was the father of the Medes; by others, of the Macedonians.

MADMANNAH, Mad-man′-nah.—A city belonging to Simeon. Josh. xv. 31. It was first given to Judah.

MADON, May′-don.—A city in Canaan, situation unknown. Josh. xi. 1; xii. 19.

MAGBISH, Mag′-bish.—One hundred and fifty-six of his children returned from the captivity. Ezra ii. 30.

MAGDALA, Mag′-da-la, *tower*, *greatness*.—A town of Palestine, in the tribe of Manasseh. Matt. xv. 39.

MAGDALENE, Mag-da-le′-ne.—See MARY MAGDALENE.

MAGDIEL, Mag′-de-el.—A prince of the Idumeans. He succeeded Mibzar. Gen. xxxvi. 43.

MAGOG, May′-gog, *roof, that dissolves*.—The son of Japheth; Gen. x. 2; generally supposed to be the father of the Scythians or Tartars.

MAGOR-MISSABIB, May′-gor-mis′-sa-bib, *terror on every side*.—The name given to Pashur, one of the Jewish priests. Jer. xx. 3.

MAGPIASH, Mag′-pe-ash.—A Levite, who sealed the covenant with Nehemiah. Neh. x. 20.

MAHALAH, May′-ha-lah, *melody*.—One of the posterity of the patriarch Manasseh. 1 Chron. vii. 18.

MAHALALEEL, Ma-hay-lay′-le-el, *he that praises God*.—The son of Cainan, of the race of Seth. He lived eight hundred and ninety-five years, and died A.M. 1290. Gen. v. 15, &c.

MAHALATH, May'-ha-lath, *melodious song, infirmity.* —1. The wife of Rehoboam, king of Judah. 2 Chron. xi. 18. 2. A daughter of Ishmael, and wife of Esau. Gen. xxviii. 9

MAHALI, May'-ha-ly.—The eldest son of Merari, and chief of the family of the Mahlites. Exod. vi. 19; Num. iii. 33.

MAHANAIM, Ma-ha-nay'-im, *the two fields or armies.* —A city of the Levites, of the family of Merari, in the tribe of Gad, on the brook Jabbok. Josh. xxi. 38; xiii. 26.

MAHANEH-DAN, May'-ha-neh-dan'.—The same as Kirjath-Jearim. Judges xviii. 12.

MAHARAI, Ma-har'-a-i.—The Netophathite, of the race of the Zarhites. He was chief of 24,000 men, who attended David as his guards in the tenth month. 2 Sam. xxiii. 28; 1 Chron. xxvii. 13.

MAHATH, May'-hath.—One of the Levites. 1 Chron. vi. 35.

MAHAZ, May'-haz.—A place mentioned in the book of Kings, and supposed to be Canaan.

MAHAZIOTH, Ma-hay'-ze-oth.—One of the sons of Heman, the king's seer. 1 Chron. xxv. 4.

MAHER-SHALAL-HASH-BAZ, May'-her-shal'-al-hash'-baz, *making speed to the spoil.*—A prophetic name mentioned by Isaiah, as a sign of the speedy destruction of Syria and Ephraim. Isai. viii. 1.

MAHLAH, Mah'-lah, *melodious song, infirmity.*—One of the daughters of Zelophehad, who received her portion in the land of promise, because her father died without male issue. Num. xxvi. 33; xxvii. 1; Josh. xvii. 3.

MAHLON, Mah'-lon, *song, infirmity.*—A son of Elimelech and Naomi. Ruth i. 2.

MAHOL, May'-hol.—Father of Ethan, Heman, Chalcol, and Darda. 1 Kings iv. 31.

MAKAZ, May'-kaz.—A city supposed to belong to the tribe of Dan. 1 Kings iv. 9.

MAKHELOTH, Mak-he'-loth.—One of the encampments of the Israelites in the wilderness. Num. xxxiii. 25.

MAKKEDAH, Mak-ke'-dah, *adoration, prostration.*— A city belonging to the tribe of Judah. Josh. xv. 41.

MAKTESH, Mak'-tesh. — A place near Jerusalem. Zeph. i. 11.

MALACHI, Mal'-a-ky, *the angel of the Lord.*—The last of the minor prophets.   See his Prophecies.

MALCHAM, Mal'-kam, *their king.*—A descendant of the patriarch Benjamin. 1 Chron. viii. 9.

MALCHIEL, Mal'-ke-el.—The son of Beriah, son of Asher, and chief of the Malchielites, in the time of Moses. Num. xxvi. 45.

MALCHIJAH or MALCHIAH, Mal-ky'-jah or Mal-ky'-ah, *the messenger of the Lord.*—1. The chief of the fifth family of the twenty-four sacerdotal families. 1 Chron. xxiv. 9.   2. One of the race of the Levites, son of Ethni. 1 Chron. vi. 40.   3. The father of Pashur. 1 Chron. ix. 12. 4. A Jew that put away his wife at the return from captivity. Neh. iii. 11.   5. The son of Rehab, chief of Beth-haccerem. Neh. iii. 14.   6. The son of a goldsmith, who contributed greatly to the rebuilding of Jerusalem. Neh. iii. 31.   7. Son of Hammelech, and keeper of the prisons at Jerusalem. Jer. xxxviii. 6.

MALCHIRAM, Mal-ky'-ram.—Son of king Jeconiah. 1 Chron. iii. 18.

MALCHOM, Mal'-kom.—The same as Milcom.

MALCHUS, Mal'-kus, *king, or kingdom.*—A servant of the high-priest Caiaphas, whose right ear Peter cut off. John xviii. 10.

MALLOTHI, Mal'-lo-thy.—One of the singers in the temple of Jerusalem. 1 Chron. xxv. 4.

MALLUCH, Mal'-luk.—The name of two Levites.
1 Chron. vi. 44 ; Ezra x. 29.

MAMMON, Mam'-mon, *riches*.—Probably the name of
a Syrian god. Matt. vi. 24.

MAMRE, Mam'-re, *rebellious, better, that changes.*—
1. An Amorite, brother of Aner and Eshcol, and friend of
Abraham. Gen. xiv. 13. 2. The same as Hebron. Gen.
xxiii. 19 ; xxxv. 27. 3. A plain near Mamre, about two
miles south of the town. Gen. xiii. 18.

MANAEN, Man'-a-en, *a comforter, he that conducts
them.*—One of the teachers in the church at Antioch, who
had been brought up with Herod the Tetrarch. Herod was
his foster-brother. Acts xiii. 1.

MANAHATH, Man'-a-hath.—One of the descendants
of the patriarch Esau. Gen. xxxvi. 23.

MANAHETHITES, Ma-nay'-heth-ites.—Of the posterity of Judah. 1 Chron. ii. 52.

MANASSEH, Ma-nas'-seh, *forgetfulness, he that is
forgotten.*—1. The eldest son of Joseph, and grandson
of the patriarch Jacob, Gen. xli. 51, born A.M. 2292.
2. The fifteenth king of Judah, the son and successor of
Hezekiah. He was twelve years old when he began to
reign, and reigned fifty-five years. 2 Kings xx. 21 ; xxi.
1, 2, &c. He was a wicked king, but was converted when
in Babylon, in prison; and, after his return to Jerusalem,
redressed, as much as possible, the evils he had caused.
3. A son of Pahath-Moab, who having married a strange
wife, put her away on his return from Babylon. Ezra
x. 30. 4. Son of Husham, under circumstances similar to
the last mentioned. Ezra x. 33.

MANASSITES, Ma-nas'-sites.—The descendants of
Manasseh, the son of Joseph. Deut. iv. 43.

MANOAH, Ma-no'-ah, *rest, a present.*—The father of
Samson, of the tribe of Dan, and of the city of Zorah.
Judges xiii. 2.

MAOCH, May'-ok.—Father of Achish, king of Gath
1 Sam. xxvii. 2.

MAON, May'-on, *house, tribe.*—A city of the tribe of Judah. Josh. xv. 55; 1 Sam. xxiii. 24, 25.

MAONITES, May'-on-ites.—Inhabitants of Maon. Judges x. 12.

MARA, May'-rah, *bitter.*—The name given to Naomi by herself. Ruth i. 20.

MARAH, May'-rah, *bitterness.*—When the Israelites came out of Egypt, and had arrived at the desert of Etham, they found the water so bitter, that neither they nor their cattle could drink of it. Exod. xv. 23. On this account they gave the name of Marah to the encampment.

MARALAH, Mar'-a-lah.—A city of the tribe of Zebulun. Josh. xix. 11.

MARAN-ATHA, Mar-a-nath'-a, *the Lord comes.*—A form of threatening or cursing among the Jews. 1 Cor. xvi. 22. See ANATHEMA.

MARCUS, Mar'-kus, *polite, shining.*—Sister's son to Barnabas. Col. iv. 10.

MARESHAH, Ma-re'-shah.—A city of the tribe of Judah. Josh. xv. 44.

MARK, Mark, *polite, shining.*—1. The same as Marcus. Supposed to have been converted by St. Peter, who calls him his son. 1 Pet. v. 13. He was the author of the Gospel under his name. 2. John Mark. Acts xii. 12.

MARMOTH, Mar'-moth.—A priest who returned from the Babylonish captivity.

MAROTH, May'-roth.—A place in Judea. Micah i. 12.

MARSENA, Mar'-se-na.—One of the seven principal officers of Ahasuerus. Esther i. 14.

MARS' HILL, Mars'-hill.—The place where the judges of Athens held their supreme council. Acts xvii. 22.

MARTHA, Mar′-tha, *who becomes bitter.*—Sister of Lazarus and Mary, and mistress of the house where our Saviour was entertained in the village of Bethany. Luke x. 38—42.

MARY, May′-re, *exalted, bitterness of the sea, mistress of the sea.*—1. The mother of our Lord Jesus Christ, and a virgin. She was of the royal race of David. Luke i. 27. 2. The mother of John Mark, a disciple of the apostles. Acts xii. 12. 3. Mary, of Cleophas. St. Jerome says, she bore the name of Cleophas either because of her father, or for some reason that cannot now be known. Others suppose, with greater probability, she was the wife of Cleophas, as our version of the New Testament makes her, by supplying *wife.* John xix. 25. It is thought she was sister of the Virgin; and that she was the mother of James the Less, of Joses, of Simon, and Judas, who in the Gospel are called the brethren of Christ. Matt. xiii. 55; xxvii. 56. 4. The sister of Lazarus and Martha; often confounded with that female sinner, spoken of Luke vii. 37—39. See John xi. 5. Mary Magdalene, so called, probably, from Magdala, a town of Galilee, of which she was a native, or where she had resided during the early part of her life. Out of her Jesus Christ cast seven devils. She is not that sinful woman mentioned Luke vii. 37. She followed Christ, and ministered to him, and attended him from Galilee to Jerusalem, and was at the foot of the cross. John xix. 25 ; Mark xv. 47.

MASCHIL, Mas′-kil, *he that instructs.*—The title of several of the Psalms : probably meaning an instructive song.

MASH, Mash.—The fourth son of Aram. Gen. x. 23.

MASHAL, May′-shal.—A city of the tribe of Asher, ceded to the Levites of Gershom's family. 1 Chron. vi. 74.

MASREKAH, Mas′-re-kah, *whistling, hissing.*—1. A duke of Edom, successor of Hadad. Gen. xxxvi. 36. 2. A town mentioned 1 Chron. i. 47.

MASSA, Mas′-sah, *temptation.*—The name of one of Ishmael's sons. Gen. xxv. 14.

MASSAH, Mas'-sah, *temptation.* — Rephidim was so called by the Israelites. Exod. xvii. 7.

MATRED, May'-tred.—The mother of Mehetabel, the wife of king Hadad. Gen. xxxvi. 39.

MATRI, May'-try, *rain, prison.*—A person of the tribe of Benjamin, chief of the family of Kish, the father of Saul. 1 Sam. x. 21.

MATTAN, Mat'-tan, *the reins, the death of them.*—1. A priest of Baal, who was killed before the altar of the false god, by order of the high-priest Jehoiada, A.M. 3126. 2 Kings xi. 18.   2. Father of Shephatiah, carried away to Babylon, A.M. 3416. Jer. xxxviii. 1.

MATTANAH, Mat'-tan-ah.—An encampment of the Israelites in the desert. Num. xxi. 18, 19.

MATTANIAH, Mat-ta-ny'-ah.—1. The chief of the ninth family of the Levites. 1 Chron. xxv. 16.   2. Zedekiah, king of Judah, so called.

MATTATHA, or MATTATHAH, Mat'-ta-thah.—1. Son of Nathan, one of the ancestors of Jesus Christ. Luke iii. 31.   2. One who returned from the Babylonish captivity, and put away his wife. Ezra x. 33.

MATTENAI, Mat-te-nay'.—One of the valiant men of king David's army; and also one who returned from captivity. Ezra x. 37.

MATTHAN, Mat'-than, *the reins, the death of them.*— The son of Eleazar, father of Jacob, and grandfather of Joseph, husband to the Virgin Mary. Matt. i. 15, 16.

MATTHAT, Mat'-that, *gift, he that gives.*—Son of Levi, and father of Heli. Luke iii. 24.

MATTHEW, Math'-yew, *given, a reward.*—An apostle and evangelist, son of Alpheus, a Galilean by birth, a Jew by religion, and a publican by profession. Mark ii. 14; Luke v. 27.   He was called by the other Evangelists by his Hebrew name Levi; but he always calls himself Matthew.   See his Gospel.

MATTHIAS, Mat-thy'-as, *the gift of the Lord.*—An apostle of Jesus Christ, but not of the number of the twelve chosen by our Lord himself. He was chosen to supply the place of Judas. Acts i. 25, 26.

MATTITHIAH, Mat-te-thy'-ah, *the gift of the Lord.*—A person of the race of Korah, head of the fourteenth family of the Levites. 1 Chron. xxv. 21.

MAZZAROTH, Maz-zay'-roth.—The Chaldee name for the twelve signs of the Zodiac. Job xxxviii. 32.

MEAH, Me'-ah.—A tower on the walls of Jerusalem. Neh. iii. 1.

MEARAH, Me-ay'-rah, *the cave.*—A place in ancient Canaan near to Sidon; also, the river Magoras, running into the Mediterranean Sea. Josh. xiii. 4.

MEBUNNAI, Me-bun'-ny.—The Hushathite, one of the valiant men of David's army. 2 Sam. xxiii. 27.

MECHERATH, Mek'-e-rath. — The birth-place of Hepher, one of David's valiant men. 1 Chron. xi. 36.

MEDAD, Me'-dad, *he that measures, the water of love.* —He and Eldad were among the elders of Israel, and prophets in the camp. Num. xi. 26.

MEDALAH, Med'-a-lah.—A city of the tribe of Zebulun.

MEDAN, Me'-dan, *judgment, process, measure, covering.* —The third son of Abraham and Keturah. Gen. xxv. 2.

MEDEBA, Med'-e-bah.—A city beyond Jordan, and in the southern parts of the tribe of Reuben. Josh. xiii. 16.

MEDES, Meeds.—The people of Media. 2 Kings xvii. 6.

MEDIA, Me'-de-a, *measure, covering, abundance.*—A country bounded on the west by Armenia and Assyria Proper, on the east by Persia, on the north by the Caspian provinces, and on the south by Susiana. It was an elevated and mountainous country, and formed a kind of pass between the cultivated parts of eastern and western Asia. It is commonly thought that it was peopled by the descendants of Madai, son of Japheth. Gen. x. 2. The Greeks maintain that it took its name from Medus, the son of Medea.

MEGIDDO, Me-gid'-do, *that declares, his precious fruit.*—A city of the tribe of Manasseh, famous for the battle fought there between Pharaoh-Nechoh and king Josiah, in which the latter was defeated and mortally wounded. Josh. xvii. 11; 2 Kings xxiii. 29.

MEHETABEL, Me-het'-a-bel, *how good is God.*—The wife of Hadar, king of Edom. Gen. xxxvi. 39.

MEHIDA, Me-hy'-da.—One whose children were of the order of the Nethinims. Ezra ii. 52.

MEHIR, Me'-her.—The son of Chelub, of the tribe of Judah. 1 Chron. iv. 11.

MEHOLATHITE, Me-hol'-ath-ite.—Barzillai was a Meholathite; but the meaning of the term is uncertain. 1 Sam. xviii. 19.

MEHUJAEL, Me-hew'-ja-el, *who proclaims God, God that blots out.*—The son of Irad, the father of Methusael, of the race of Cain. Gen. iv. 18.

MEHUMAN, Me-hew'-man.—A chief of the eunuchs or officers of king Ahasuerus. Esther i. 10.

MEHUNIM, Me-hew'-nim.—One whose children were of the order of the Nethinims. Ezra ii. 50

ME-JARKON, Me-jar'-kon.—A city belonging to the tribe of Dan. Josh. xix. 46.

MEKONAH, Mek'-o-nah.—A city of the tribe of Judah. Neh. xi. 28.

MELATIAH, Mel-a-ty'-ah.—One who returned from the Babylonish captivity. Neh. iii. 7.

MELCHI, Mel′-ky, *king.*—1. Son of Janna, and father of Levi, in the genealogy of Christ. Luke iii. 24. 2. The son of Addi, and father of Neri, in the genealogy of Christ. Luke iii. 28.

MELCHI-SHUA, Mel-ke-shu′-ah, *my king is a saviour.* —The third son of Saul: he was killed, with his father, in the battle of Gilboa. 1 Sam. xxxi. 2.

MELCHIZEDEK, Mel-kiz′-ze-dek, *king of righteousness.* —King of Salem, and priest of the most high God, to whom Abraham gave tithes. Heb. vii. 1, 2. An eminent type of Christ.

MELEA, Me-le′-a.—Son of Menan, and father of Eliakim, one of the ancestors of our Saviour. Luke iii. 31.

MELECH, Me′-lek, *king.*—Second son of Micah, and grandson of Jonathan, son of king Saul. 1 Chron. viii. 35.

MELICU, Me′-le-ku.—The same person as Mulluch, the priest. Neh. xii. 14.

MELITA, Mel′-e-ta, *affording honey.*—An island in the Mediterranean Sea, now called Malta. It lies between Africa and Sicily, is about twenty miles long, and twelve broad, and was formerly reckoned as a part of Africa, but now belongs to Europe. Acts xxviii. 1.

MELZAR, Mel′-zar, *a steward.*—One who was appointed to guard the prophet Daniel. Dan. i. 11.

MEMPHIS, Mem′-fis, *by the mouth.*—The ancient capital of Egypt. Hosea ix. 6.

MEMUCAN, Me-mew′-kan, *impoverished, to prepare, certain, true.*—One of the seven principal counsellors of Ahasuerus. Esther i. 14—16.

MENAHEM, Men′-a-hem, *comforter, who conducts them.*—The sixteenth king of Israel. He was the son of Gadi, and revenged the death of his master Zechariah by that of Shallum, son of Jabesh, who had usurped the crown of Israel. 2 Kings xv. 14. A.M. 3232.

165

MENAN, Me'-nan.—Son of Mattatha, and father of Melea, mentioned Luke iii. 31.

MENE, Me'-ne.—A Chaldean word, signifying *he has numbered or counted.* See Dan. v. 25.

MEONENIM, Me-on'-e-nim.—A place mentioned Judges ix. 37.

MEONOTHAI, Me-on'-o-thay.—A son of Othniel, father of Ophrah, of the tribe of Judah. 1 Chron. iv. 13, 14.

MEPHAATH, Mef'-a-ath.—A city in the tribe of Reuben, ceded to the Levites of the family of Merari. Josh. xiii. 18.

MEPHIBOSHETH, Me-fib'-bo-sheth, *out of my mouth proceeds reproach.*—1. The son of Saul and his concubine Rizpah. 2 Sam. xxi. 8, 9. 2. The son of Jonathan. 2 Sam. iv. 4, &c.; ix. 6, &c.

MERAB, Me'-rab, *he that fights, he that multiplies.*— The eldest daughter of king Saul. 1 Sam. xiv. 49; xviii. 17—19.

MERAIAH, Mer-a-i'-ah.—A Jewish priest in Zerubbabel's time. Neh. xii. 12.

MERAIOTH, Me-ray'-yoth.—The son of Ahitub, high-priest of the Jews. 1 Chron. ix. 11.

MERARI, Mer'-a-ry, *bitter, to provoke.*—The third son of Levi, and father of Mahali and Mushi. Exod. vi. 19.

MERATHAIM, Mer-a-thay'-im.—Part of the Baby-lonish empire. Jer. l. 21.

MERCURIUS, Mer-kew'-re-us.—Derived from a Latin word which signifies to *buy* or *sell,* because Mercury presided over merchandise. His Greek name is Hermes, *orator or interpreter.* He was a false god, the son of Jupiter and Maia, and the messenger of the other deities. See Acts xiv. 12.

MERED, Me'-red.—A son of Ezra. 1 Chron. iv. 17.

MEREMOTH, Mer'-e-moth.—A priest among those that returned from Babylon. Ezra viii. 33.

MERES, Me'-rees.—A prince of the court of Ahasuerus. Esther i. 14.

MERIBAH, Mer'-re-bah, *dispute, quarrel.*—Rephidim was so called by the Israelites. Exod. xvii. 7.

MERIBAH-KADESH, Mer'-re-bah-kay'-desh, *the strife of holiness.*—A place where the Israelites murmured in the wilderness. Deut. xxxii. 51.

MERIB-BAAL, Me-rib'-ba-al, *rebellion, he that resists Baal, and strives against the idol.*—The son of Jonathan, and father of Micah. 1 Chron. viii. 34; ix. 40. The same as MEPHIBOSHETH. 2 Sam. iv. 4.

MERODACH, Mer'-ro-dak, *bitter, contrition ;* in Syriac, *the little lord.*—An ancient king of Babylon, who was placed among the gods, and worshipped by the Babylonians. Jer. l. 2.

MERODACH-BALADAN, Mer'-ro-dak-bal'-la-dan, *who creates contrition, the son of death, of thy vapour.*—A king of Babylon, who having heard that Hezekiah had been miraculously healed, and that the sun had gone backward, congratulated him with presents. Isai. xxxix.

MEROM, Me'-rom, *eminences, elevations.*—Waters of the most northern and smallest of the three lakes which are supplied by the river Jordan. Josh. xi. 5.

MERONOTHITE, Me-ron'-o-thite.—A person mentioned 1 Chron. xxvii. 30.

MEROZ, Me'-roz, *secret, leanness.*—A place in the neighbourhood of the brook Kishon. Judges v. 23.

MESHA, Me'-shah.—1. A mountain. Gen. x. 30. 2. A king of the Moabites. 2 Kings iii. 4. 3. The eldest son of Hezron, son of Caleb, the son of Jephunneh. 1 Chron. ii. 42.

MESHACH, Me'-shak, *that draws with force, that surrounds the waters.*—The Chaldean name given to Mishael. Dan. i. 7.

MESHECH, Me′-shek, *who is drawn by force, shut up, surrounded.*—The sixth son of Japheth. Gen. x. 2.

MESHELEMIAH, Mesh-el-e-my′-ah, *peace, perfection, retribution of the Lord.*—Father of Zechariah, a Levite, and porter of the temple. 1 Chron. ix. 21.

MESHEZABEEL, Mesh-ez′-a-beel.—A Levite who sealed the covenant with Nehemiah. Neh. x. 21.

MESHILLEMITH, Mesh-il′-le-mith.—The father of Meshullam, the priest. 1 Chron. ix. 12.

MESHILLEMOTH, Mesh-il′-le-moth.—One of the posterity of the patriarch Ephraim. Neh. xi. 13.

MESHOBAB, Me-sho′-bab.—A prince of the tribe of Simeon. 1 Chron. iv. 34.

MESHULLAM, Me-shul′-lam.—The name of several men of whom we know nothing but their names.

MESHULLEMETH, Me-shul′-le-meth.—The wife of Manasseh, king of Judah, daughter of Haruz, of the city of Jotbah. 2 Kings xxi. 19.

MESOPOTAMIA, Mes-o-po-tay′-me-a, *between two rivers.*—A large province lying between the Euphrates and the Tigris. It is much celebrated in Scripture as being the first dwelling of men, both before and after the deluge. Deut. xxiii. 4.

MESSIAH, Mes-sy′-ah, *anointed.* — A name given principally by way of eminence to Jesus Christ.

MESSIAS, Mes-sy′-as.—The same as MESSIAH. John iv. 25.

METERUS, Me-te′-rus.—One who returned from the Babylonish captivity.

METHEG-AMMAH, Me′-theg-am′-mah, *bridle of bondage.*—Supposed to be the city of Gath, in Philistia. 2 Sam. viii. 1.

METHUSAEL, Me-thew′-sa-el, *who demands his death.* —A descendant of Cain. Gen. iv. 18.

METHUSELAH, Me-thew'-se-lah, *he has sent his death.*—The son of Enoch, and father of Lamech. Gen. v. 21. The oldest man.

MEUNIM, Me-yew'-nim.—One whose children were of the order of the Nethinims. Neh. vii. 52.

MEZAHAB, Mez'-a-hab.—The mother of Matred. Gen. xxxvi. 39.

MIAMIN, My'-a-min.—One who returned from the Babylonish captivity. Ezra x. 25.

MIBHAR, Mib'-har.—One of king David's valiant men. 1 Chron. xi. 38.

MIBSAM, Mib'-sam.—One of the sons of Ishmael. Gen. xxv. 13.

MIBZAR, Mib'-zar.—Successor to Teman, in the principality of Edom. Gen. xxxvi. 42.

MICAH, My'-kah, *poor, humble, who strikes, is there.*— 1. The son of Mephibosheth, the father of Pithon and others. 1 Chron. viii. 34. 2. A man of the tribe of Ephraim, son of a rich and superstitious widow. See Judges xvii., xviii. 3. The Morasthite, or of Moresa, the sixth of the minor prophets. He was contemporary with Isaiah.

MICAIAH, My-kay'-yah, *who is like to God? the lowliness of God.*—The son of Imlah, of the tribe of Ephraim, and a prophet of the Lord. 1 Kings xxii. 13, &c.

MICHA, My'-kah, *poor, humble.*—One who sealed the covenant with Nehemiah. Neh. x. 11.

MICHAEL, My'-ka-el, *who is like to God? the lowliness of God.*—1. The archangel who presided over the Jewish nation. Dan. x. 13; Rev. xii. 7; Jude 9. 2. The father of Sethur, of the tribe of Asher. Num. xiii. 13. 3. One of the valiant men who took part with David against Saul. 1 Chron. xii. 20. 4. The son of king Jehoshaphat. 2 Chron. xxi. 2.

MICHAH, My' kah, *poor, humble.*—A son of Uzziel, and father of Shamir. 1 Chron. xxiv. 24.

MICHAIAH, My-kay′-yah.—The son of Gemariah. Jer. xxxvi. 11.

MICHAL, My′-kal, *who is it that has all? who is perfect?* —Daughter of king Saul, and wife of David. 2 Sam. iii. 13.

MICHMAS, Mik′-mas, *he that strikes, the poor taken away.*—A person who returned from the Babylonish captivity. Ezra ii. 27.

MICHMASH, Mik′-mash, *he that strikes, the poor taken away.*—The name of a city in Palestine, in the tribe of Ephraim. 1 Sam. xiii. 5.

MICHMETHAH, Mik′-me-thah.—A city belonging to the half-tribe of Manasseh, on this side Jordan. Josh. xvi. 6.

MICHRI, Mik′-ry.—The name of a Benjamite. 1 Chron. ix. 8.

MICHTAM, Mik′-tam, *a golden song.*—The title of the fifty-sixth Psalm.

MIDDIN, Mid′-din.—A city of Palestine. Josh. xv. 61.

MIDIAN, Mid′-de-an, *judgment, measure, covering.*— The fourth son of Abraham and Keturah. Gen. xxv. 2. The Midanites mentioned Num. xxv. 6, 15, were descended from this person. The land of Midian extended from the east of the land of Moab, on the east of the Dead Sea, southward along the Elanitic gulf of the Red Sea, stretching into Arabia: it further passed to the south of the land of Edom, into the peninsula of Mount Sinai.

MIGDAL-EL, Mig′-da-lel.—A city in the tribe of Naphtali. Josh. xix. 38.

MIGDAL-GAD, Mig′-dal-gad, *the tower of Gad.*—A city of the tribe of Judah. Josh. xv. 37.

MIGDOL, Mig′-dol, *a tower, greatness.*—A place or tower near which the Israelites encamped when they came out of Egypt. Exod. xiv. 2.

MIGRON, Mig′-ron, *fear, a barn, from the throat.*—A village near Gibeah. 1 Sam. xiv. 2.

MIJAMIN, Mid'-ja-min.—The name of a priest. 1 Chron. xxiv. 9

MIKLOTH, Mik'-loth.—1. Son of Jehiel or Abi-Gibeon, and father of Shimeah. 1 Chron. viii. 32; ix. 37. 2. One of the captains of David's army. 1 Chron. xxvii. 4.

MIKNEIAH, Mik-ny'-ah.—A Levite, who was a porter in the temple at Jerusalem. 1 Chron. xv. 21.

MILALAI, Mil-a-lay'.—The name of a priest. Neh. xii. 36.

MILCAH, Mil'-kah, *queen*.—1. The daughter of Haran, sister of Lot, wife of Nahor, niece of Abraham, and mother of Bethuel. Gen. xi. 29; xxii. 20. 2. A daughter of Zelophehad. Num. xxxvi. 11.

MILCOM, Mil'-kom, *their king*.—The god of the Ammonites, the same as Moloch. 1 Kings xi. 5.

MILETUS, My-le'-tus, *red, scarlet*.—A town in Asia Minor, in the province of Caria, the birth-place of Thales. Acts xx. 15.

MILLO, Mil'-lo, *fulness, repletion*.—1. A deep valley between the old city Jebus, or Jerusalem, and the city of David, built upon Mount Sion. 1 Kings ix. 15. 2. Probably a citizen of Shechem; otherwise the name of some part of that city. Judges ix. 6.

MINIAMIN, Me-ny'-a-min.—A Levite. 2 Chron. xxxi. 15.

MINNI, Min'-ny, *disposed, reckoned*.—A province of Armenia. Jer. li. 27.

MINNITH, Min'-nith, *counted, prepared*. — A city beyond Jordan, situated four miles from Heshbon. Judges xi. 33; Ezek. xxvii. 17.

MIPHKAD, Mif'-kad.—The name of a gate of the city of Jerusalem. Neh. iii. 31.

MIRIAM, Mir'-e-am, *exalted, bitterness of the sea, mistress of the sea*.—The sister of Moses and Aaron, and daughter of Amram and Jochebed. She was older than Moses; born A.M. 2424. Exod. xv. 20.

MIRMA, Mir'-mah.—One of the posterity of Benjamin. 1 Chron. viii. 10.

MISGAB, Mis'-gab, *the high fort or rock.*—Supposed to be a city of the Moabites. Jer. xlviii. 1.

MISHAEL, Mish'-a-el, *asked for, lent, God takes away.* —One of the three companions of Daniel. Dan. i. 7.

MISHAL, My'-shal.—A city of Palestine, in the tribe of Asher. Josh. xxi. 30.

MISHAM, My'-sham.—A descendant of Benjamin. 1 Chron. viii. 12.

MISHEAL, My'-she-al.—A city in the tribe of Asher. Eusebius says near Mount Carmel. Josh. xix. 26.

MISHMA, Mish'-mah.—The fifth son of Ishmael. Gen. xxv. 14.

MISHMANNAH, Mish-man'-nah.—A person who resorted to David at Ziklag. 1 Chron. xii. 10.

MISHRAITES, Mish'-ra-ites.—A family mentioned 1 Chron. ii. 53.

MISPERETH, Mis'-pe-reth.—One who returned from the Babylonish captivity. Neh. vii. 7.

MISREPHOTH-MAIM, Mis'-re-foth-may'-im, *the burnings of the waters, furnaces where metals are melted.*—A city mentioned Josh. xi. 8; supposed to be Sarepta.

MITHCAH, Mith'-kah.—An encampment of the Israelites in the wilderness. Num. xxxiii. 28, 29.

MITHREDATH, Mith'-re-dath.—One who signed the letter to Artaxerxes, king of Persia, to hinder the Jews from building the walls of Jerusalem. Ezra iv. 7.

MITYLENE, Mit-e-lee'-ne, *purity, press.*—The capital of the island of Lesbos. Acts xx. 14.

MIZAR, My'-zar, *little.*—A hill mentioned Psal. xlii. 6.

MIZPAH, Miz'-pah, *a sentinel, speculation, that waits for.*—1. A city in the tribe of Gad. Gen. xxxi. 49. 2. A city in the tribe of Benjamin. 1 Sam. xv. 22.

MIZPAR, Miz'-par.—One who returned from the Babylonish captivity. Ezra ii. 2.

MIZPEH, Miz'-peh, *a sentinel, speculation, that waits for.*—1. A country at the foot of Hermon. Josh. xi. 3. 2. A city in the tribe of Judah, Josh. xv. 38, to the south of Jerusalem.

MIZRAIM, Miz'-ra-im, *tribulations, in straits.*—Son of Ham, and father of Ludim, Anamim, Lehabim, Naphtuhim, Pathrusim, and Casluhim. Gen. x. 6, 13. He was the progenitor of the Egyptians, whence the country of Egypt is frequently called by this name.

MIZZAH, Miz'-zah.—The son of Reuel, and grandson of Esau. Gen. xxxvi. 13.

MNASON, Nay'-son, *a diligent seeker, betrother, an exhorter.*—An old disciple, a Jew by birth. St. Paul lodged at his house in Jerusalem. Acts xxi. 16.

MOAB, Mo'-ab, *of a father.*—The son of Lot and his eldest daughter. Gen. xix. 37. He was the father of the Moabites, who dwelt eastward of the Dead Sea.

MOLADAH, Mol'-a-dah, *birth, generation.*—A city of the tribe of Simeon. Josh. xv. 26.

MOLECH or MOLOCH, Mo'-lek, or Mo'-lok, *king.*— A god of the Ammonites. Lev. xviii. 21; xx. 2—5.

MOLI, Mo'-ly.—A son of Levi.

MOLID, Mo'-lid.—One of the posterity of Caleb. 1 Chron. ii. 29.

MORASTHITE, Mo'-ras-thite.—Micah the prophet was so called because he was from Morasthi, a place in the southern part of Judea. Jer. xxvi. 18.

MORDECAI, Mor'-de-kay, *contrition, bitter bruising;* in Syriac, *pure myrrh.*—The son of Jair, of the race of Saul, and one of the chief of the tribe of Benjamin. He was carried captive by Nebuchadnezzar, A.M. 3416. His history is contained in the book of Esther.

MOREH, Mo'-reh.—A place on the west side of the river Jordan. Gen. xii. 6.

MORESHETH-GATH, Mor'-esh-eth-gath'.—Supposed to be the king of Assyria, to whom the Philistine cities sent presents. Micah i. 14.

MORIAH, Mo-ry'-ah, *bitterness or fear of the Lord.*—A mountain on which Abraham was going to offer his son, and on which the temple of Solomon was afterwards built. 2 Chron. iii. 1.

MOSERA, Mo-se'-ra, *erudition, discipline, bond.*—One of the encampments of the Israelites in the wilderness. Deut. x. 6.

MOSEROTH, Mo-se'-roth.—The same as MOSERA. Num. xxxiii. 30.

MOSES, Mo'-zez, *taken out of the water.*—The son of Amram and Jochebed. His father and mother were of the tribe of Levi. The lawgiver of Israel, and the author of the Pentateuch. He was born A.M. 2433; and died 2553, in the one hundred and twentieth year of his age.

MOZA, Mo'-za.—The son of Zimri, of king Saul's family. Also the son of Caleb. 1 Chron. ii. 46.

MOZAH, Mo'-zah.—A city of Palestine. Josh. xviii. 26.

MUPPIM, Mup'-pim.—One of the sons of Benjamin. Gen. xlvi. 21.

MUSHI, Mew'-shy, *he that touches, withdraws himself.*—The son of Merari, chief of the family of the Levites, named Mushites. Num. iii. 20.

MYRA, My'-ra, from a Greek word, signifying, "*I flow, pour out, weep.*"—A city of Lycia. Acts xxvii. 5.

MYSIA, Mish'-e-a, *criminal, abominable.*—A province in Asia Minor. Acts xvi. 7, 8.

N

NAAM, Nay'-am.—Son of Caleb. 1 Chron. iv. 15.

NAAMAH, Nay'-a-mah.—1. Daughter of Lamech and Zillah. Gen. iv. 22. 2. An Ammonitess, wife of Solomon, and mother of Rehoboam. 1 Kings xiv. 21. 3. A city from whence Zophar, one of Job's friends, came. Job ii. 11.

NAAMAN, Nay'-a-man, *beautiful, agreeable, that prepares himself to motion.*—1. A son of Benjamin. Gen. xlvi. 21. 2. A son of Bela, and grandson of Benjamin. 1 Chron. viii. 4. 3. General of the army of Benhadad, king of Syria. 2 Kings v. 1, &c. This man was cured of the leprosy by the prophet Elisha.

NAARAI, Nay'-a-ry.—One of the valiant men of David's army. 1 Chron. xi. 37.

NAARAN, Nay'-a-ran.—A city of Ephraim. 1 Chron. vii. 28.

NAARATH, Nay'-a-rath.—A city of the tribe of Ephraim. Josh. xvi. 7.

NAASHON, Na-ash'-on, *that foretells, serpent.*—Aaron's brother-in-law, the son of Amminadab. Exod. vi. 23.

NAASSON, Na-as'-son.—The same as NAASHON. Matt. i. 4.

NABAL, Nay'-bal, *fool, senseless.*—A rich churlish man, of the tribe of Judah, and race of Caleb. See 1 Sam. xxv. 3.

NABOTH, Nay'-both, *words, prophecies, fruits.*—An Israelite of the city of Jezreel, who lived under Ahab, and who was murdered by Jezebel's orders, that Ahab might possess his vineyard. See 1 Kings xxi.

NACHOR, Nay'-kor.—The individual at whose thrashing-floor the oxen stumbled in drawing the cart in which the ark had been put. Luke iii. 34.

NADAB, Nay'-dab, *free and voluntary gift, prince.*—1. The son of Aaron, and brother to Abihu. See Lev. x. 1, &c. 2. The son of Jeroboam, king of Israel. He succeeded his father, A.M. 3050. 1 Kings xv. 25, &c.

NAGGE, Nag'-ge, *brightness*.—One of the ancestors of Joseph, the husband of the Virgin Mary. Luke iii. 25.

NAHALIEL, Na-hay'-le-el.—An encampment of the Israelites in the wilderness. Num. xxi. 19.

NAHALLAL, Na-hal'-lal.—A city of Zebulun. Josh. xix. 15.

NAHAM, Nay'-ham.—A descendant of Judah. 1 Chron. iv. 19.

NAHAMANI, Na-ham'-a-ny.—One who returned from the Babylonish captivity. Neh. vii. 7.

NAHARI, Na-har'-i, *my nostrils, hoarse, hot.* — A native of Beeroth, a person of great valour, and armour-bearer to Joab. 2 Sam. xxiii. 37.

NAHASH, Nay'-hash, *snake, one that foretells, brass.*— 1. A king of the Ammonites, who attacked Jabesh-gilead, a month after the election of Saul to be king of Israel. 1 Sam. xi. 2. King of the Ammonites, and a friend of David, probably the son of the last mentioned. 2 Sam. x. 2. 3. The father of Abigail and Zeruiah. 2 Sam. xvii. 25. 4. The father of Shobi, the friend of David. 2 Sam. xvii. 27.

NAHATH, Nay'-hath.—The son of Reuel, and grandson to Esau. Gen. xxxvi. 13.

NAHBI, Nah'-by.—Son of Vophsi, one of the spies. Num. xiii. 14.

NAHOR, Nay'-hor, *hoarse, hot, angry.*—The son of Serug; was born A.M. 1849, and died at the age of one hundred and forty-eight years: he was the grandfather of Abraham. Gen. xi. 22—24. 2. The son of Terah, and brother of Abraham. Gen. xi. 26.

NAHSHON, Nah'-shon, *that foretells, serpent.*—Aaron's brother-in-law. Exod. vi. 23. The son of Amminadab, head of the tribe of Judah, at the time when the children of Israel came out of Egypt. Num. vii. 12, 17.

NAHUM, Nay'-hum, *comforter, penitent, their guide.*— The seventh of the twelve lesser prophets, a native of Elkosh, a little village of Galilee.

NAIN, Nay'-in, *beauty, pleasantness.*—A city of Palestine, where Jesus Christ restored the widow's son to life. Luke vii. 11.

NAIOTH, Nay'-yoth, *beauties, habitations.*—A place near Rama, to which David withdrew to avoid Saul. 1 Sam. xix. 23.

NAOMI, Nay'-o-my, *beautiful, agreeable.*—The wife of Elimelech. See the book of Ruth.

NAPHISH, Nay'-fish, *the soul, he that refreshes himself, that respires:* in Syriac, *that multiplies.*—A son of Ishmael. Gen. xxv. 15.

NAPHTALI, Naf'-ta-ly, *comparison, likeness, that struggles.*—The sixth son of Jacob, by Bilhah, Rachel's handmaid. Gen. xxx. 8. Also a town of Palestine.

NAPHTUHIM, Naf'-tu-him.—The fourth son of Mizraim, the son of Ham, the patriarch. Gen. x. 13.

NARCISSUS, Nar-sis'-sus, *astonishment.*—One whose household was greeted by St. Paul. Rom. xvi. 11.

NATHAN, Nay'-than, *who gives or is given.*—1. The son of David and Bathsheba, the father of Mattatha. Luke iii. 31; 1 Chron. iii. 5. 2. A prophet of the Lord who appeared in Israel in the time of king David, and had a great share in the confidence of this prince. 2 Sam. vii. 3, &c. 3. The father of Igal. 2 Sam. xxiii. 36. 4. One of the chief of the Jews that returned from captivity with Ezra. Ezra viii. 16.

NATHANAEL, Na-than'-a-el, *the gift of God.*—A disciple of Christ. John i. 45, 46.

NAUM, Nay'-um.—See NAHUM. Luke iii. 25.

NAZARENE, Naz-a-reen', *kept, flower.*—An inhabitant of Nazareth. Matt. ii. 23.

NAZARETH, Naz'-a-reth, *separated, sanctified.* — A small city in the tribe of Zebulun, in Lower Galilee, celebrated as the residence of Christ during the first thirty years of his life. Luke ii. 51.

NEAH, Ne'-ah.—A city in the tribe of Zebulun. Josh. xix. 13.

NEAPOLIS, Ne-ap'-po-lis, *new city.*—A city of Macedonia. Acts xvi. 11.

NEARIAH, Ne-a-ry'-ah.—One of the sons of Ishi, and one of those who drove out the Amalekites from Mount Seir, and occupied their country. 1 Chron. iv. 42.

NEBAI, Neb'-a-i.—A Hebrew of rank. Neh. x. 19.

NEBAIOTH, Ne-bay'-yoth, *prophecies, fruits.*—The first son of Ishmael, and grandson of Abraham and Hagar. Gen. xxv. 13. He is thought to be the father of the Nabathean Arabians. Isai. lx. 7.

NEBAJOTH, Ne-bay'-joth.—The same as NEBAIOTH. Gen. xxv. 13.

NEBALLAT, Ne-bal'-lat.—A city of Palestine. Neh. xi. 34.

NEBAT, Ne'-bat, *that beholds.*—The father of Jeroboam, the first king of the ten tribes, and the author of the revolt against the house of David. 1 Kings xi. 26.

NEBO, Ne'-bo, *that speaks, prophesies, fructifies.*—1. A city in the tribe of Reuben. Num. xxxii. 38. 2. The name of a city of Judah. Ezra ii. 29. 3. The name of a mountain beyond Jordan, where Moses died. Deut. xxxii. 49. 4. The name of an idol of the Babylonians. Isai. xlvi. 1.

NEBUCHADNEZZAR, Neb-ew-kad-nez'-zar, *tears and groans of judgment :* surnamed *the Great.*—He was the son and successor of Nabopolassar, king of Babylon. He ascended the throne A.M. 3399; and died A.M. 3442, having reigned forty-three years. This is the king so much celebrated in Scripture. See the book of Daniel.

NEBUSHASBAN, Neb-ew-shas'-ban. — One of the generals of Nebuchadnezzar's army. Jer. xxxix. 13.

NEBUZARADAN, Neb-ew-zar′-a-dan, *fruits or pro-phecies of judgment, winnowed, spread.* — A general of Nebuchadnezzar's army, and a chief officer of his house-hold. 2 Kings xxv. ; Jer. xxxix.

NECHO, Ne′-ko, *lame, who was beaten.*—A king of Egypt, who carried his arms as far as the Euphrates, and conquered Carchemish. 2 Chron. xxxv. 20.

NEDABIAH, Ned-a-by′-ah, *the vow of the Lord, the prince of the Lord.*—One of the posterity of David. 1 Chron. iii. 18.

NEHELAMITE, Ne-hel′-a-mite, *dreamer, vale, brook.* —Shemaiah, a false prophet of Judah, was a Nehelamite, that is, of Nehelam. Jer. xxix. 24.

NEHEMIAH, Ne-he-my′-ah, *consolation, rest, conduct of the Lord.*—He was the son of Hachaliah, born at Babylon during the captivity. Neh. i. 1, &c.   See the book of Nehemiah.

NEHUM, Ne′-hum, *a comforter, penitent, leader of them.*—One who returned from captivity. Neh. vii. 7.

NEHUSHTA, Ne-hush′-tah, *snake, soothsayer.*—The daughter of Elnathan, and mother to Jehoiachin. 2 Kings xxiv. 8.

NEHUSHTAN, Ne-hush′-tan, *which is of brass or copper, a trifle of brass.*—The name which king Hezekiah gave to the serpent of brass which Moses had made. 2 Kings xviii. 4.

NEIEL, Ne′-e-el, *commotion, moving of God.*—A city in the tribe of Asher. Josh. xix. 27.

NEKEB, Ne′-keb, *a pipe.*—A city in the tribe of Naph-tali. Josh. xix. 33.

NEKODA, Ne-ko′-da, *painted, inconstant, made crooked.* —One whose children were of the order of the Nethinims. Ezra ii. 48.

NEMUEL, Nem-yew′-el, *the sleeping of God.*—1. A son of Eliab, of the tribe of Reuben, and brother to Dathan and Abiram. Num. xxvi. 9. 2. The son of Simeon, and father of the Nemuelites. Num. xxvi. 12.

NEPHEG, Ne'-feg, *weak, slack.*—The son of David. 2 Sam. v. 15.

NEPHISH, Ne'-fish, *a soul.*—A country of Canaan, against which Reuben warred. 1 Chron. v. 19.

NEPHISHESIM, Ne-fish'-e-sim, *diminished, torn in pieces.*—One whose children were of the order of the Nethinims. Neh. vii. 52.

NEPHTHALIM, Nef'-tha-lim, *comparison, likeness, that fights.*—The same as NAPHTALI. A town of Palestine, near Thisbe. Matt. iv. 13.

NEPHTOAH, Nef'-to-ah, *open, or an opening.*—The name of a fountain in the tribe of Benjamin. Josh. xv. 9.

NEPHUSIM, Ne-few'-sim. *diminished, torn in pieces.*— One whose children were of the order of the Nethinims. Ezra ii. 50.

NER, Ner, *lamp, brightness, land newly tilled.*—The son of Abiel, and father of Abner, the general of Saul's armies. 1 Sam. xiv. 50, 51.

NEREUS, Ne'-re-us, *lamp, brightness.* — One whom St. Paul saluted. Rom. xvi. 15.

NERGAL, Ner'-gal, *searching out, a footman.*—A god of the Cuthites. 2 Kings xvii. 30.

NERGAL-SHAREZER, Ner'-gal-sha-re'-zer, *overseer of the treasury.*—A general of Nebuchadnezzar's army. Jer. xxxix. 3.

NERI, Ne'-ry, *light or candle of the Lord.*—The son of Melchi. Luke iii. 27.

NERIAH, Ne-ry'-ah, *light or lamp of the Lord.*—The father of the prophet Baruch. Jer. xxxii. 12.

NETHANEEL, Ne-than'-e-el, *the gift of God.*—1. Son of Zuar, head of the tribe of Issachar, at the time of the coming up out of Egypt. Num. i. 8 ; vii. 18, 19. 2. The fourth son of Jesse, and brother of David. 1 Chron. ii. 14.

3. Son of Obededom, and of the race of the priests. 1 Chron. xv. 24 ; xxvi. 4.   4. A doctor of the law, who was sent by Jehoshaphat to several cities of his empire to instruct the people. 2 Chron. xvii. 7.   5. Father of Shemaiah, a Levite. 1 Chron. xxiv. 6.   6. A Levite in the time of Josiah. 2 Chron. xxxv. 9.   7. One who returned from the Babylonish captivity. Ezra x. 22.

NETHANIAH, Neth-a-ny'-ah, *the gift of the Lord.*— The father of Ishmael, who slew Gedaliah.   2 Kings xxv. 23.   2. A Levite, head of the fifth band of musicians. 1 Chron. xxv. 2, 12.

NETHINIMS, Neth'-in-ims, *given, offered, rewarded.*— Servants who had been given up to the service of the tabernacle and temple, to perform the meanest and most laborious services therein, in supplying wood and water. Josh. ix. 27 ; Ezra viii. 20.

NETOPHAH, Ne-to'-fah, *dropping down from the head, the bending of the mouth.*—A city and country between Bethlehem and Anathoth. Ezra ii. 22 ; Neh. vii. 26.

NETOPHATHI, Ne-tof'-a-thy.—A country in Judea. Neh. xii. 28.

NETOPHATHITE, Ne-tof'-a-thite.—An inhabitant of Netophathi. Jer. xl. 8 ; 1 Chron. ix. 16.

NEZIAH, Ne-zy'-ah, *a conqueror, everlasting, strong.*— One whose children were of the order of the Nethinims. Ezra ii. 54.

NEZIB, Ne'-zib, *standing, a standing-place, a plant.*— A city of Palestine, in the tribe of Judah, in the valley. Josh. xv. 43.

NIBHAZ, Nib'-haz, *that fructifies, to prophesy, to speak.* —A god of the Avites. 2 Kings xvii. 31.

NIBSHAN, Nib'-shan, *a speech, prophecy, the springing forth of a tooth.*—A city of Judah, place uncertain. Josh. xv. 62.

NICANOR, Ny-kay'-nor, *a conqueror, victorious.*—One of the first deacons that was appointed at Jerusalem, soon after the descent of the Holy Ghost. Acts vi. 5.   There is another Nicanor often mentioned in the book of Maccabees, the son of Patroclus, who returned from Rome with Antiochus Epiphanes, and had a great share in the favour of this prince.

NICODEMUS, Nik-o-de′-mus, *innocent blood:* in Greek, *the victory of the people.*—A disciple of Jesus Christ, a Jew by nation, and a Pharisee. John iii. 1, &c.

NICOLAITANES, Nik-o-lay′-e-tans. — Followers of Nicolas. Heretics in the first age of the church. Rev. ii. 15.

NICOLAS, Nik′-o-las, *conqueror of the people.*—He was first a proselyte of Antioch; afterwards he embraced Christianity, and was one of the most zealous and holy among the first Christians. He afterwards fell into errors, as some say, and originated the sect of the Nicolaitanes: this is, however, very uncertain. Acts vi. 5.

NICOPOLIS, Ny-kop′-o-lis, *the city of victory.*—A city of Epirus, on the gulf of Ambracia. Tit. iii. 12. There is another Nicopolis in Thrace, on the borders of Macedonia.

NIGER, Ny′-jer, *black, dark.*—The surname of Simeon, one of the teachers in the church of Antioch. Acts xiii. 1.

NIMRAH, Nim′-rah, *a leopard, rebellion, bitterness, change.*—A city in the tribe of Gad, or Reuben, situated to the east of the Dead Sea. Num. xxxii. 3.

NIMRIM, Nim′-rim, *a leopard, rebellion.*—See NIMRAH. Jer. xlviii. 34; Isai. xv. 6.

NIMROD, Nim′-rod, *rebellious, an apostate.*—The sixth son of Cush, a mighty hunter. Gen. x. 8, 9.

NIMSHI, Nim′-shy, *rescued from danger, that touches.* —The father of Jehu, king of Israel. 1 Kings xix. 16.

NINEVE, Nin′-e-ve, *agreeable dwelling.*—See NINEVEH.

NINEVEH, Nin′-e-veh, *agreeable dwelling.*—The capital of Assyria, founded by Asshur, the son of Shem. Gen. x. 11. It was one of the largest and most ancient cities in the world, situated on the banks of the Tigris. In the time of Jonah, who was sent there in the reign of Jeroboam II., its circuit was a three days' journey. Jonah iii. 3.

NINEVITES, Nin′-e-vites.—The inhabitants of Nineveh. Luke xi. 30.

NISAN, Ny′-san, *banner, a miracle.*—The first month of the sacred year of the Jews, answering to our March, but the seventh month of the civil year. Neh. ii. 1.

NISROCH, Nis′-rok, *flight, standard, proof.*—A god of the Assyrians. 2 Kings xix. 37; Isai. xxxvii. 38.

NO, or NO-AMMON, No, No-am′-mon, *a stirring up, a forbidding.*—The dwelling of Ammon or Ham. A city of Egypt, probably Diospolis, in the Delta. See Jer. xlvi. 25.

NOADIAH, No-a-dy′-ah, *witness of the Lord.*—The name of a Levite. Ezra viii. 33.

NOAH, No′-ah, *repose, rest, consolation.*—1. The son of Lamech, born A.M. 1056. Amidst the general corruption of the human race, he only was found righteous, Gen. vi. 9; and was saved with his family in the ark, when God destroyed all the inhabitants of the antediluvian world. 2. A daughter of Zelophehad. Num. xxvi. 33.

NOB, Nob, *prophecy, discourse.*—A sacerdotal city of the tribe of Benjamin or Ephraim. See 1 Sam. xxi., xxii.

NOBAH, No′-bah, *that barks or yelps.*—A city beyond Jordan. It took its name from an Israelite of the same name, who made a conquest of it. Num. xxxii. 42.

NOD, Nod, *vagabond, fugitive.*—The country to which Cain withdrew after he had slain his brother. It is difficult to ascertain where it was. Gen. iv. 16.

NODAB, No′-dab, *vowing of his own accord, principal.* —A country bordering upon Iturea and Idumea, but now unknown. 1 Chron. v. 19.

NOE, No′-e.—The same as Noah. Matt. xxiv. 37. See Noah.

NOGAH, No′-gah, *brightness, clearness.*—The name of one of David's sons. 1 Chron. iii. 7.

NOHAH, No'-hah, *resting, a guide.*—The fourth son of the patriarch Benjamin. 1 Chron. viii. 2.

NOPH, Noff, *honeycomb, a sieve, that drops.*—A celebrated city of Egypt, the residence of the ancient kings of Egypt: the same as Memphis. Isai. xix. 13.

NOPHAH, No'-fah, *fearful, binding.*—A city of the Moabites, which afterwards belonged to the Amorites, and lastly to the Israelites. Num. xxi. 30.

NUN, Nun, *son, posterity, durable.*—The son of Elishamah, and father of Joshua. Num. xiii. 8, 16.

NYMPHAS, Nim'-fas, *a bride, spouse, bridegroom.*—A person mentioned Col. iv. 15.

O

OBADIAH, Ob-a-dy'-ah, *servant of the Lord.*—1. A valiant man of David's army who came to join him in the wilderness. 1 Chron. xii. 9.   2. One whom king Jehoshaphat sent as an itinerant teacher. 2 Chron. xvii. 7.   3. One who signed the covenant. Neh. x. 5.   4. The prophet. He is thought by some to be the person mentioned 1 Kings xviii. 3, &c., the governor of Ahab's house, who concealed and fed the prophets whom Jezebel would have destroyed. And others say he was that Obadiah whom Josiah made overseer of the works of the temple. 2 Chron. xxxiv. 12. His prophecy is contained in one chapter.

OBAL, O'-bal, *inconvenience of old age, flowing.*—The eighth son of Joktan. Gen. x. 28.

OBED, O'-bed, *a servant, a workman.*—1. The son of Boaz and Ruth, father of Jesse, and grandfather of David. Ruth iv. 17.   2. The son of Ephlal, and father of Jehu, of the tribe of Judah. 1 Chron. ii. 37.

OBED-EDOM, O'-bed-e'-dom, *the servant of Edom.*—Son of Jeduthun, a Levite, 1 Chron. xvi. 38, and the father of Shemaiah and others. 1 Chron. xvi. 5. The Lord blessed him for the ark resting under his roof. 2 Sam. vi. 10, 11.

OBIL, O'-bil, *that weeps, deserves to be bewailed, ancient.* — An Ishmaelite, master of David's camels. 1 Chron. xxvii. 30.

OBOTH, O'-both, *dragons, fathers, desires.* — An encampment of the Israelites in the wilderness. Num. xxi. 10; xxxiii. 43.

OCRAN, Ok'-ran, *disturber.*—The father of Pagiel. Num. i. 13.

ODED, O'-ded, *sustaining, lifting up.*—1. Father of the prophet Azariah. 2 Chron. xv. 1. 2. A prophet of the Lord. 2 Chron. xxviii. 9.

OG, Og, *a cake, bread baked in the ashes.*—A giant of the race of the Rephaim, and king of Bashan. Deut. iii. 11; Num. xxi. 33.

OHAD, O'-had, *praising, confessing.*—The third son of Simeon, and one who went down into Egypt with his grandfather. Gen. xlvi. 10.

OHEL, O'-hel, *tent, tabernacle, brightness.* — Son of Zerubbabel, and descendant of Josiah. 1 Chron. iii. 20.

OLYMPAS, O-lim'-pas, *heavenly.*—A believer of distinguished piety. Rom. xvi. 15.

OMAR, O'-mar, *he that speaks, bitter.*—Son of Eliphaz, and grandson of Esau. Gen. xxxvi. 11.

OMEGA, O-meg'-a.—The last letter of the Greek alphabet. It is used as a title of Christ, and, associated with Alpha, denotes his perfection and eternity.

OMRI, Om'-ry, *a sheaf of corn, rebellion, bitter.*—1. General of the army of Elah, king of Israel, and his successor when he heard that his master was murdered. 1 Kings xvi. 9, 16, &c., A.M. 3075. 2. The son of Michael, of the tribe of Issachar. 1 Chron. xxvii. 18.

ON, On, *pain, force, iniquity.*—An image worshipped in Egypt; or a city, probably Heliopolis. Gen. xli. 45, 50; xlvi. 20.

185

ONAM, O'-nam, *sorrow, strength, the iniquity of them.*
—The son of Shobal. Gen. xxxvi. 23.

ONAN, O'-nan, *pain, strength, iniquity.*—A son of the patriarch Judah. Gen. xxxviii. 4, 8, &c.

ONESIMUS, O-nes'-se-mus, *profitable, useful.*—A Phrygian by nation, and slave to Philemon, who ran away, and was converted at Rome. Philem. 10.

ONESIPHORUS, On-e-sif'-fo-rus, *who brings profit.*—An individual highly commended by St. Paul, for his benevolence towards him while he was a prisoner at Rome. 2 Tim. i. 16, 17.

ONO, O'-no, *grief, strength, iniquity of him.*—A city in the tribe of Benjamin. 1 Chron. viii. 12.

OPHEL, O'-fel, *tower, obscurity.*—A wall and tower in Jerusalem. 2 Chron. xxvii. 3.

OPHER, or OPHIR, O'-fer, *ashes, a making fruitful.*—1. Son of Joktan. Gen. x. 29. 2. A country much celebrated in Scripture, and peopled by Ophir, the son of Joktan. It is uncertain where it was: some conjecture India, others Ceylon, others Socotra. It is connected with Tarshish, and Solomon's ships traded thither. 1 Kings xxii. 48; 2 Chron. xx. 36. They sailed from Eziongeber, a port of the Red Sea.

OPHNI, Of'-ny, *fleeting, weariness, folding together.*—A city in the tribe of Benjamin. Josh. xviii. 24.

OPHRAH, Of'-rah, *dust, a fawn, lead.*—A city in the tribe of Benjamin. Josh. xviii. 23.

OREB, O'-reb, *a raven, mixture, the evening.*—One of the princes of Midian, slain on the rock Oreb. Judges vii. 25.

OREN, O'-ren, *a coffer, rejoicing, the slander of them.*—The son of Jerahmeel, of the posterity of Judah. 1 Chron. ii. 25.

ORION, O-ry'-on.—A constellation of the heavens. Job ix. 9.

ORNAN, Or'-nan, *that rejoices, their bow or ark.*—1 Chron. xxi. 15. See ARAUNAH.

ORPAH, Or'-pah, *a neck, skull, nakedness of the mouth.*
—A Moabitish female. Ruth i. 4.

OSEE, O'-see.—See HOSEA. Rom. ix. 25.

OSHEA, O'-she-a.—See JOSHUA. Num. xiii. 8.

OTHNI, Oth'-ny, *my time, my hour.*—Son of Shemaiah,
a valiant man in David's army. 1 Chron. xxvi. 7.

OTHNIEL, Oth'-ne-el, *the hour of God.*—Son of
Kenaz, of the tribe of Judah, Caleb's brother. Josh. xv. 17.

OZEM, O'-zem, *that fasts, their eagerness.*—The sixth
son of Jesse. 1 Chron. ii. 15.

OZIAS, O-zy'-as.—Son of Joram. Matt. i. 8.

OZNI, Oz'-ny, *an ear, my hearing, a goldsmith's balance.*
—The son of Gad, and head of the family of the Oznites.
Num. xxvi. 16.

P

PAARAI, Pay'-a-ray, *a gaping, an opening.*—The
Arbite, a valiant man of David's army. 2 Sam. xxiii. 35.

PADAN-ARAM, Pay'-dan-ay'-ram, *of the field of Syria.*
—A large country, which the Seventy render Mesopotamia.
Gen. xxv. 20.

PADON, Pay'-don, *his redemption, the yoke of an ox.*—
One whose children were Nethinims. Ezra ii. 44.

PAGIEL, Pay'-je-el, *prevention, or prayer of God.*—
The son of Ocran, who made his offering at the tabernacle.
Num. vii. 72.

PAHATH-MOAB, Pay'-hath-mo'-ab.—A duke of Moab.
The name of a place in the country of the Moabites. Ezra
ii. 6; viii. 4.

PAI, Pay'-i, *howling, sighing, appearing.*—A city in the
land of Moab, but uncertain where. 1 Chron. i. 50.

PALAL, Pay'-lal, *thinking, judging.*—One who repaired
the walls of Jerusalem. Neh. iii. 25.

187

PALESTINE. Pal'-es-tine, *strewed or covered with ashes or dust.*—Properly the country of the Philistines, extending from Gaza south, to Lydda north. In a more general sense it is the land of promise, or Canaan, or the land of Judea: it was about two hundred miles long, and eighty in the main breadth.

PALESTINA, Pal-es-ty'-na.—See PALESTINE. Exod. xv. 14; Isai. xiv. 29.

PALLU, Pal'-lew, *marvellous, hidden, wonderful.*—One of the sons of Reuben. Num. xxvi. 8.

PALLUITES, Pal'-lew-ites.—The descendants of Pallu. Num. xxvi. 5.

PALTI, Pal'-ty, *deliverance, flight, banishment.*—The son of Raphu, and one of the spies. Num. xiii. 9.

PALTIEL, Pal'-te-el, *deliverance, banishment of God.*—The son of Azzan, of the tribe of Issachar, and one of the commissioners appointed to divide the land. Num. xxxiv. 26.

PALTITE, Pal'-tite.—A descendant of Palti. 2 Sam. xxiii. 26.

PAMPHYLIA, Pam-fil'-le-a, *a nation made up of every tribe.*—A province of Asia Minor. Acts xxvii. 5. Its southern boundary is the Mediterranean Sea; its northern, Pisidia; its western, Lycia; and its eastern, Cilicia. Acts xiii. 13.

PANNAG, Pan'-nag.—Some regard it as the name of a place, and others as an article of merchandise. Ezek. xxvii. 17.

PAPHOS, Paf'-os, *which boils, is hot.*—A city of Cyprus, lying on the western coast of the island, where Venus had her most ancient and most famous temple. Acts xiii. 6.

PARAH, Pay'-rah, *a cow, increasing, stirring up.*—A city in the tribe of Benjamin. Josh. xviii. 23.

PARAN, Pay'-ran, *beauty, glory, ornament.* — 1. A desert of Arabia Petrea, to the south of Judea, and to the north-east of the gulf Elanitis. Gen. xiv. 6; xxi. 21; Num. x. 12. 2. A city of Arabia Petrea, situate at three days' journey from Elah, towards the east. 3. Also a mountain. Deut. xxxiii. 2.

PARBAR, Par'-bar.—A gate or building belonging to Jerusalem. 1 Chron. xxvi. 18.

PARMASHTA, Par-mash'-tah, *the breaking of a foundation, a bull of one year old.*—The seventh son of Haman. Esther ix. 9.

PARMENAS, Par'-me-nas, *that abides and is permanent.* —One of the first seven deacons of the Christian church. Acts vi. 5.

PARNACH, Par'-nak, *a bull, smiting, broken.*—One of the posterity of Zebulun. Num. xxxiv. 25.

PAROSH, Pay'-rosh, *a flea, fruit of the moth, a goat.*— One whose children, to the number of two thousand one hundred and seventy-two, returned from the Babylonish captivity. Ezra ii. 3; x. 25.

PARSHANDATHA, Par-shan'-da-thah, *revelation of impurities, of his trouble.*—The eldest son of Haman. Esther ix. 7.

PARTHIANS, Par'-the-ans, *horsemen.*—The same with the Persians, known by the name of Elamites till after the time of Cyrus. They were called Persians in the time of the prophets; and Parthians, about the time of our Saviour. Acts ii. 9.

PARUAH, Par'-u-ah, *flourishing, that flies away.*— The father of Jehoshaphat. 1 Kings iv. 17.

PARVAIM, Par-vay'-im.—Supposed to be Peru, or Ceylon. 2 Chron. iii. 6.

PASACH, Pay'-sak, *thy broken piece, thy diminishing.*— A descendant of Asher. 1 Chron. vii. 33.

189

PASDAMMIM, Pas-dam′-min, *a portion or diminishing of blood.*—A place in Palestine. 1 Chron. xi. 13.

PASEAH, Pa-se′-ah, *a passing over, a halting.*—One whose children were Nethinims. 1 Chron. iv. 12; Neh. iii. 6.

PASHUR, Pash′-ur, *that extends the hole, whiteness.*—One whose children, to the number of one thousand two hundred and forty-seven, returned from captivity. Ezra ii. 38.

PATARA, Pat′-a-ra, *trodden underfoot, white-limed, bringing death.*—A maritime city of Lycia, at which St. Paul touched. Acts xxi. 1.

PATHROS, Path′-ros, *mouthful of dew, or dough, persuasion, of decay.*—A city and canton of Egypt, mentioned Isai. xi. 11 ; Jer. xliv. 1, 15.

PATHRUSIM, Path-rew′-sim.—The fifth son of Mizraim, Gen. x. 14, and the progenitor of the people called by that name.

PATMOS, Pat′-mos, *mortal.*—An island in the Ægean Sea, whither St. John was banished, A.D. 94. Rev. i. 9.

PATROBAS, Pat′-ro-bas, *paternal, that pursues the steps of a father.*—A disciple of the Apostles. Rom. xvi. 14.

PAU, Pay′-ew, *that cries aloud, appears.*—A city of Edom. Gen. xxxvi. 39.

PAUL, Paul, *a worker.*—His former name, Saul, means a *destroyer.* He was a native of the city of Tarsus in Cilicia, of the tribe of Benjamin, a Pharisee by profession. He was first a persecutor, and afterwards a disciple of Christ, and an apostle to the Gentiles. See the Acts of the Apostles.

PEDAHEL, Ped′-a-hel, *the redemption of God.*—Son of Ammihud, of the tribe of Naphtali. One of the commissioners for dividing the Holy Land. Num. xxxiv. 28.

PEDAHZUR, Ped'-ah-zur, *saviour, strong, powerful, stone of redemption.*—The father of Gamaliel, head of the tribe of Manasseh. Num. i. 10.

PEDAIAH, Ped-a-i'-ah, *redemption of the Lord.*—1. The grandmother of Jehoiakim, king of Judah. 2 Kings xxiii. 36. 2. Father of Zerubbabel and Shimei. 1 Chron. iii. 18.

PEKAH, Pe'-kah, *he that opens or is at liberty.*—The son of Remaliah, general of the army of Pekahiah, king of Israel: he conspired against his master. 2 Kings xv. 25.

PEKAHIAH, Pek-a-hy'-ah, *it is the Lord that opens.*— Son and successor of Menahem, king of Israel: he reigned but two years. 2 Kings xv. 22, 23.

PEKOD, Pe'-kod, *noble, a ruler.*—A city. Jer. l. 21.

PELAIAH, Pel-a-i'-ah, *the miracle or secret of the Lord.*—The principal Levite who signed the covenant with Nehemiah. Neh. x. 10.

PELALIAH, Pel-a-ly'-ah, *a thinking on the Lord, entertaining the Lord.*—The son of Amzi, a priest. Neh. xi. 12.

PELATIAH, Pel-a-ty'-ah, *let the Lord deliver.*—1. An individual who subdued the Amalekites on the mountains of Seir. 1 Chron. iv. 42. 2. The son of Benaiah, a prince of the people, who lived in the time of Zedekiah, king of Judah. Ezek. xi. 1, &c.

PELEG, Pe'-leg, *a division.*—Son of Eber; born A.M. 1757. Gen. x. 25; xi. 16.

PELET, Pe'-let, *deliverance.*—The son of Azmaveth, one of David's valiant men. 1 Chron. xii. 3.

PELETH, Pe'-leth, *decay, destruction.*—The father of On. Num. xvi. 1.

PELETHITES, Pe'-leth-ites, *judges, destroyers.*—These and the Cherethites were famous in the reign of David for their valour. 2 Sam. viii. 18.

PELON, Pe'-lon, *hid, concealed.*—A city of Judea.

PELONITE, Pel'-on-ite.—A citizen of Pelon. 1 Chron. xi. 36.

PENIEL, Pe-ny'-el, *face or vision of God.*—A city beyond Jordan, near the ford or brook Jabbok. It took its name from the circumstance recorded Gen. xxxii. 24.

PENINNAH, Pe-nin'-nah, *precious stone.*—The second wife of Elkanah, the father of Samuel. 1 Sam. i. 2.

PEOR, Pe'-or, *gaping, opening.*—A mountain beyond Jordan, near Nebo and Pisgah. See Num. xxv. 3; Deut. iv. 3.

PERAZIM, Per'-a-zim, *irruption.*—A mountain of Palestine, where the Philistines were defeated. Isai. xxviii. 21.

PERESH, Pe'-resh, *a horseman, casting out to be slain.*—The son of Machir. 1 Chron. vii. 16.

PERES, or PEREZ, Pe'-rez, *divided, Persian.*—The name of one of Solomon's captains. 1 Chron. xxvii. 3. It was one of the words written on the palace-wall of Belshazzar. Dan. v. 28.

PEREZ-UZZAH, Pe'-rez-uz'-zah, *the division of Uzzah,* or *the strength of Uzzah.*—The place where Uzzah was struck dead for touching the ark. 2 Sam. vi. 8.

PERGA, Per'-ga, *very earthy.*—A city of Pamphylia in Asia. Acts xiii. 13.

PERGAMOS, Per'-ga-mos, *height, elevation.*—A city of Troas, very considerable in the time of John the Evangelist. Rev. ii. 12.

PERIDA, Pe-ry'-da, *separation, division.*—A person mentioned Neh. vii. 57.

PERIZZITES, Per'-iz-zites, *dispersed, dwelling in unwalled villages.*—The ancient inhabitants of Palestine, mixed with the Canaanites. Gen. xiii. 7; Josh. xvii. 15.

PERSIA, Per'-she-a, *that cuts, nail, horseman, dividing a horse-hoof.*—An ancient kingdom of Asia, bounded on the north by Media, on the west by Susiana, on the east by Carmania, and on the south by the Persian Gulf. Esther i. 3.

PERSIS, Per'-sis, *breaking, dividing, nail, horseman.*—A Roman lady, whom St. Paul salutes in his Epistle to the Romans. Rom. xvi. 12.

PERUDA, Per-yew'-da, *separation, division.*—A person that came up from captivity. Ezra ii. 55.

PETER, Pe'-ter, *a stone.*—One of Christ's apostles. He was the son of Jonas, and brother to Andrew. John i. 42. His first name was Simon; but when our Saviour called him to the apostleship, he changed it to Cephas.

PETHAHIAH, Peth-a-hy'-ah, *the Lord, opening the gate of the Lord.*—He was the head of the nineteenth family of the sacerdotal order. 1 Chron. xxiv. 16.

PETHOR, Pe'-thor, *a table.*—A city of Mesopotamia, of which the prophet Baalam was a native. Deut. xxiii. 4.

PETHUEL, Pe-thew'-el, *mouth or persuasion of God.*—The father of the prophet Joel. Joel i. 1.

PEULTHAI, Pe-ul'-thay, *my works.*—The eighth son of Obed-edom. 1 Chron. xxvi. 5.

PHALEC, Fay'-lek, *division.*—One in the genealogy of Christ. Luke iii. 35.

PHALTI, Fal'-ty, *deliverance, flight.*—The son of Laish, who married Michal, after Saul had taken her away from David. 1 Sam. xxv. 44; 2 Sam. iii. 15; xxi. 8; vi. 23.

PHANUEL, Fa-new'-el, *seeing God, vision of God.*—A person of the tribe of Aser, the father of a holy widow and prophetess called Anna. See Luke ii. 36—38.

PHARAOH, Fay'-ro, *that disperses, that discovers.*—A common name of the kings of Egypt. We meet with it very early. See Gen. xii. 15. Josephus says, that all the kings from Menæus, builder of Memphis, down to the time of Solomon, for more than 3300 years, had this name. In the Egyptian language it means *king.* There are ten kings of this name referred to in the Scriptures. 1. He who reigned when Abraham and Sarah went down into Egypt. 2. The one who reigned when Joseph was prime-minister. 3. He that persecuted the Israelites. Exod. i. 8. 4. He that was drowned in the Red Sea. 5. He that gave protection to Hadad, son of the king of Edom. 6. He who gave his daughter in marriage to Solomon, king of Israel. 1 Kings iii. 1. 7. Shishak, who entertained Jeroboam in his dominions. 8. He with whom Hezekiah made a league. 9. Pharaoh-Necho, who made war with Josiah. 10. Pharaoh-Hophra, who entered into an alliance with Zedekiah.

PHAREZ, Fay'-rez, *division, rupture.*—Son of Judah and Tamar. Gen. xxxviii. 29.

PHARISEES, Far'-re-sees, *a division, or set apart.*—A sect of the Jews, of whom frequent mention is made in the Gospels. See Matt. xv. 1—9; xxiii. 13—33; Luke xi. 39—52.

PHAROSH, Fay'-rosh.—One who returned from the Babylonish captivity. Ezra viii. 3.

PHARPAR, Far-'par, *that produces fruit, the fall of the bull.*—A river of Damascus, an arm of the river Barrady, or Chrysorrhoas, which waters the city of Damascus. 2 Kings v. 12.

PHASEAH, Fay'-se-ah.—One whose children were Nethinims. Neh. vii. 51.

PHEBE, Fe'-be, *shining, clear.*—A deaconess of the church at Cenchrea. Rom. xvi. 1, 2.

PHENICE, Fe-ny'-se, *red, purple, palm-tree.*—A port in the island of Crete, to the west. Acts xxvii. 12.

PHICOL, Fy'-col, *the mouth of all, perfection.*—General of the army of Abimelech, king of Gerar. Gen. xxi. 22.

PHILADELPHIA, Fil-a-del'-fe-a, *the love of a brother.* —A city of Lydia, at the foot of Mount Tmolus, about twenty-four miles east of Sardis, and seventy-two from Smyrna. Rev. iii. 7.

PHILEMON, Fy-le'-mon, *that embraced, or is affectionate.*—A citizen of Colosse, in Phrygia, converted to the Christian faith. St. Paul addressed a letter to him respecting his slave Onesimus. See Epistle to Philemon.

PHILETUS, Fy-le'-tus, *amiable, beloved.*—A heretic in the early church. 2 Tim. ii. 17.

PHILIP, Fil'-ip, *a warrior, a lover of horses.*—1. The same as HEROD PHILIP, which see. 2. Philip the apostle, a native of Bethsaida, in Galilee. John i. 43, 44; Luke vi. 14; Matt. x. 3; John vi. 5—7. 3. The second of the seven deacons chosen by the apostles after our Saviour's resurrection. Acts vi. 5.

PHILIPPI, Fil-lip'-py, *lovers of horses.*—One of the principal cities of Macedonia, lying on the north-west of Neapolis. It took its name from Philip, king of Macedon, by whom it was repaired and beautified. Acts xvi. 12.

PHILIPPIANS, Fil-lip'-pe-ans.—The inhabitants of Philippi. St. Paul addressed an epistle to them.

PHILISTIA, Fil-lis'-te-a.—The country of the Philistines. Psal. lxxxvii. 4.

PHILISTIM, Fil-lis'-tim.—Philistia is so called, Gen. x. 14.

PHILISTINES, Fil-lis'-tines, *those that dwell in villages.*—A people of Palestine, who came from the isle of Caphtor, frequently named in Scripture. Josh. xiii. 2, 3; 2 Chron. xxi. 16, &c.

PHILOLOGUS, Fil-lol'-o-gus, *a lover of learning.*—A person to whom St. Paul sends his salutation. Rom. xvi. 15.

PHINEHAS, Fin'-e-has, *a bold countenance.*—1. Son of Eleazar, and grandson of Aaron. He was the third high-priest of the Jews, and discharged his office from A.M. 2571 to 2590. See Num. xxv. 7, &c. 2. Son of Eli, the high-priest, and brother to Hophni. 1 Sam. i. 3.

PHLEGON, Fle'-gon, *zealous, burning.*—A person saluted by St. Paul, Rom. xvi. 14.

PHRYGIA, Fridj'-e-a, *dry, barren.*—A country of Asia. Acts ii. 10; xvi. 6.

PHURAH, Few'-rah, *that bears fruit, that grows.*—The servant of Gideon, who went with him to spy the camp of the Midianites. Judges vii. 10, 11.

PHUT, Fut.—The third son of Ham. Gen. x. 6. Also a place frequently mentioned by the prophets.

PHUVAH, Few'-vah, *a pair of bellows.*—One of the sons of Issachar. Gen. xlvi. 13.

PHYGELLUS, Fy-jel'-lus, *a fugitive.*—A Christian of Asia, who was at Rome when Paul was, and forsook him in his necessity. 2 Tim. i. 15.

PHYLACTERIES, Fy-lak'-te-riz, *things to be particularly observed.*—Rolls of parchment, on which were written certain words of the law, and which the Jews wore on their forehead, &c. See Exod. xiii. 9—16; Matt. xxiii. 5.

PI-BESETH, Py'-be-seth, *dispute from the mouth.*— A city in Egypt. Ezek. xxx. 17.

PI-HAHIROTH, Py-ha-hy'-roth, *the mouth or pass of Hiroth, the opening of liberty.*—One of the encampments of the Israelites in the wilderness. Exod. xiv. 2.

PILATE, Py'-lat, *who is armed with a dart.*—Pontius Pilate was probably of Rome, and was sent to govern Judea in the room of Gratus, A.D. 26 or 27. He governed for ten years. See Luke xiii. 1, &c. He condemned Jesus Christ. See the Gospels.

PILDASH, Pil'-dash.—A son of Nahor. Gen. xxii. 22.

PILEHA, Pil'-e-hah.—One of the chief priests who signed the covenant with Nehemiah. Neh. x. 24.

PILTAI, Pil'-tay.—A descendant of Levi. Neh. xii. 17.

PINON, Py'-non, *a pearl, a gem.*—A duke of Edom. Gen. xxxvi. 41.

PIRAM, Py'-ram, *a wild ass of them, cruelty of them.*—The king of Jarmuth, who came to the assistance of Adoni-zedec, king of Jerusalem, and was conquered by Joshua. See Josh. x. 3, 24—27.

PIRATHON, Pir'-a-thon, *his dissipation, deprivation;* in Syriac, *his vengeance.*—A city in the tribe of Ephraim, in the mountain of Amalek. Judges xii. 15.

PISGAH, Pis'-gah, *a hill, eminence, fortress.*—A mountain beyond Jordan, in the country of Moab. Nebo, Pisgah, and Abarim make but one chain of mountains near Mount Peor. Num. xxi. 20.

PISIDIA, Pis-sid'-e-a, *pitch, pitchy.*—A province of Asia Minor. Acts xiii. 14; xiv. 24.

PISON, Py'-son, *changing, doubling, extended.*—One of the four great rivers that watered paradise. Gen. ii. 11.

PISPAH, Pis'-pah, *a mouth diminished.*—One of the posterity of Asher. 1 Chron. vii. 38.

PITHOM, Py'-thom, *their mouthful, bit, consummation.*—One of the cities that the Israelites built for Pharaoh in Egypt during their servitude. Exod. i. 11.

POLLUX, Pol'-luks, *a boxer.*—See CASTOR. Acts xxviii. 11.

PONTIUS PILATE, Pon'-she-us Py'-lat, *marine, belonging to the sea.*—See PILATE.

PONTUS, Pon'-tus, *the sea.*—A province of Asia Minor. 1 Pet. i. 1.

PORATHA, Por'-a-thah, *fruitful.*—A son of Haman, who suffered with his father. Esther ix. 8.

PORCIUS FESTUS, Por'-she-us Fes'-tus.—The successor of Felix in the government of Judea. Acts xxiv. 27.

POTIPHAR, Pot'-te-far, *bull, fat bull.*—An officer of Pharaoh, king of Egypt, and general of his troops, to whom Joseph was sold. Gen. xxxvii. 36.

POTI-PHERAH, Po-tif′-e-rah, *that scatters abroad, or diminishes the fat.*—A priest of On, in Egypt, Joseph's father-in-law. Gen. xli. 45.

PRISCA, Pris′-kah, *ancient.*—A Christian woman. 2 Tim. iv. 19.

PRISCILLA, Pris-sil′-lah, *ancient.*—A Christian woman, who with her husband was at Corinth when Paul came thither, and had the honour of entertaining him. Acts xviii. 1, 2, &c.

PROCHORUS, Prok′-o-rus, *he that presides over the chairs.*—One of the first seven deacons. Acts vi. 5.

PTOLEMY, Tol′-e-me, *a furrow, an assembly of waters, warlike.*—A name borne by all the kings of Egypt from Ptolemy, the son of Lagus.

PUA, or PUAH, Pew′-a, *a mouth, a corner, a bush of hair.*—1. Son of Issachar, and head of the family of Punites. Num. xxvi. 23. 2. Father of Tola, of the tribe of Issachar. Judges x. 1. 3. One of the two Hebrew midwives, whom Pharaoh commanded to destroy all the male children. Exod. i. 15.

PUBLIUS, Pub′-le-us, *common.*—The governor of Melita. Acts xxviii. 7, 8.

PUDENS, Pew′-dens, *shame-faced.*—He is mentioned 2 Tim. iv. 21.

PUL, Pull, *bean, destruction.*—King of Assyria. He came into the land of Israel in the time of Menahem, king of the ten tribes. 2 Kings xv. 19.

PUNON, Pew′-non, *precious stone, that beholds.*—A station of the Israelites in the wilderness. Num. xxxiii. 42.

PUR, Pur, *lot.*—A solemn feast of the Jews, instituted in memory of the lots cast by Haman. Esther iii. 7.

PURIM, Pew′-rim, *lots.*—Plural of Pur.

PUTEOLI, Pew-tee′-o-ly.—A city in Campania in Italy. Acts xxviii. 13.

PUTIEL, Pew′-te-el, *the fatness of God.*—The father-in-law of Eleazar, the son of Aaron. Exod. vi. 25.

198

Q.

QUARTUS, Quar'-tus, *the fourth.*—A disciple, mentioned Rom. xvi. 23.

R.

RAAMAH, Ray'-a-mah, *greatness, thunder, evil, bruising.*—The fourth son of Cush. Gen. x. 7. His descendants peopled a country of Arabia, from whence they brought to Tyre spices, precious stones, and gold. Ezek. xxvii. 22.

RAAMIAH, Ra-a-my'-ah, *thunder of the Lord, evil from the Lord.*—One who returned from the Babylonish captivity. Neh. vii. 7.

RAAMSES, Ra-am'-ses, *thunder, he that destroys evil.*—A city built by the Hebrews, during their servitude in Egypt. Exod. i. 11.

RABBAH, Rab'-bah, *powerful, contentious.*—A city mentioned by Joshua, chap. xv. 60.

RABBATH, Rab'-bath, *powerful, contentious.* — The same as RABBAT-AMMON. The capital city of the Ammonites, situated beyond Jordan. Deut. iii. 11.

RABBATH-MOAB, Rab'-bath-mo'-ab.—The capital city of the Moabites. See AR.

RABBI, Rab'-by, *excellent, master.*—A title of dignity among the Hebrews. Matt. xxiii. 7.

RABBITH, Rab'-bith. A city in the tribe of Issachar. Josh. xix. 20.

RABMAG, Rab'-mag, *one who overthrows a multitude, chief of the magicians.*—The name of a Babylonish prince. Jer. xxxix. 3.

RABSARIS, Rab'-sa-ris, *master, set over eunuchs.*—A prince of Babylon. 2 Kings xviii. 17.

RABSHAKEH, Rab'-sha-keh, *chamberlain, cup-bearer of the prince.*—A term of dignity. He was sent by Sennacherib, king of Assyria, to summon Hezekiah to surrender Jerusalem. 2 Kings xviii. 17.

RACA, Ray'-ka, a Syriac word which signifies *empty, vain, beggarly, foolish.*—Matt. v. 22.

RACHAB, Ray'-kab, *proud, strong, enlarged.*—The wife of Salmon, and mother of Booz. Matt. i. 5.

RACHAL, Ray'-kal, *to whisper, injurious, an apothecary.* —A city in the tribe of Judah. 1 Sam. xxx. 29.

RACHEL, Ray'-tchel, *a sheep.*—The daughter of Laban, sister of Leah, and wife of Jacob. Gen. xxix. 6. The prophet Jeremiah and St. Matthew have put Rachel for the tribes of Ephraim and Manasseh, the children of Joseph, the son of Rachel. Jer. xxxi. 15; Matt. ii. 18.

RADDAI, Rad'-da-i, *ruling.*—The fifth son of Jesse, and brother of David. 1 Chron. ii. 14.

RAGAU, Ray'-gaw, *a companion, his shepherd, breaking asunder.*—The name of one of our Lord's ancestors. Luke iii. 35.

RAGUEL, Ra-gew'-el, *shepherd or friend of God.*—The father-in-law of Moses. Num. x. 29.

RAHAB, Ray'-hab, *proud, strong, quarrelsome.*—1. The name of the person who entertained the spies. Josh. ii. 1, &c. 2. A country or city. Psalm lxxxvii. 4; lxxxix. 10.

RAHAM, Ray'-ham, *mercy, compassion, a friend.*—A son of Shema, a descendant of Judah. 1 Chron. ii. 44.

RAKEM, Ray'-kem, *void, pictures.*—One of the posterity of Manasseh. 1 Chron. vii. 16.

RAKKATH, Rak'-kath, *emptiness, spittle.*—A fenced city belonging to the tribe of Naphtali. Josh. xix. 35.

RAKKON, Rak'-kon, *void, vain, diverse pictures, mountain of lamentations.*—A city of the tribe of Dan. Josh. xix. 46.

RAM, Ram, *high, casting away.*—1. The son of Hezron, and father of Amminadab, of the tribe of Judah. 1 Chron. ii. 9. 2. Ram is also put for Aram. Job xxxii. 2.

RAMAH, Ray'-mah, *elevated, who rejects.*—1. A city of Benjamin, Josh. xviii. 25, situated between Gaba and Bethel. 2. A city in the tribe of Naphtali, on the frontiers of Asher. Josh. xix. 29, 36.

RAMATHAIM, Ray-math-ay'-im, *elevated, who rejects.* —A city of Palestine, on the road from Joppa to Jerusalem. 1 Sam. i. 1.

RAMATHITE, Ray'-math-ite, *lofty, exalted, cast away.* —An inhabitant of Ramath. 1 Chron. xxvii. 27.

RAMATH-LEHI, Ray'-math-le'-hy, *elevation of the jaw-bone.*—A city of the Philistines. Judges xv. 17.

RAMATH-MIZPEH, Ray'-math-mis'-peh, *the elevation of a sentinel.*—A city of Palestine, in the tribe of Gad. Josh. xiii. 26.

RAMESES, Ra-me'-ses, *thunder, he that destroys evil.*— A city of lower Egypt, to the east of the river Nile. Exod. xii. 37.

RAMIAH, Ray-my'-ah, *exaltation of the Lord.*—One who returned from the Babylonish captivity. Ezra x. 25.

RAMOTH, Ray'-moth, *seeing death, high places.*—A city in the mountains of Gilead. 1 Kings iv. 13. It belonged to the tribe of Gad, and is frequently called Ramoth-Gilead.

RAPHA, Ray'-fah, *relaxation, physic, a giant.*—1. A descendant of Benjamin. 1 Chron. viii. 2. 2. The name of a son of Binea. 1 Chron. viii. 37.

RAPHU, Ray'-fu, *cured, comforted.*—Num. xiii. 9. See RAPHA.

REAIAH, or REAIA, Re-a-i'-ah, *the vision of the Lord.* —1. The son of Shobal, father of Jahath, and grandson to the patriarch Judah. 1 Chron. iv. 2. 2. The son of Micah, father of Baal. 1 Chron. v. 5. 3. One whose children returned from Babylon. Neh. vii. 50.

REBA, Re'-bah, *the fourth, a square, that stoops.*—One of the princes of the Midianites. Num. xxxi. 8. He perished in the war with Moses.

REBEKAH, Re-bek'-kah, *fat, fed, quarrel appeased.*—A daughter of Bethuel, wife of Isaac, and mother of Esau and Jacob. Gen. xxv. 21, 22.

RECHAB, Re'-kab, *square, chariot, rider.*—1. One of the assassins of Ishbosheth, the son of Saul. 2 Sam. iv. 2. 2. The father of Jonadab, and founder of the order of the Rechabites. Some suppose he was of the tribe of Judah; others, a Levite or priest. Jer. xxxv.

RECHABITES, Re'-kab-ites.—The posterity of Rechab. Jer. xxxv.

RECHAH, Re'-kah.—A city of Judea, but uncertain where it was situated. 1 Chron. iv. 12.

REELAIAH, Re-el-i'-ah, *a shepherd of the Lord, or a companion to the Lord himself.*—One of the race of the priests who returned t' Jerusalem with Zerubbabel. Ezra ii. 2.

REGEM, Re'-gem, *stoning, purple.*—A son of Jahdai, of the posterity of Judah. 1 Chron. ii. 47.

REGEM-MELECH, Re-gem'-me-lek, *stoning the king, purple of the king.*—One of a deputation to the priests and prophets at Jerusalem, to know if they were still to fast and mortify themselves on the fifth month of the sacred year, in commemoration of the destruction of the city of Jerusalem. Jer. lii. 12, 13; Zech. vii. 2, 3.

REHABIAH, Re-ha-by'-ah, *the breath of the Lord, the street of the Lord.*—The eldest son of Eliezer. 1 Chron. xxiii. 17. He and his brethren were Levites, and treasurers of the temple.

REHOB, Re'-hob, *breadth, extent.*—1. The father of Hadadezar, king of Zobah, of Syria. 2 Sam. viii. 3. 2. A city of the tribe of Asher, given for a dwelling to the Levites of the family of Gershom. Josh. xix. 28.

REHOBOAM, Re-ho-bo'-am, *who sets the people at liberty, space of the people.*—The son and successor of Solomon: his mother was Naamah, an Ammointish woman whom Solomon had married. 1 Kings xiv. 21. He was forty-one years of age when he began to reign: he died A.M. 3046, having reigned seventeen years in Jerusalem.

REHOBOTH, Re-ho'-both, *spaces, places.* — 1. The name of a well which Isaac dug. Gen. xxvi. 22.   2. The name of a city built by Asshur. Gen. x. 11.

REHUM, Re'-hum, *compassionate, friendly.* — 1. A Levite, son of Bani: he returned from Babylon with Zerubbabel. Ezra ii. 2; Neh. iii. 17.   2. The chancellor of Artaxerxes, king of Persia. Ezra iv. 8, 9, 17, 23.

REI, Re'-i, *my shepherd, companion, friend.*—One of the officers in David's army, who adhered to the party of Solomon against Adonijah. 1 Kings i. 8.

REKEM, Re'-kem, *void, vain, divers pictures.*—1. One of the princes of Midian who was put to death by Phinehas, son of the high-priest Eleazar. Num. xxxi. 8.   2. The son of Hebron, and brother of Korah. 1 Chron. ii. 43.   3. A city of the tribe of Benjamin. Josh. xviii. 27.

REMALIAH, Rem-a-ly'-ah, *the exaltation of the Lord.* —The father of Pekah, king of Israel. 2 Kings xv. 25.

REMETH, Re'-meth, *highly, cast away.*—A city in the tribe of Issachar. Josh. xix. 21.

REMMON, Rem'-mon, *greatness, a pomegranate.*—A city in the tribe of Simeon.   The same as RIMMON. Josh. xix. 7.

REMMON-METHOAR, Rem'-mon-meth'-o-ar. — A city bordering on the tribe of Zebulun. Josh. xix. 13.

REMPHAN, Rem'-fan, *prepared, set in array.*—The name of an idol, which some suppose to be Saturn. Amos v. 26; Acts vii. 43.

REPHAEL, Re'-fa-el, *the medicine of God.*—One of the porters of the temple of Jerusalem. 1 Chron. xxvi. 7.

REPHAH, Re'-fah, *the releasing the snare.*—The son of Beriah. 1 Chron. vii. 25.

REPHAIAH, Ref-a-i'-ah, *the medicine of the Lord, the recreating of the Lord.*—The son of Tola, and grandson of Issachar. 1 Chron. vii. 2.

REPHAIMS, Ref'-a-ims, *giant, physician, relaxed.*—1. The Rephaim were ancient giants of the land of Canaan. Gen. xiv. 5. 2. A valley famous in Joshua's time. Josh. xv. 8; xviii. 16.

REPHIDIM, Ref'-id-im, *beds, places of rest.*—It was a station or encampment of the Israelites. Exod. xvii. 1.

RESEN, Re'-sen, *a bridle or bit.*—A city of Assyria, built by Asher, between Nineveh and Calah. Gen. x. 12.

RESHEPH, Re'-shef. — One of the posterity of the patriarch Ephraim. 1 Chron. vii. 25.

REU, Re'-u, *his shepherd, companion, friend.*—The son of Peleg, born A.M. 1787: he was the father of Serug. Gen. xi. 18, 20.

REUBEN, Rew'-ben, *who sees the son, or vision of the son.*—The eldest son of Jacob and Leah; born A.M. 2252. Gen. xxix. 32.

REUEL, Re-yew'-el, *shepherd, or friend of God.*—A son of Esau and Bashemath, the daughter of Ishmael. Gen. xxxvi. 4, 17.

REUMAH, Rew'-mah, *high, elevated.*—A concubine of Nahor, the brother of Abraham. Gen. xxii. 24.

REZEPH, Re'-zeff, *a pavement, burning coal.*— A city of Syria. 2 Kings xix. 12; Isai. xxxvii. 12.

REZIA, Re-zy'-ah, *a messenger.*—A son of Ulla, of the tribe of Asher. 1 Chron. vii. 39.

REZIN, Re'-zin, *voluntary, a messenger, a runner.*—A king of Syria, who made an alliance with Pekah, son of Remaliah, to invade the dominions of Ahaz, king of Judah. 2 Kings xv. 37; xvi. 5, 6.

REZON, Re'-zon, *lean, small, secret, prince.*—The son of Eliadah, who revolted from his master Hadadezer, king of Zobah. 1 Kings xi. 23.

RHEGIUM, Re′-je-um, *rupture, fracture.*—A city of Italy, in the kingdom of Naples. St. Paul landed there on his way to Rome, A. D. 61. Acts xxviii. 13, 14.

RHESA, Re′-sah, *will, course, a meeting, a head.*—One in the genealogy of Christ. Luke iii. 27.

RHODA, Ro′-dah, *a rose.*—A servant who lived with Mary the mother of John Mark. Acts xii. 13.

RHODES, Roads, *a rose.*—An island lying south of the province of Caria in Asia Minor, and among the Asiatic Islands is next in importance to Cyprus and Lesbos. Acts xxi. 1.

RIBAI, Ry′-bay, *strife, chiding, multiplying.* — The father of Ittai, of the tribe of Benjamin. 2 Sam. xxiii. 29.

RIBLAH, Rib′-lah, *quarrel, that increases or spreads.* —A city of Syria, in the country of Hamath. 2 Kings xxv. 6, 20, 21.

RIMMON, Rim′-mon, *a pomegranate, exalted.*—1. A city of Zebulun. 1 Chron. vi. 77.   2. A rock to which the children of Benjamin retreated after their defeat. Judges xx. 45.   3. The name of an idol of the people of Damascus. 2 Kings v. 18.   4. The Beerothite, the father of Baanah and Rechab, the murderers of king Ishbosheth. 2 Sam. iv. 5, 9.

RIMMON-PAREZ, Rim′-mon-pay′-rez.—An encampment of the Israelites in the wilderness. Num. xxxiii. 19.

RINNAH, Rin′-nah, *song, rejoicing.*—A descendant of the patriarch Judah. 1 Chron. iv. 20.

RIPHATH, Ry′-fath, *medicine, release.* — The second son of Gomer, and grandson of Japheth. Gen. x. 3.

RISSAH, Ris′-sah, *watering, distillation, dew.*— An encampment of the Israelites in the wilderness. Num. xxxiii. 21, 22.

RITHMAH, Rith′-mah, *a juniper-tree, a sound, a noise.* —An encampment of the Israelites in the desert. Num. xxxiii. 18.

RIZPAH, Riz'-pah, *stretched out.*—The daughter of Aiah, and a concubine of king Saul. 2 Sam. iii. 7.

ROGELIM, Ro-ge'-lim, *foot, footmen, searching out, an accuser, custom.*—A place in Gilead, beyond Jordan, where Barzillai lived. 2 Sam. xvii. 27.

ROHGAH, Roh'-gah.—A descendant of the patriarch Asher. 1 Chron. vii. 34.

ROME, Rome, *strength, power.*—A large city of Italy, founded by Romulus and Remus, 750 years before Christ, towards the end of the reign of Hezekiah. Acts ii. 10.

RUFUS, Rew'-fus, *red.*—The son of Simon the Cyrenian, who assisted our Saviour in carrying his cross to Mount Calvary: Mark xv. 21: whether the same as the person mentioned Rom. xvi. 13, is uncertain.

RUHAMAH, Rew'-ha-mah, *having obtained mercy.*—A name given to those Israelites who had not bowed the knee to Baal. See Hosea ii. 1.

RUMAH, Rew'-mah, *exalted, rejected.*—The name of a place mentioned 2 Kings xxiii. 36.

RUTH, Rooth, *satisfied, filled.*—A Moabitish female, married to Boaz. See the book of Ruth. Her name is in the genealogy of the Saviour. Matt. i. 5.

S

SABACHTHANI, Sa-bak-thay'-ny, *thou hast forsaken me.*—One of the last words of Christ. Matt. xxvii. 46.

SABAOTH, Sab'-a-oth, *armies.*—Rom. ix. 29; James v. 4.

SABEANS, Sa-be'-ans, *captivity, conversion, old age.*—A people of Arabia, descended from Suba. See Job i. 15.

SABTAH, Sab'-tah.—The third son of Cush. Gen. x. 7.

SABTECHAH, Sab'-te-kah, *that surrounds.*—The fifth son of Cush. Gen. x. 7.

SACAR, Say′-kar.—An officer of David. 1 Chron. xi. 35.

SADDUCEES, Sad′-dew-sees, *just, justified.*—A sect among the Jews, so called from their founder Sadoc. They taught that there was no resurrection, nor future state, neither angel, nor spirit. Matt. xxii. 23; Acts xxiii. 8.

SADOC, Say′-dok, *just, justified.*—The son of Azor. Matt. i. 14.

SALA, Say′-lah, *branches, mission.*—One in the genealogy of Christ. Luke iii. 35.

SALAH, Say′-lah, *mission, branches, that spoils.*—The son of Arphaxad; or the son of Cainan, and grandson of Arphaxad. See Gen. xi. 12—15; Luke iii. 36.

SALAMIS, Sal′-a-mis, *shaken, tossed, beaten.*—Once a famous city in the isle of Cyprus, opposite to Seleucia on the Syrian coast: here St. Paul preached, A. D. 45. Acts xiii. 5.

SALATHIEL, Sa-lay′-the-el, *I have asked of God.*—Son of Jeconiah, and father of Zorobabel. See 1 Chron. iii. 17. He died in Babylon during the captivity. He was also the son of Neri, probably by adoption, or by having married the heiress of Neri's family. Luke iii. 27.

SALCAH, Sal′-kah.—A city in the country of Bashan. Deut. iii. 10; 1 Chron. v. 11.

SALEM, Say′-lem, *peace.*—1. Jerusalem. Psal. lxxvi. 2. 2. A city of the Shechemites. Gen. xxxiii. 18.

SALIM, Say′-lim, *fox, fist, path.*—The place where John baptized, near Jordan. John iii. 23.

SALLAI, Sal′-la-i.—A person that came up from captivity. Neh. xi. 8.

SALLU, Sal′-lew.—A Benjamite. 1 Chron. ix. 7.

SALLUM, Sal′-lum.—A son of king Josiah.

SALMA, Sal'-mah.—One of Caleb's posterity. 1 Chron. ii. 51.

SALMON, Sal'-mon, *peaceable, perfect, that rewards.*— The son of Nashon: he married Rahab, by whom he had Boaz. 1 Chron. ii. 11, 51, 54; Ruth iv. 20, 21.

SALMONE, Sal-mo'-ne, *peaceable.*—A city and sea-port in the island of Crete. Acts xxvii. 7.

SALOME, Sa-lo'-me, *peaceable, or peacemaker.*—The name of several Jewish women. 1. Of the daughter of Herodias and Herod Philip, who at the instigation of her mother asked the head of John the Baptist. 2. The wife of Zebedee, and mother of St. James the Greater, and St. John the Evangelist. She was one of those holy women that attended upon Christ. See Matt. xxvii. 56; xx. 20—22; Mark xv. 40.

SALU, Say'-lu, *exaltation.*—The father of Zimri, of the tribe of Simeon. Num. xxv. 14.

SAMARIA, Sa-may'-re-a, *his guard, prison, or diamond.* —The capital city in the ten tribes that revolted from the house of David: it was built by Omri, king of Israel. It took the name of Samaria from Shemer, the person of whom the hill was bought on which it was built. 1 Kings xvi. 24.

SAMARITANS, Sa-mar'-e-tans.—Inhabitants of Samaria. John iv. 9.

SAMGAR-NEBO, Sam'-gar-ne'-bo.—A prince of Babylon. Jer. xxxix. 3.

SAMLAH, Sam'-lah, *raiment, his left hand, his name.*— A king of Edom. Gen. xxxvi. 36.

SAMOS, Say'-mos, *full of gravel.*—An island in the Archipelago, on the coast of Asia Minor. Acts xx. 15.

SAMOTHRACIA, Sam-o-thray'-she-a.—An island in the Ægean Sea, so called, because it was peopled by Samians and Thracians. Acts xvi. 11.

SAMSON, Sam'-son, *his son, his service, here the second time.*—The son of Manoah, of the tribe of Dan. Judges xiii. 24. He was born A.M. 2843, and was a Nazarite from his infancy.

SAMUEL, Sam'-u-el, *heard or asked of God.*—The son of Elkanah and Hannah, of the tribe of Levi, and family of Kohath: he was born A.M. 2833. 1 Sam. i. 1, &c. He was an eminent prophet, historian, and the seventeenth judge of Israel: he died in the ninety-eighth year of his age. It is doubtful whether he was a priest: he wore an ephod, anointed kings, and offered sacrifices, but he was not of the race of Aaron.

SANBALLAT, San-bal'-lat, *bush, or enemy in secret.*—The governor of the Samaritans, and an enemy to the Jews. Neh. ii. 10, 19.

SANSANNAH, San-san'-nah.—A city in Judea. Josh. xv. 31.

SAPH, Saff, *rushes, end, threshold.*—A person of the race of the giants. 2 Sam. xxi. 18.

SAPHIR, Saf'-fir, *a city.*—A city in Judea. Micah i. 11.

SAPPHIRA, Saf-fy'-ra, *that tells, that writes books.*—A Christian woman that perished by the hand of God. Acts v. 1, &c.

SARA, SARAH, Say'-rah, or SARAI, Say'-ray, *lady, princess of the multitude.*—1. The wife of Abraham, and his sister, having the same father, but not the same mother. Gen. xx. 12. 2. A daughter of Asher. Num. xxvi. 46.

SARAIAH, Sa-ra-i'-ah, *my prince of the Lord.*—One of the posterity of Judah.

SARAPH, Say'-raff.—The name of a person mentioned 1 Chron. iv. 22.

SARDIS, Sar'-dis, *prince, or song of joy, what remains;* in Syriac, *a pot or kettle.*—A city of Asia Minor, formerly the capital of Crœsus, king of the Lydians. Rev. iii. 1, &c.
209

SARDITES, Sar'-dites.—Descendants of Sered. Num. xxvi. 26.

SARDIUS, Sar'-de-us.—A gem in the breast-plate of the high-priest. Exod. xxviii. 17.

SARDONYX, Sar'-do-nicks.—A precious stone. Rev. xxi. 20.

SAREPTA, Sa-rep'-ta, *a goldsmith's shop, where metals are used to be melted and tried.*—A city of Sidon. Luke iv. 26.

SARGON, Sar'-gon, *who takes away protection, who takes away the garden:* in Syriac, *nuts, snares.*—A king of Assyria. Isai. xx. 1.

SARID, Say'-rid.—A city. Josh. xix. 10, 12.

SARON, Say'-ron, *his field, plain, song.*—A country. Acts ix. 35.

SARSECHIM, Sar-se'-kim, *master of the wardrobe, of the perfumes.*—A captain or prince in the service of the king of Babylon. Jer. xxxix. 3.

SARUCH, Say'-ruk, *a branch, layer, twining.*—One of the ancestors of Jesus Christ. Luke iii. 35.

SATAN, Say'-tan, *contrary, adversary, an accuser.*—A name applied in Scripture to the devil, or the chief of the fallen angels.

SAUL, Sawl, *demanded, sepulchre, destroyer.*—1. The king of Idumea. Gen. xxxvi. 37. 2. The son of Kish, of the tribe of Benjamin, the first king of the Israelites. 1 Sam. ix. 1, 2, &c. 3. Paul the apostle, so called prior to his conversion.

SCEVA, Se'-vah, *disposed, prepared.*—A Jew, and chief of the priests. Acts xix. 14—16.

SCYTHIAN, Sith'-e-an, *tanner, leather-dresser.*—An inhabitant of Scythia, a large country in the north of Europe and Asia. Col. iii. 11.

SEBA, Se'-bah, *drunkard, that surrounds :* in Syriac, *old man.*—The son of Cush. Gen. x. 7. Also a country. Psal. lxxii. 10.

SEBAT, Se'-bat, *twig, sceptre, bride.*—The name of a month among the Hebrews. Zech. i. 7.

SECACAH, Sek'-a-kah.—A city of Judah. Josh. xv. 61.

SECHU, Se'-kew.—A place in Judea, within which Ramah was. 1 Sam. xix. 22.

SECUNDUS, Se-kun'-dus, *the second.*—A disciple, of whose life and death we have no particulars. Acts xx. 4.

SEGUB, Se'-gub, *fortified, raised.*—1. The son of Hezron. 1 Chron. ii. 21, &c. 2. The younger son of Hiel, who died at the setting up of the gates of Jericho. 1 Kings xvi. 34; Josh. vi. 26.

SEIR, Se'-er, *hairy, demon, tempest, barley.*—1. The Horite, whose dwelling was in the mountains of Seir, east and south of the Dead Sea. Gen. xiv. 6; Deut. ii. 12. His descendants reigned here. Gen. xxxvi. 20—30. 2. Mountains near the Dead Sea. Deut i. 2. 3. A mountain on the frontiers of the tribe of Judah and Dan. Josh. xv. 10.

SEIRATH, Se'-e-rath.—A place in the land of Moab, not far from Bethel and Gilgal. Judges iii. 26.

SELA, Se'-la, *a rock.*—A place in Palestine. Isai. xvi. 1.

SELA-HAMMAH-LEKOTH, Se'-la-ham-mah-le'-koth, *the rock of divisions.*—A place in Judea, where Saul returned from pursuing David. 1 Sam. xxiii. 28.

SELED, Se'-led.—A son of Nadab. 1 Chron. ii. 30.

SELEUCIA, Se-lew'-she-a, *beaten by waves, runs as a river.*—A city of Syria, situated on the Mediterranean Sea. Acts xiii. 4.

SEMACHIAH, Sem-a-ky'-ah. — A Levite. 1 Chron. xxvi. 7.

211

SEMEI, Sem'-e-i, *hearing, obeying.*—One in the genealogy of Christ. Luke iii. 26.

SENAAH, Sen'-a-ah.—One whose children returned from captivity. Ezra ii. 35.

SENEH, Se'-neh, *bush.*—A rock mentioned in Jonathan's history. 1 Sam. xiv. 4.

SENIR, Se'-nir, *a sleeping candle, a changing.*—A part of Canaan. 1 Chron. v. 23.

SENNACHERIB, Sen-na-ke'-rib, *bush, of the destruction of the sword, of drought.*—The king of Assyria, son and successor of Shalmaneser: he began to reign A.M. 3290, and reigned only four years. See 2 Kings xix. 7, 20, 37.

SEORIM, Se-o'-rim.—The fourth of the twenty-four families of priests. 1 Chron. xxiv. 8.

SEPHAR, Se'-far, *a book, scribe:* in Syriac, *a haven.*— A mountain of the east, near Armenia. See Gen. x. 30.

SEPHARAD, Sef'-ar-ad, *a book, descending, ruling.*—A place in Judea. Obadiah 20.

SEPHARVAIM, Sef-ar-vay'-im, *two books, two scribes.* —A country of Assyria. 2 Kings xvii. 24, 31. Its situation cannot now be accurately discovered. Also a city. Isai. xxxvii. 13.

SEPHARVITES, Se'-far-vites.—Inhabitants of Sepharvaim. 2 Kings xvii. 31.

SERAH, Se'-rah, *lady of scent, song, the morning.*—The sister of the sons of Asher. Gen. xlvi. 17.

SERAIAH, Se-ra-i'-ah, *prince of the Lord.*—1. David's secretary. 2 Sam. viii. 17.   2. The father of Joab. 1 Chron. iv. 14.   3. The son of Asiel. 1 Chron. iv. 35.   4. A high-priest. Jer. lii. 24.   5. One that returned from captivity. Ezra ii. 2.   6. A native of Netophah. 2 Kings xxv. 23. 7. The son of Neriah. Jer. li. 59, 61.

SERGIUS-PAULUS, Ser'-je-us-Paw'-lus, *a maker of nets.*—The pro-consul or governor of the island of Cyprus. Acts xiii. 7—12.

SERUG, Se'-rug, *branch, layer, twining.*—The son of Reu. Gen. xi. 20—22; 1 Chron. i. 26.

SETH, Seth, *set up, put, who puts.*—The son of Adam and Eve, born A.M. 130. Gen. v. 3—8.

SETHUR, Se'-thur.—One of the spies. Num. xiii. 13.

SHAALABBIN, Shay-al-ab'-bin, *beholding the heart.*—A city of Palestine, in the tribe of Dan. Josh. xix. 42.

SHAALBIM, Shay-al'-bim, *that beholds the heart; or fist, or hand.*—A city in Judea. Judges i. 35. See 2 Sam. xxiii. 32.

SHAAPH, Shay'-aff.—One of Caleb's posterity. 1 Chron. ii. 47.

SHAARAIM, Shay-a-ray'-im, *gales, valuation, hairs, barley, tempests, demons.*—A city. 1 Chron. iv. 31.

SHAASHGAZ, Shay-ash'-gaz, *he that passes the fleece.*—A chamberlain of Ahasuerus. Esther ii. 14.

SHABBETHAI, Shab-beth'-a-i.—A Levite who assisted Ezra in the reformation. Ezra x. 15.

SHACHIA, Shak'-e-a.—One of the chiefs of the tribe of Benjamin. 1 Chron. viii. 10.

SHADRACH, Shay'-drak, *tender nipple, tender field.*—A name given to Hananiah, one of Daniel's companions. Dan. i. 7.

SHAGE, Shay'-ge.—One of David's worthies. 1 Chron. xi. 34.

SHAHAZIMAH, Shay-haz'-e-mah.—A city on the borders of Issachar. Josh. xix. 22.

SHALEM, Shay'-lem, *fox, fist, path.*—A city of Shechem. Gen. xxxiii. 18.

SHALIM, Shay'-lim, *fox, fist, path.*—A country of Judea. 1 Sam. ix. 4.

SHALISHA, Shal'-e-sha, *three, the third, prince.*—A city about fifteen miles from Diospolis. 1 Sam. ix. 4.

SHALLECHETH, Shal'-le-keth, *a casting out.*—The name of one of the gates of Jerusalem. 1 Chron. xxvi. 16.

SHALLUM, Shal'-lum, *perfect, peaceable.*—1. The son of Jabesh. 2 Kings xv. 10—15. 2. Son of Tikvah. 2 Kings xxii. 14. 3. Son of Sisamai. 1 Chron. ii. 40. 4. Father of Mibsam. 1 Chron. iv. 25. 5. Son of Josiah. 1 Chron. iii. 15. 6. Son of Zadok. 1 Chron. vi. 12, 13. 7. Son of Kore. 1 Chron. ix. 19, 31.

SHALLUN, Shal'-lun.—Son of Colhozeh. Neh. iii. 15.

SHALMAI, Shal'-ma-i, *peaceable.*—A Nethinim. Ezra ii. 46.

SHALMAN, Shal'-man, *peaceable, perfect, that rewards.* —A general that spoiled Beth-arbel. Hosea x. 14.

SHALMANESER, Shal-ma-ne'-ser, *peace, tied, perfection and retribution.*—The king of Assyria, who succeeded Tiglath-pileser, and had Sennacherib for his successor. See 2 Kings xvii. 3 ; xviii. 9.

SHAMA, Shay'-mah, *loss, desolation, astonishment.*— Son of Hothan. 1 Chron. xi. 44. He is called Shammah, 2 Sam. xxiii. 25; Shammoth, 1 Chron. xi. 27.

SHAMARIAH, Sham-a-ry'-ah.—A son of Rehoboam. 2 Chron. xi. 19.

SHAMED, Shay'-med.—One of the chief men of Benjamin. 1 Chron. viii. 12.

SHAMER, Shay'-mer.—One of the family of Kohath. 1 Chron. vi. 46.

SHAMGAR, Sham'-gar, *named a stranger, he is here a stranger, surprise of the stranger.*—One of the judges of Israel. Judges iii. 31.

SHAMHUTH, Sham'-huth, *desolation, astonishment.*— One of David's men. 1 Chron. xxvii. 8.

SHAMIR, Shay'-mir, *prison, bush, lees.*—The name of two cities; one in Judah, Josh. xv. 48; the other in Ephraim. Judges x. 1.

SHAMMA, Sham'-mah, *loss, desolation, astonishment.*— A son of Asher. 1 Chron. vii. 37.

SHAMMAH, Sham'-mah, *loss, desolation, astonishment.* —1. A son of Reuel. Gen. xxxvi. 13.   2. A son of Jesse. 1 Sam. xvi. 9.

SHAMMAI, Sham'-ma-i.—Son of Rekem, and father of Maon. 1 Chron. ii. 44.

SHAMMUA, Sham-mew'-a, *one that is heard or obeyed.* —Son of Zaccur, and one of the spies. Num. xiii. 4.

SHAMSHERAI, Sham-she-ray'-i.—One of the chiefs of the tribe of Benjamin. 1 Chron. viii. 26.

SHAPHAM, or SHAPHAN, Shay'-fam, or Shay'-fan, *a rabbit, rat, their lip.*—The son of Azaliah, secretary of the temple in the time of king Josiah. 2 Kings xxii. 3, 9, 10, &c.

SHAPHAT, Shay'-fat, *a judge, judging.*—1. One of the spies. Num. xiii. 5.   2. Father of Elisha.   1 Kings xix. 16, 19.   3. Son of Shemaiah. 1 Chron. iii. 22.   4. Son of Adlai. 1 Chron. xxvii. 29.

SHAPHER, Shay'-fer.—One of the encampments in the wilderness. Num. xxxiii. 23.

SHARAI, Shar'-a-i, *my lord, my song.*—One who had married a strange wife in Babylon. Ezra x. 40.

SHARAR, Shay'-rar.—The father of Ahiam. 2 Sam. xxiii. 33.

SHAREZER, Sha-re'-zer, *overseer of the treasury.*—The second son of Sennacherib, who assisted to murder his father. 2 Kings xix. 37.

SHARON, Shay'-ron, *his plain, field, song.*—There are three cantons in Palestine known by this name. It became proverbial of any place of beauty or fertility. See Isai. xxxiii. 9. Sharon, or Lasharon, a city whose king was taken and put to death by Joshua. Josh. xii. 18.

SHARUHEN, Sha-rew'-hen.—A city. Josh. xix. 6.

SHASHAI, Shash'-a-i.—One that had married a strange wife in Babylon. Ezra x. 40.

SHASHAK, Shay′-shak, *a bag of linen, the sixth bag.*— One of the chief men of the tribe of Benjamin. 1 Chron. viii. 25.

SHAUL, Shay′-ul.—The son of Simeon. Num. xxvi. 13; Gen. xlvi. 10.

SHAVEH, Shay′-veh, *the plain, that makes equality.*— A valley of Judea, near Jerusalem. Gen. xiv. 17.

SHAVSHA, Shav′-sha, *a secretary.*—One of David's officers. 1 Chron. xviii. 16.

SHEAL, She′-al.—The son of Bani. Ezra x. 29.

SHEALTIEL, She-al′-te-el, *I have asked of God.*—The father of Zerubbabel. Ezra iii. 2.

SHEARIAH, She-a-ry′-ah, *gate or tempest of the Lord.* —A descendant of Saul. 1 Chron. viii. 38.

SHEAR-JASHUB, She-ar-jay′-shub, *the remnant shall return.*—The son of Isaiah. Isai. vii. 3.

SHEBA, She′-ba, *captivity, compassing about, repose, old age.*—1. A son of Raamah. Gen. x. 7. 2. The son of Joktan. Gen. x. 28. 3. Son of Jokshan. Gen. xxv. 3. 4. A queen who came to visit Solomon. 1 Kings x. 1; Matt. xii. 42. 5. A city of the tribe of Simeon. Josh. xix. 2. 6. A son of Abihail, of the tribe of Gad. 1 Chron. v. 13. 7. Son of Bichri of the tribe of Benjamin. 2 Sam. xx. 1.

SHEBAM, She′-bam.—A city beyond Jordan. Num. xxxii. 3.

SHEBANIAH, Sheb-a-ny′-ah, *the Lord that converts, that recalls from captivity, that understands.*—A priest in the time of David, who assisted in bringing the ark to Jerusalem. 1 Chron. xv. 24.

SHEBARIM, Sheb′-a-rim.—A place near Ai and Bethel. Josh. vii. 5.

SHEBAT, She′-bat.—The fifth month of the civil year of the Hebrews, and the eleventh of the ecclesiastical year.

SHEBER, She'-ber.—Son of Caleb. 1 Chron. ii. 48.

SHEBNA, Sheb'-nah, *who rests himself, who is now captive.*—Secretary to king Hezekiah. 2 Kings xviii. 18; Isai. xxii. 15, &c.

SHEBUEL, Sheb'-u-el.—The eldest son of Gershom, son of Moses. 1 Chron. xxiii. 16.

SHECHANIAH, Shek-a-ny'-ah.—The name of several persons mentioned in Scripture. 1 Chron. iii. 21; Neh. vi. 18; Ezra viii. 3, 5.

SHECHEM, She'-kem, *portion, the back, shoulders.*—1. The son of Gilead, and chief of the family of the Shechemites. Num. xxvi. 31. 2. The son of Hamor, and prince of the Shechemites. Gen. xxxiv. 1, 2, &c. 3. A city of Samaria, near the parcel of ground which Jacob bought of Hamor, the father of Shechem, and gave to his son Joseph. Gen. xlviiii. 22. It is also called *Sechem, Sichem, Sychem,* and *Sychar* in the New Testament; afterwards Neapolis; now Nablous, Naplous, Napolose, Napolosa.

SHEDEUR, Shed'-e-ur, *field, destroyer of fire.*—A chief of the tribe of Reuben. Num. i. 5.

SHEHARIAH, She-ha-ry'-ah.—One of the chief men of the tribe of Benjamin. 1 Chron. viii. 26.

SHELAH, She'-lah, *that breaks, that undresses.*—A son of Judah. Gen. xxxviii. 11.

SHELANITES, She'-lan-ites.—The descendants of Shelah. Num. xxvi. 20.

SHELEMIAH, Shel-e-my'-ah, *God is my perfection, my happiness.*—1. One who had married a strange wife in Babylon. Ezra x. 39. 2. A priest. Neh. xiii. 13.

SHELEPH, She'-lef, *who draws out.*—A son of Joktan. Gen. x. 26.

SHELESH, She'-lesh.—A son of Helem. 1 Chron. vii. 35.

SHELOMI, Shel'-o-my, *peace, happiness.*—One of the commissioners for dividing the land of Canaan. Num. xxxiv. 27.

SHELOMITH, Shel'-o-mith, *peaceable, perfect.*—1. The daughter of Dibri, of the tribe of Dan, and mother to the blasphemer mentioned Lev. xxiv. 11. 2. Daughter of Zerubbabel. 1 Chron. iii. 19. 3. Son of Shimei, a Levite. 1 Chron. xxiii. 9. 4. Son of Izhar, a Levite. 1 Chron. xxiii. 18. 5. Daughter of Rehoboam. 2 Chron. xi. 20. 6. Son of Zichri. 1 Chron. xxvi. 25.

SHELOMOTH, Shel'-o-moth.—One of the Kohathites. 1 Chron. xxiv. 22.

SHELUMIEL, She-lew'-me-el, *happiness, retribution of God.*—Son of Zurishaddai, prince of the tribe of Simeon. Num. i. 6; vii. 36.

SHEM, Shem, *name, renown, he that places.*—A son of Noah. Gen. vi. 10. He was born A. M. 1557.

SHEMA, She'-mah.—1. A city in the tribe of Judah. Josh. xv. 26. 2. The fourth son of Hebron. 1 Chron. ii. 43. 3. Son of Joel. 1 Chron. v. 8.

SHEMAAH, Shem'-a-ah. — The father of Joash. 1 Chron. xii. 3.

SHEMAIAH, Shem-a-i'-ah, *that obeys the Lord.*—1. Father of Shimri, of the tribe of Simeon. 1 Chron. iv. 37. 2. Son of Joel, of the tribe of Reuben. 1 Chron. v. 4. 3. A prophet of the Lord, who was sent to Rehoboam. 1 Kings xii. 22. There are thirteen other persons of this name mentioned in Scripture, respecting whom something may be known by consulting the subjoined texts. 1 Chron. iii. 22; ix. 14, 16; xv. 8, 11; xxiv. 6; 2 Chron. xvii. 8; xxix. 14; xxxi. 15; xxxv. 9; Ezra viii. 16; Neh. vi. 10; Jer. xxix. 24—32; xxxvi. 12.

SHEMARIAH, Shem-a-ry'-ah, *God is my guard, diamond.*—1. A friend of David. 1 Chron. xii. 5. 2. One who had married a strange wife in Babylon. Ezra x. 32.

SHEMEBER, Shem'-e-ber, *name of force, fame of the strong.*—The king of Zeboiim. Gen. xiv. 2, &c.

SHEMER, She'-mer, *guardian, thorn.*—The person who sold to Omri the mount on which Samaria was built. 1 Kings xvi. 24.

SHEMIDA, She-my'-da, *name of knowledge, that puts knowledge, the science of the heavens.*—The son of Gilead. Num. xxvi. 32.

SHEMINITH, Shem'-e-nith, *the eighth.*—The title of several Psalms.

SHEMIRAMOTH, She-mir'-a-moth, *the height of the heavens, the elevation of a name.*—A Levite, and porter of the temple. 1 Chron. xv. 18.

SHEMUEL, She-mew'-el.—A son of Ammihud. Num. xxxiv. 20.

SHEN, Shen, *tooth, change, he that sleeps.*—The name of a place in Judea. 1 Sam. vii. 12.

SHENAZAR, She-nay'-zar.—One of the successors of Jeconiah. 1 Chron. iii. 18.

SHENIR, She'-nir, *lantern, light, that sleeps, he that shows.*—A name of Mount Hermon. Deut. iii. 9.

SHEPHAM, She'-fam.—A city of Syria, perhaps the same as Apamea. Num. xxxiv. 10, 11.

SHEPHATIAH, or SHEPHATHIAH, Shef-a-ty'-ah, or Shef-a-thy'-ah, *the Lord that judges.*—1. A son of David and Abital. 2 Sam. iii. 4. 2. Son of Reuel. 1 Chron. ix. 8. 3. One of David's worthies. 1 Chron. xii. 5. 4. Son of Maachah. 1 Chron. xxvii. 16. 5. Son of Jehoshaphat. 2 Chron. xxi. 2. 6. One whose children returned from Babylon. Ezra ii. 57. 7. Son of Mattan. Jer. xxxviii. 1.

SHEPHO, She'-fo.—Son of Shobal. Gen. xxxvi. 23.

SHEPHUPHAN, She-few'-fan. — The son of Bela. 1 Chron. viii. 5.

SHERAH, She'-rah. — The daughter of Beriah, who built Beth-horon. 1 Chron. vii. 24.

SHEREBIAH, Sher-e-by'-ah.—A Levite. Ezra viii. 18.

SHERESH, She'-resh.—A descendant of Manasseh. 1 Chron. vii. 16.

SHEREZER, She-re′-zer.—One sent into the house of God to make inquiries when the captives were in Babylon. Zech. vii. 2.

SHESHACH, She′-shak, *bag of flax, the sixth bag.*— The name by which Jeremiah points out Babylon. Jer. xxv. 26; li. 41. Sheshach was probably an idol worshipped in Babylon.

SHESHAI, She′-shay.—A giant of the race of Anak. Josh. xv. 14.

SHESHAN, She′-shan.—A son of Ishi. 1 Chron. ii. 31.

SHESHBAZZAR, Shesh-baz′-zar, *joy in tribulation, or of vintage.*—A prince of Judah, thought to be the same as Zerubbabel. Ezra i. 8.

SHETH, Sheth.—The same as SETH. 1 Chron. i. 1; Gen. iv. 25.

SHETHAR, She′-thar.—An officer of Ahasuerus. Esther i. 14.

SHETHAR-BOZNAI, She′-thar-boz′-nay-i, *that makes to rot and corrupt.*—An officer of the king of Persia. Ezra v. 6.

SHEVA, She′-vah, *vanity, elevation, tumult, fame.*— Secretary to king David. 2 Sam. xx. 25.

SHIBBOLETH, Shib′-bo-leth, *burden, ear of corn.* — A word used by the Gileadites to test an Ephraimite. Judges xii. 6.

SHIBMAH, Shib′-mah.—A city of the tribe of Reuben. Num. xxxii. 38.

SHICRON, Shy′-kron, *drunkenness, his wages.*—A city of Judea. Josh. xv. 11.

SHIGGAION, Shig-gay′-yon, *the reproof of falsehood, a song of trouble.*—The title of Psalm vii.

SHIGIONOTH, She-gy′-o-noth, *according to variable tunes.*—A musical note or instrument. Hab. iii. 1.

220

SHIHON, Shy′-on.—A city of Palestine. Josh. xix. 19.

SHIHOR-LIBNATH, Shy′-hor-lib′-nath.—A city of Judea. Josh. xix. 26.

SHILHI, Shil′-hy.—The grandfather of Jehoshaphat. 1 Kings xxii. 42.

SHILHIM, Shil′-him.—A city of Judah. Josh. xv. 32.

SHILLEM, Shil′-lem.—A son of Naphtali, Gen. xlvi. 24; head of the great family of the Shillemites. Num. xxvi. 49.

SHILOAH, Shy-lo′-ah, *sent, dart, branch.*—A small brook running through Jerusalem, at the foot of Mount Sion. Isai. viii. 6.

SHILOH, Shy′-loh, *sent, the apostle, peace, abundance.* —1. The prophetic name of Christ. Gen. xlix. 10. 2. A celebrated city in the tribe of Ephraim, twelve miles from Shechem. Josh. xviii., xix., xxi.

SHILONI, Shy-lo′-ny.—One of the captivity, chosen to dwell at Jerusalem. Neh. xi. 5.

SHILONITES, Shy-lo′-nites.—Children of Shiloni. 1 Chron. ix. 5.

SHILSHAH, Shil′-shah.—One of the descendants of Asher. 1 Chron. vii. 37.

SHIMEA, Shim′-e-ah, *that hears, that obeys.*—A prince. 1 Chron. vi. 39.

SHIMEAH, Shim′-e-ah, *that hears, that obeys.*—A brother of David. 2 Sam. xiii. 32.

SHIMEAM, Shim′-e-am, *that hears.*—A descendant of Saul. 1 Chron. ix. 38.

SHIMEATH, Shim′-e-ath, *my reputation.*—The name of the mother of one who slew Joash. 2 Kings xii. 21.

SHIMEATHITES, Shim′-e-ath-ites. — Belonging to Caleb's descendants. 1 Chron. ii. 55.

SHIMEI, Shim'-me-i, *that hears, name of the heap, my reputation.*—1. The son of Gera, a kinsman of king Saul. 2 Sam. xvi. 5, 6, &c. 2. David's vine-keeper. 1 Chron. xxvii. 27. 3. A Levite, who put away his wife. Ezra x. 23.

SHIMEON, Shim'-e-on.—One who put away his wife. Ezra x. 31. The same as SIMEON.

SHIMHI, Shim'-hy.—A descendant of Benjamin. 1 Chron. viii. 21.

SHIMI, Shy'-my.—The son of Gershon. Exod. vi. 17.

SHIMITES, Shim'-ites.—Descendants of Shimi. Num. iii. 21.

SHIMMA, Shim'-mah.—Brother of David. 1 Chron. ii. 13.

SHIMON, Shy'-mon.—Father of Ammon. 1 Chron. iv. 20.

SHIMRATH, Shim'-rath. — Son of Shimhi, and a descendant of Benjamin. 1 Chron. viii. 21.

SHIMRI, Shim'-ry.—A son of Shemaiah, one of the posterity of Simeon. 1 Chron. iv. 37.

SHIMRITH, Shim'-rith.—A Moabitish woman. 2 Chron. xxiv. 26.

SHIMRON, Shim'-ron. 1. A son of Issachar. Num. xxvi. 24. 2. A city in Zebulun. Josh. xix. 15. 3. Shimron-meron, a city. Josh. xii. 20.

SHIMRONITES, Shim'-ron-ites.—Persons belonging to the tribe of Issachar. Num. xxvi. 24.

SHIMSHAI, Shim'-shay, *my sun.*—One who wrote a letter to Artaxerxes against the Jews who were rebuilding Jerusalem. See Ezra iv. 8.

SHINAB, Shy'-nab.—King of Admah. Gen. xiv. 2.

SHINAR, Shy'-nar, *the watching of him that sleeps, change of the city.*—A province of Babylonia, where they undertook to build the tower of Babel. Gen. xi. 2; x. 10.

SHIPHI, Shy'-fy.—A prince of the posterity of Simeon. 1 Chron. iv. 37.

SHIPHMITE, Shif'-mite. — From SHIPHI. 1 Chron. xxvii. 27.

SHIPHRAH, Shif'-rah, *handsome, trumpet, that does good.*—A midwife in Egypt. Exod. i. 15.

SHIPHTAN, Shif'-tan.—Father of Kemuel. Num. xxxiv. 24.

SHISHA, Shy'-shah.—Father of Ahiah. 1 Kings iv. 3.

SHISHAK, Shy'-shak, *present of the bag, of the pot, of the thigh.*—A king of Egypt, who declared war against Rehoboam. 2 Chron. xii. 2, 3, &c.

SHITRAI, Shit'-ra-i. — David's shepherd. 1 Chron. xxvii. 29.

SHITTAH, Shit'-tah, *that turns away, scourges, rods.*— A tree, perhaps the box. Isai. xli. 19.

SHITTIM, Shit'-tim, *that turns away, scourges, rods.*— A kind of wood. Num. xxv. 1.

SHIZA, Shy'-zah.—One of David's worthies. 1 Chron. xi. 42.

SHOA, Sho'-ah, *tyrants.*—One joined with the Chaldeans, of whom it was foretold that they should come against Aholibah, or Jerusalem. Ezek. xxiii. 23.

SHOBAB, Sho'-bab, *returned, turned back.*—A son of David. 2 Sam. v. 14.

SHOBACH, Sho'-bak, *your bonds, your nets, his captivity : in Syriac, a dove-house.*—General of the army of Hadarezer, king of Syria, defeated by David. 2 Sam. x. 16—19.

SHOBAI, Sho'-bay-i, *bonds.*—One of the race of priests. Ezra ii. 42.

SHOBAL, Sho'-bal.—A son of Caleb. 1 Chron. ii. 50.

SHOBEK, Sho'-bek.—A prince mentioned Neh. x. 24.

SHOBI, Sho'-by, *returned.*—A friend of David. 2 Sam. xvii. 27.

SHOCHOH, Sho'-koh, *defence, a bough.*—A city of Palestine. 1 Sam. xvii. 1

SHOHAM, Sho'-ham.—A descendant of Levi. 1 Chron. xxiv. 27.

SHOMER, Sho'-mer.—The father of one of the murderers of Joash. 2 Kings xii. 21.

SHOPHACH, Sho'-fak.—A captain of the Syrian host, whom David slew. 1 Chron. xix. 18.

SHOPHAN, Sho'-fan.—A city of Gad. Num. xxxii. 35.

SHOSHANNIM, Sho-shan'-nim, *lilies of the testimony.*—A word in the title of the forty-fifth, sixty-ninth, and eightieth Psalms: probably a musical instrument.

SHUA, and SHUAH, Shoo'-ah, *pit, crying, humiliation.*—1. Brother of Chelub. 1 Chron. iv. 11. 2. Daughter of Heber. 1 Chron. vii. 32. 3. The sixth son of Abraham. Gen. xxv. 2. 4. The mother of Er, Onan, and Shelah. Gen. xxxviii. 2, &c.

SHUAL, Shoo'-al, *fox, hand, fist, traces, way.*—A country in the land of Israel. 1 Sam. xiii. 17. The situation cannot now be ascertained.

SHUBAEL, Shoo'-ba-el.—Son of Amram. 1 Chron. xxiv. 20.

SHUHAM, Shoo'-ham.—A descendant of Dan. Num. xxvi. 42.

SHUHAMITES, Shoo'-ham-ites.—Children of Shuham.

SHUHITE, Shoo'-hite.—Bildad, the Shuhite, was probably a descendant of Shuah, the son of Abraham. Job ii. 11.

SHULAMITE, Shoo'-lam-ite, *peaceable, perfect, that recompenses.*—A name applied to the church, and taken from the name of Solomon's wife. Cant. vi. 13.

SHUMATHITES, Shoo'-ma-thites.—One of the six families that came out of Kirjath-jearim. 1 Chron. ii. 53.

SHUNAMMITE, Shoo'-nam-mite.—A woman of Shunem. A name given to several women. 1 Kings i. 3; 2 Kings iv. 12.

SHUNEM, Shoo'-nem, *their change, their sleep.*—A city belonging to the tribe of Issachar, five miles south of Tabor. Josh. xix. 18.

SHUNITES, Shoo'-nites.—Posterity of Shuni. Num. xxvi. 15.

SHUPHAM, Shoo'-fam.—A prince in Israel. Num. xxvi. 39.

SHUPHAMITES, Shoo'-fam-ites.—Children of Shupham. Num. xxvi. 39.

SHUPPIM, Shup'-pim.—A descendant of Benjamin. 1 Chron. xxvi. 16.

SHUR, Shur, *wall, ox.*—A city of Arabia, also a desert. Gen. xvi. 7; Exod. xv. 22; 1 Sam. xv. 7; xxvii. 8.

SHUSHAN, Shoo'-shan, *lily, rose, joy.*—The capital of the country of Elam or Persia. Dan. viii. 2, 3. It was here Daniel had some of his visions. See Esther i. 1, 2, &c.; Neh. i. 1.

SHUTHALITES, Shoo'-thal-ites.—Children of Shuthelah.

SHUTHELAH, Shoo'-the-lah, *plant, verdure, moist pot.*—A son of Ephraim. Num. xxvi. 35.

SIA, Sy'-a.—One who returned from Babylon. Ezra ii. 44.

SIBBECHAI, Sib'-be-kay.—One of David's worthies, who slew the giant Saph. 2 Sam. xxi. 18; 1 Chron. xx. 4.

SIBBOLETH, Sib'-bo-leth. See SHIBBOLETH.

SIBMAH, Sib'-mah, *conversion, captivity, old age, rest.*—A city of Reuben. Isai. xvi. 8.

SIBRAIM, Sib'-ray-im.—A city at the extremity of Canaan, between Hamath and Damascus. Ezek. xlvii. 16.

SICHAR, Sy'-kar.—See SHECHEM.

225

SICHEM, Sy'-kem.—See SHECHEM.

SIDDIM, Sid'-dim.—A vale which is now the Dead Sea. Gen. xiv. 3.

SIDON, Sy'-don, *hunting, fishing, venison.*—The eldest son of Canaan, and founder of the city of that name. Gen. x. 15; Josh. xi. 8; xix. 28. It is situated on the Mediterranean.

SIHON, Sy'-hon, *rooting out, conclusion.*—A king of the Amorites, who was defeated by Moses. Num. xxi. 21, &c.

SIHOR, Sy'-hor, *black, trouble, early in the morn.*—A name given to the Nile, because its waters were often black or troubled. Josh. xiii. 3.

SILAS, Sy'-las, *considering, marking.*—He accompanied St. Paul in visiting the churches of Syria and Cilicia. Acts xv. 22.

SILLA, Sil'-lah.—A place, probably near Jerusalem. 2 Kings xii. 20.

SILOA, Sil'-o-ah.—The same as SHILOAH.

SILOE, Sil'-o-e.—The same as SILOA.

SILVANUS, Sil-vay'-nus, *one who loves the woods.*—An individual whom Paul associates with him in the Epistle to the Thessalonians. 1 Thess. i. 1.

SIMEON, Sim'-e-on, *that hears or obeys.*—The son of Jacob and Leah; Gen. xxix. 33; born A.M. 2253. 2. A pious aged man, who was waiting for the incarnation of Christ, and at length embraced him in the temple. Luke ii. 25. 3. Son of Judah. Luke iii. 30.

SIMON, Sy'-mon, *that hears or obeys.*—1. A Cyrenian, who was compelled to bear the cross of Christ after him. Matt. xxvii. 32. 2. A Canaanite, an apostle of Christ. Luke vi. 15; Acts i. 13. 3. The brother of our Lord. Matt. xiii. 55; Mark vi. 3. 4. The Pharisee in whose house Jesus dined. Luke vii. 36, 37, &c. 5. The leper who dwelt in Bethany. 6. Peter. 7. The father of Judas Iscariot. John vi. 71. 8. He that was surnamed Niger Acts xiii. 1. See NIGER. 9. The tanner. Acts. ix. 43. 10. Simon Magus, or the sorcerer. Acts viii. 18—24.

SIMRI, Sim'-ry.—A porter of the temple. 1 Chron. xxvi. 10.

SIN, Sin, *bush.*—A city and desert to the south of the Holy Land, in Arabia Petrea. Exod. xvi. 1 ; xvii. 1.

SINAI, Sy'-na, or Si'-na-i, *bush :* in Syriac, *enmity.*— A celebrated mountain in Arabia Petrea, on which God gave the law to Moses. Exod. xix. 1, &c.

SINIM, Sin'-im, *the south country.*—The name of Pelusium, a city in Egypt.

SINITES, Sin'-ites.—The descendants of the eighth son of Canaan. Gen. x. 17.

SION, Sy'-on, *noise, tumult.*—One of the names of Mount Hermon. Deut. iv. 48.

SIPHMOTH, Siff'-moth.—A place to which David sent spoil. 1 Sam. xxx. 28.

SIPPAI, Sip'-pay.—The name of a giant. 1 Chron. xx. 4.

SIRAH, Sy'-rah, *turning aside, rebellion.*—A well near Jerusalem. 2 Sam. iii. 26.

SIRION, Sir'-re-on, *a breast-plate, deliverance.*—Mount Hermon. Deut. iii. 9.

SISAMAI, Sis-am'-ma-i.—One of Sheshan's posterity. 1 Chron. ii. 40.

SISERA, Sis'-se-ra, *that sees a horse or swallow.*—The general of the army of Jabin, king of Hazor. Judges iv. 2, &c.

SITNAH, Sit'-nah, *hatred.*—A well in Gerar. Gen. xxvi. 21.

SIVAN, Sy'-van, *bush, thorn.*—The Babylonish name of a Jewish month, answering to our May and June. Esther viii. 9.

SMYRNA, Smer'-nah, *myrrh.*—A city of Asia Minor, on the Archipelago, having a fine harbour. See Rev. ii. 8, 9, 10.

SO, So, *measure for grain.*—A king of Egypt, who made an alliance with Hoshea, king of Israel. 2 Kings xvii. 4.

SOCHO, So'-koh, *tents, tabernacles.*—There were two cities of this name, the Upper and the Lower. 1 Chron. iv, 18.

SOCOH, So'-koh, *tents, tabernacles.*—A city of Judah. Josh. xv. 35.

SODI, So'-dy, *my secret.*—The father of Gadiel, one of the spies. Num. xiii. 10.

SODOM, Sod'-om, *their secret, their lime, their cement.* —The capital of Pentapolis, which was for some time the residence of Lot, and was destroyed by fire from heaven. Gen. xiii. 12, 13.

SODOMITES, Sod'-om-ites.—Inhabitants of Sodom. See also 1 Kings xiv. 24.

SOLOMON, Sol'-o-mon, *peaceable, perfect, one who recompenses.*—The son of David and Bathsheba : born A.M. 2971. He was beloved of God, and selected to build the temple ; and was one of the best kings of Israel. He began to reign when about eighteen years of age, and reigned forty years. 2 Sam. xii. 24. He died A.M. 3029.

SOPATER, So'-pa-ter, *who defends his father.*—A Christian of Berea. Acts xx. 4.

SOPHERETH, Sof'-e-reth.—One who returned from Babylon. Ezra ii. 55.

SOREK, So'-rek, *hissing, a colour inclining to yellow.*— The name of a brook that passed through the tribe of Dan; and also a valley where Delilah, Samson's mistress, dwelt. Judges xvi. 4. It was famous for choice wines.

SOSIPATER, So-sip'-a-ter, *who saves his father.*—A kinsman of St. Paul. Rom. xvi. 21.

SOSTHENES, Sos'-the-nees, *a strong and powerful saviour.*—Chief of the synagogue at Corinth. Acts xviii. 17. 2. A Christian whom Paul associated with him in his address to the Corinthians. 1 Cor. i. 1.

SOTAI, So'-ta-i.—One who returned from Babylon. Ezra ii. 55.

SPAIN, Spane, *rare, precious.*—A large country of Europe, lying to the south-west. Rom. xv. 24.

STACHYS, Stay'-kis, *spike.*—A disciple mentioned by St. Paul, Rom. xvi. 9.

STACTE, Stak'-te.—The gum which distils from myrrh-trees. Exod. xxx. 34.

STEPHANAS, Stef'-fa-nas, *a crown, crowned.*—The name of one of the principal Christians at Corinth, whom St. Paul baptized. 1 Cor. i. 16.

STEPHEN, Ste'-ven, *a crown, crowned.*—One of the seven deacons chosen as narrated Acts vi. 5, 6. He was the first martyr for Christ. Acts vii.

SUAH, Sew'-ah.—A descendant of Asher. 1 Chron. vii. 36. The same as SHUAH.

SUCCOTH, Suk'-koth, *tents, tabernacles.*—1. The first encampment of the Israelites. Exod. xii. 37. 2. A city beyond Jordan, near the brook Jabbok. Gen. xxxiii. 17; Josh. xiii. 27.

SUCCOTH-BENOTH, Suk'-koth-be'-noth, *tents of young women.*—Places of prostitution built by the Babylonians in Samaria. 2 Kings xvii. 30.

SUKKIIMS, Suk'-ke-ims, *covered, shadowed.*—A people of Africa. 2 Chron. xii. 3.

SUR, Sur, *that withdraws, or departs.*—The name of a gate of the temple. 2 Kings xi. 6.

SUSANCHITES, Soo'-san-kites.—A people of Persia. Ezra iv. 9.

SUSANNA, Su-zan'-nah, *a lily, a rose, joy.*—A holy woman, an attendant on our Saviour. Luke viii. 2, 3.

SUSI, Soo'-sy, *horse, swallow, moth.*—The father of one of the spies. Num. xiii. 11.

SYCHAR, Sy'-kar.—See SHECHEM.

SYENE, Sy-e′-ne, *bush :* in Syriac, *enmity.*—A city in the southern frontiers of Egypt, between Thebes and the cataracts of the Nile. Ezek. xxix. 10.

SYNTYCHE, Sin′-te-ke, *that speaks or discourses.*—A Christian in the church at Philippi, who had some disagreement with Euodias. Phil. iv. 2.

SYRACUSE, Sir′-a-kewse, *that draws violently.*—A city of Sicily, situated on the east side of the island. Acts xxviii. 12.

SYRIA, Sir′-re-a, *sublime, deceiving.*—In Hebrew, it is called Aram, from the patriarch Aram. It is a country of Asia, having the Mediterranean on the west, Mount Taurus on the north, the Euphrates and Arabia on the east, and to the south, Judea. Antioch was its capital. 2 Sam. viii., x.

SYRO-PHENICIA, Sy′-ro-fe-nish′-e-a, *purple, drawn to.*—Phenicia, properly so called, of which Sidon was the capital. In the gospel, the Canaanitish woman is called a Syrophenician, because she was of Phenicia, which was then looked upon as part of Syria. Mark vii. 26.

T

TAANACH, Tay′-a-nak, *who humbles or answers thee.*—A city of Palestine. Josh. xii. 21.

TAANATH-SHILOH, Tay′-a-nath-shy′-loh.—A place in Palestine. Josh. xvi. 6.

TABBAOTH, Tab′-ba-oth, *goodness.* — A Nethinim. Ezra ii. 43.

TABBATH, Tab′-bath, *good, goodness.*—A place; but where, cannot be correctly ascertained. Judges vii. 22.

TABEAL, Tay′-be-al, *good God.*—Isai. vii. 6.

TABEEL, Tay′-be-el, *good God.*—One who joined in writing to Artaxerxes against the Jews. Ezra iv. 7.

TABERAH, Tab'-e-rah, *burning.*—An encampment in the wilderness. Num. xi. 3.

TABITHA, Tab'-e-thah, *clear-sighted.* — Also called Dorcas. A pious woman who resided at Joppa. Acts ix. 36. She was raised from death by St. Peter.

TABOR, Tay'-bor, *choice :* in Syriac, *contrition.* 1. A mountain not far from Kadesh, in the tribe of Issachar. 1 Sam. x. 3. 2. A city on the summit of this mountain, given to the Levites. 1 Chron. vi. 77.

TABRIMON, Tab'-re-mon, *good pomegranate.*—The son of Hezion, and father of Benhadad, king of Damascus. 1 Kings xv. 18.

TADMOR, Tad'-mor, *palm-tree, change.*—A city built by Solomon, afterwards called Palmyra, situated in the wilderness of Syria, upon the borders of Arabia Deserta. 1 Kings ix. 18.

TAHAN, Tay'-han.—Son of Ephraim. Num. xxvi. 35.

TAHAPANES, or TAHPANHES, Ta-hap'-pa-nes, or Tah'-pan-hes, *secret temptation.*—A city of Egypt. Jer. ii. 16 ; xliii. 7.

TAHATH, Tay'-hath.—An encampment of the Hebrews in the wilderness. Num. xxxiii. 26, 27.

TAHPENES, Tah'-pe-nes, *standard, flight.*—A queen of Egypt. 1 Kings xi. 19, 20.

TAHTIM-HODSHI, Tah'-tim-hod'-shy.—A place in Palestine, but uncertain where. 2 Sam. xxiv. 6.

TALITHA CUMI, Tal'-e-thah-kew'-my, *Young woman, arise.*—See Mark v. 41.

TALMAI, Tal'-may, *my furrow, heap of waters.*— 1. Son of Anak, a giant. Num. xiii. 22. 2. King of Geshur. 2 Sam. iii. 3.

TALMON, Tal'-mon.—A Levite. 1 Chron. ix. 17.

TAMAH, Tay'-mah.—A Nethinim. Neh. vii. 55.
231

TAMAR, Tay'-mar, *a palm, palm-tree.*—1. Daughter-in-law to the patriarch Judah, wife to Er. Gen. xxxviii. 6. 2. Daughter of David, and sister of Amnon. 2 Sam. xiii. 2. 3. Daughter of Absalom. 2 Sam. xiv. 27. 4. A city of Judea, near the Dead Sea. Ezek. xlvii. 19.

TAMMUZ, Tam'-muz, *abstruse, concealed.*—1. The name of a Jewish month. 2. The name of a pagan Deity. Ezek. viii. 14.

TANACH, Tay'-nak, *who humbles or answers thee.*— A city in the half-tribe of Manasseh, on this side of Jordan. Josh. xxi. 25.

TANHUMETH, Tan'-hu-meth, *consolation, repentance.* —A Netophathite, left in Judea at the captivity. 2 Kings xxv. 23.

TAPHATH, Tay'-fath, *little girl.*—A daughter of Solomon. 1 Kings iv. 11.

TAPPUAH, Tap'-pu-ah.—A city on the frontiers of Manasseh, but belonging to Ephraim. Josh. xvii. 8.

TARAH, Tay'-rah.—An encampment of the Israelites in the wilderness. Num. xxxiii. 27.

TARALAH, Tar'-a-lah.—A city of Benjamin. Josh. xviii. 27.

TAREA, Tay'-re-a.—A son of Micah. 1 Chron. viii. 35.

TARPELITES, Tar'-pe-lites, *ravishers, wearied.*—A people named, Ezra iv. 9.

TARSHISH, Tar'-shish, *contemplation of the marble.*— 1. The second son of Javan. Gen. x. 4. 2. A Persian nobleman. Esther i. 14.

TARSUS, Tar'-sus, *winged, feathered.*—The capital city of Cilicia, and the native place of St. Paul. Acts ix. 11.

TARTAK, Tar'-tak, *chained, bound, shut up.*—A deity of the Avites. 2 Kings xvii. 31.

TARTAN, Tar'-tan, *that searches the gift of the turtle.* —An officer of Sennacherib. 2 Kings xviii. 17.

TATNAI, Tat'-na-i, *that gives.*—Governor of Samaria, and of the provinces on this side Jordan. Ezra v. 6.

TEBAH, Te'-bah, *murder, a cook.*—The son of Nahor, Abraham's brother. Gen. xxii. 24.

TEBALIAH, Teb-a-ly'-ah.—A porter of the temple. 1 Chron. xxvi. 11.

TEBETH, Te'-beth.—The fourth month of the civil year of the Hebrews. Esther ii. 16.   It is said that on the tenth of this month the Jews fast in abhorrence of the translation of the Scriptures from Hebrew into Greek, by the command of Ptolemy Philadelphus.

TEHAPHNEHES, Te-haf'-ne-hes.—See TAHAPANES. Ezek. xxx. 18.

TEHINNAH, Te-hin'-nah.—One of the sons of Rechah. 1 Chron. iv. 12.

TEKEL, Te'-kel, *weight.*—See Dan. v. 25.

TEKOA, Te-ko'-ah, *sound of the trumpet.*—A city in the tribe of Judah. 2 Chron. xi. 6.

TEKOITES, Te-ko'-ites.—The inhabitants of Tekoa. Neh. iii. 5.

TEL-ABIB, Tel'-a-bib, *a heap of new grain.*—A place mentioned Ezek. iii. 15.

TELAH, Te'-lah.—A descendant of Ephraim. 1 Chron. vii. 25.

TELAIM, Tel'-a-im. — A place in Judea, to which Saul gathered the people when about to fight Amalek. 1 Sam. xv. 4.

TELASSAR, Te-las'-sar.—A place mentioned Isai. xxxvii. 12.

TELEM, Te'-lem.—A city mentioned Josh. xv. 24.

TELHARESHA, Tel-ha-re'-shah.—A place in which several Israelites had dwelt during the captivity. Neh. vii. 61.

TELHARSA, Tel-har'-sah, *heap, suspension of the plough, or of the head.*—A place in which Jews had dwelt during the captivity. Ezra ii. 59.

TEL-MELAH, Tel′-me-lah, *heap, or salt of the mariners.*
—A place where Jews had dwelt during the Babylonish
captivity. Neh. vii. 61.

TEMA, Te′-mah, *admiration, perfection.*—Son of Ishmael. Gen. xxv. 15.

TEMAN, Te′-man, *the south.*—The grandson of Esau.
Gen. xxxvi. 15. Also a place.

TEMANI, Tem′-a-ny.—A country of Edom. Gen.
xxxvi. 34.

TEMANITES, Te′-man-ites.—Inhabitants of Teman,
or posterity of Teman. 1 Chron. i. 45.

TEMENI, Tem′-e-ny.—A descendant of Ashur.
1 Chron. iv. 6.

TERAH, Te′-rah, *to breathe, to scent, to blow.*—The son
of Nahor, and father of Abraham, Nahor, and Haran.
Born A.M. 1878. Gen. xi. 24.

TERAPHIM, Ter′-a-fim, *images, idols.*—Gen. xxxi. 19;
xxxv. 4.

TERESH, Te′-resh.—One of the chamberlains of king
Ahasuerus. Esther ii. 21.

TERTIUS, Ter′-she-us *the third.*—An amanuensis of
St. Paul. Rom. xvi. 22.

TERTULLUS, Ter-tul′-lus, *a liar, an impostor.*—An
advocate who pleaded against St. Paul before Felix. Acts
xxiv. 1—9.

THADDÆUS, Thad-de′-us, *that praises.*—A surname
of Jude. Matt. x. 3.

THAHASH, Thay′-hash, *he that makes haste or keeps
silence.*—Son of Nahor. Gen. xxii. 24.

THAMAH, Thay′-mah, *that blots out or suppresses.*—
A Nethinim. Ezra ii. 53.

THARA, Thay′-rah.—One of the genealogy of Christ.
Luke iii. 34.

THARSHISH, Thar'-shish.—1. A son of Bilhan. 1 Chron. vii. 10. 2. A country to which Solomon sent fleets, and famous for its traffic. 1 Kings x. 22.

THEBEZ, The'-bez, *muddy, silk.*—A city of Ephraim. Judges ix. 50.

THELASAR, The-las'-ar, *that unbinds and grants the suspension.*—A place in Assyria. 2 Kings xix. 12.

THEOPHILUS, The-of'-fe-lus, *a friend of God.*—A person to whom St. Luke addressed his Gospel and the Acts. Acts i. 1 ; Luke i. 3.

THESSALONICA, Thes-sa-lo-ny'-kah, *victory against the Thessalians.*—A celebrated city of Macedonia, and capital of that kingdom. Acts xvii. 1—4, &c.

THEUDAS, Thew'-das, *a false teacher.*—An insurrectionist in Judea, who was slain. Acts v. 36.

THOMAS, Tom'-as, *a twin.*—One of the apostles. See Matt. x. 3 ; Luke vi. 15.

THUMMIM, Thum'-mim, *perfections.*—The use of Urim and Thummim among the Jews was to consult God in difficult cases ; but with the exact mode we are not acquainted. Exod. xxviii. 30; Ezra ii. 63.

THYATIRA, Thy-a-ty'-rah, *a sweet sacrifice of labour, or sacrifice of contrition.*—A city in the frontiers of Mysia and Lydia. Acts xvi. 14; Rev. ii. 18, 19.

TIBERIAS, Ty-be'-re-as, *good vision.*—The sea of Galilee. John vi. 1.

TIBERIUS, Ty-be'-re-us.—An emperor of Rome, who reigned when Pilate was governor of Judea. Luke iii. 1.

TIBHATH, Tib'-hath.—A city of Syria. 1 Chron. xviii. 8.

TIBNI, Tib'-ny, *straw, understanding.*—A traitor in Judea. See 1 Kings xvi. 21.

TIDAL, Ty'-dal, *that breaks the yoke.*—He is styled King of nations. Gen. xiv. 1.

TIGLATH-PILESER, or TILGATH-PILNESER, Tig'-lath-py-le'-zer, or Til'-gath-pil-ne'-zer, *that takes away, captivity, miraculous.*—King of Assyria, and son and successor of Sardanapalus. He began to reign in Nineveh A.M. 3257. 1 Chron. v. 6; 2 Kings xv. 29.

TIKVAH, or TIKVATH, Tik'-vah, or Tik'-vath, *hope, a congregation.*—The father-in-law of Huldah, the prophetess. 2 Kings xxii. 14; 2 Chron. xxxiv. 22.

TILON, Ty'-lon.—A descendant of Judah. 1 Chron. iv. 20.

TIMÆUS, Ty-me'-us, *perfect, admirable.*—The father of blind Bartimeus. Mark x. 46.

TIMNA, or TIMNAH, Tim'-nah, *image, enumeration.* —1. Concubine to Eliphaz, Esau's son. Gen. xxxvi. 12. 2. One of the posterity of Esau. Gen. xxxvi. 40; 1 Chron. i. 36. 3. A city in the tribe of Judah. Josh. xv. 10, 57. 4. A city of the Philistines. Judges xiv. 2.

TIMNATH-SERAH, Tim'-nath-see'-rah, *image of the morning.*—A city of Ephraim. Josh. xix. 50.

TIMON, Ty'-mon, *honourable.*—One of the seven deacons. Acts vi. 5.

TIMOTHEUS, Ti-mo'-the-us, *honoured of God, valued of God.*—Commonly called Timothy, a disciple of St. Paul. He was of Lystra, in Lycaonia; his father being a Gentile, and his mother a Jewess. 2 Tim. i. 5; Acts xvi. 1. He was first bishop of the church at Ephesus, and St. Paul addressed two epistles to him.

TIMOTHY, Tim'-o-the.—See TIMOTHEUS.

TIPHSAH, Tiff'-sah, *passage, passover.*—A city of the tribe of Ephraim. 1 Kings iv. 24.

TIRAS, Ty'-ras.—The seventh son of Japheth. Gen. x. 2.

TIRATHITES, Ty'-rath-ites.—One of the families of scribes that dwelt at Jabez. 1 Chron. ii. 55.

TIRHAKAH, Tir'-ha-kah, *inquirer, law made dull.*—King of Ethiopia, or the land of Cush, bordering upon Palestine and Egypt. 2 Kings xix. 9.

TIRHANAH, Tir'-ha-nah.—A son of Caleb. 1 Chron. ii. 48.

TIRIA, Tir'-e-a.—A descendant of Judah. 1 Chron. iv. 16.

TIRSHATHA, Tir'-sha-thah, *that overturns the foundation:* in Syriac, *that beholds the time.*—A title of governor. Ezra ii. 63.

TIRZAH, Tir'-zah, *benevolent, pleasant.*—1. A daughter of Zelophehad. Num. xxvi. 33. 2. A city in the tribe of Ephraim, which was the royal seat of the kings of the ten tribes till the building of Samaria. 2 Kings xv. 14, 16.

TISHBITE, Tish'-bite, *that makes captives, that dwells.*—A name given to Elijah, from the name of the town Thisbe, in Gilead, beyond Jordan. 1 Kings xvii. 1.

TISRI, Tis'-ry.—The first Hebrew month of the civil year, and the seventh of the sacred year.

TITUS, Ty'-tus, *honourable.*—A disciple of St. Paul. He was a Gentile by birth and religion, but after his conversion was called St. Paul's son. Gal. ii. 3; Titus i. 4. St. Paul addressed an epistle to him, and he was a bishop of Crete.

TOAH, To'-ah, *a weapon.*—A Levite. 1 Chron. vi. 34.

TOB, Tob, *good, goodness.*—A country of Palestine, lying beyond Jordan, in the northern part of Manasseh. Judges xi. 3, 5.

TOB-ADONIJAH, Tob-a-do-ny'-jah, *the good Lord is my master.*—A Levite. 2 Chron. xvii. 8.

TOBIAH, To-by'-ah, *the Lord is good.*—1. An Ammonite, and enemy to the Jews, who strenuously opposed the rebuilding of the temple. Neh. ii. 10: iv. 3; vi. 1, &c. 2. The son of Nekoda. Ezra ii. 60.

237

TOBIJAH, To-by′-jah, *the Lord is good.*—1. A Levite. 2 Chron. xvii. 8. 2. One who gave to Zechariah an offering of gold, &c., for the temple. Zech. vi. 10, 14.

TOCHEN, To′-ken.—A city of Simeon. 1 Chron. iv. 32.

TOGARMAH, To-gar′-mah, *which is all bone, strong.*— The third son of Gomer. Gen. x. 3.

TOHU, To′-hew, *that lives, or declares.*—Son of Zuph. 1 Sam. i. 1.

TOI, To′-i, *that wanders.*—The king of Hamath. 2 Sam. viii. 9, 10.

TOLA, To′-lah, *worm, scarlet.*—1. The tenth judge of Israel. Judges x. 1. 2. The eldest son of Issachar. Num. xxvi. 23.

TOLAD, To′-lad, *nativity.*—A city of Simeon. 1 Chron. iv. 29.

TOPAZ, To′-paz.—A precious stone in the breast-plate of the Jewish high-priest. Exod. xxviii. 17.

TOPHEL, To′-fel, *ruin, folly, insipid.*—A place near which Moses delivered the Deuteronomy. Deut. i. 1.

TOPHET, To′-fet, *a drum, betraying.*—A valley where sacrifices were offered to Moloch. See Isai. xxx. 33 ; Jer. vii. 31.

TOU, To′-yew.—The same as Toi.

TRACHONITIS, Trak-o-ny′-tis.—A large province, having Arabia Deserta to the east, Batanea to the west, Iturea to the south, and the country of Damascus to the north. Luke iii. 1.

TROAS, Tro′-as, *penetrated.*—A city of Phrygia, or of Mysia, in the Hellespont. Acts xvi. 8 ; xx. 5, 6.

TROGYLLIUM, Tro-jil′-le-um.—A city in the isle of Samos, in the Archipelago, on the coast of Asia Minor. Acts xx. 15.

TROPHIMUS, Trof'-e-mus, *well educated.*—A disciple, originally a Gentile by religion, and an Ephesian by birth. Acts xx. 4.

TRYPHENA, Try-fee'-nah, *delicate.*—A pious woman. Rom. xvi. 12.

TRYPHOSA, Try-fo'-sah, *thrice shining.* — A pious woman. Rom. xvi. 12.

TUBAL, Tew'-bal, *the earth, confusion.*—The fifth son of Japheth. Gen. x. 2.

TUBAL-CAIN, Tew'-bal-kane', *worldly possession, jealous of confusion.*—The son of Lamech and Zillah. Gen. iv. 19—22.

TYCHICUS, Tik'-e-kus, *casual, happening.*—A disciple often employed in conveying letters to several churches. Acts xx. 4; Eph. vi. 21, 22.

TYRANNUS, Ty-ran'-nus, *a prince, one that reigns.*— A person in whose school St. Paul preached at Ephesus. Acts xix. 9.

TYRE, Tire, *strength.*—A large city of Phœnicia, allotted to the tribe of Asher. Josh. xix. 29. It is supposed to have been built by a colony of Sidonians, and hence was called the daughter of Zidon. Isai. xxiii. 12.

TYRUS, Ty'-rus.—The same as TYRE.

U

UCAL, Yew'-kal, *power, prevalency.*—A contemporary of Agur, who desired his instructions. Prov. xxx. 1.

UEL, Yew'-el.—One who put away his strange wife. Ezra x. 34.

ULAI, Yew'-la-i, *strength.*—A river dividing the province of Luscana in Persia from Elam. Dan. viii. 2.

ULAM, Yew'-lam, *the porch, their strength.*—A descendant of Saul. 1 Chron. vii. 16.

ULLA, Ul'-lah, *elevation, holocaust, leaf.*—A descendant of Asher. 1 Chron. vii. 39.

UMMAH, Um'-mah.—A city of Asher. Josh. xix. 30.

UNNI, Un'-ny, *poor, afflicted.*—A Levite. 1 Chron. xv. 18.

UPHARSIN, Yew-far'-sin, *division.*—See Dan. v. 25.

UPHAZ, Yew'-faz, *gold of Phasis or Pison.*—A place supposed to be Ophir by some. Jer. x. 9.

UR, Ur, *fire, light.*—A city of Chaldea, from which Abraham came forth. Gen. xi. 28.

URBANE, Ur'-ba-ne, *civil, courteous.*—A person mentioned Rom. xvi. 9. Nothing certain is known of him.

URI, Yew'-ry, *my light or fire.*—The father of Bezaleel. Exod. xxxi. 2.

URIAH, Yew-ry'-ah, *the Lord is my light or fire.*—The husband of Bathsheba, and a general in David's army, whose death David plotted. 2 Sam. xi. 3.

URIAS, Yew-ry'-as, *the Lord is my light or fire.*—The same as URIAH. Matt. i. 6.

URIEL, Yew'-re-el, *God is my light or fire.*—1. A Levite in the time of David. 1 Chron. vi. 24. 2. The grandfather of king Abijah. 2 Chron. xiii. 2.

URIJAH, Yew-ry'-jah, *the Lord is my light or fire.*—1. A chief priest under Ahaz. 2 Kings xvi. 10, 11. 2. A prophet, son of Shemaiah of Kirjath-jearim. Jer. xxvi. 20, 21.

URIM, Yew'-rim, *lights.*—See THUMMIM.

UTHAI, Yew'-tha-i.—The son of Ammihud. 1 Chron. ix. 4.

UZ, Uz, *counsel*: in Syriac, *to fix.*—1. The eldest son of Aram, and grandson of Shem. Gen. x. 23. 2. A Horite. Gen. xxxvi. 28. 3. Uz, the country of Job. Job i. 1.

UZAI, Yew'-za-i.—One who repaired the walls of Jerusalem. Neh. iii. 25.

UZAL, Yew'-zal.—The sixth son of Joktan. Gen. x. 27.

UZZA, Uz'-zah, *strength, a goat.*—The son of Abinadab, who perished for his officiousness in touching the ark. 2 Sam. vi. 3—7; 1 Chron. xv. 13.

UZZEN-SHERAH, Uz'-zen-she'-rah, *ear of the flesh or of the parent.*—A city of Ephraim, built by Sherah, the daughter of Beriah. 1 Chron. vii. 22—24.

UZZI, Uz'-zy, *my strength, my kid.*—The son of Bukki, the sixth high-priest of the Hebrews: he was succeeded by Eli, A.M. 2848. 1 Chron. vi. 5.

UZZIAH, Uz-zy'-ah, *the strength of the Lord.*—The same as Azariah, king of Judah. 2 Kings xv. 13.

UZZIEL, Uz-zy'-el, *the strength of God.*—The son of Kohath, a Levite. Exod. vi. 18.

UZZIELITES, Uz-zy'-el-ites.—The posterity of Uzziel. Num. iii. 27.

V

VAJEZATHA, Va-jez'-a-thah.—One of Haman's sons. Esther ix. 9.

VANIAH, Va-ny'-ah.—One who had married a strange wife in Babylon. Ezra x. 36.

VASHNI, Vash'-ny, *the second.*—The eldest son of Samuel. 1 Chron. vi. 28.

VASHTI, Vash'-ty, *that drinks, thread.*—The queen of Ahasuerus. Esther i. 9.

VOPHSI, Vof'-sy, *fragment, diminution.*—Father of one of the spies sent to view the land. Num. xiii. 14.

Z

ZAANAN, Zay'-a-nan, *the country of flocks.*—A city of Palestine. Micah i. 11.

ZAANANNIM, Zay-a-nan'-nim, *movings.*—A boundary of the tribe of Naphtali. Josh. xix. 33.

ZAAVAN, Zay'-a-van.—One of the children of Ezer. Gen. xxxvi. 27.

ZABAD, Zay'-bad, *a dowry.*—One who assisted in the murder of Joash, king of Judah. 2 Chron. xxiv. 26.

ZABBAI, Zab'-bay.—Son of Bebai. Ezra x. 28.

ZABDI, Zab'-dy, *portion, dowry.*—A Benjamite. Josh. vii. 1.

ZABDIEL, Zab'-de-el, *dowry of the Lord.*—A captain of king David. 1 Chron. xxvii. 2.

ZABUD, Zay'-bud.—Son of Nathan. 1 Kings iv. 5.

ZABULON, Zab'-u-lon, *dwelling, habitation.*—The same as ZEBULUN.

ZACCAI, Zak'-kay-i.—One whose children returned from the Babylonish captivity. Ezra ii. 9.

ZACCHÆUS, Zak-ke'-us, *pure, justified.*—The chief of the publicans, who was converted by Christ. Luke xix. 1, &c.

ZACCUR, Zak'-kur.—1. A descendant of Reuben. Num. xiii. 4. 2. A Levite. Neh. xiii. 13. 3. The son of Imri. Neh. iii. 2.

ZACHARIAH, ZACHARIAS, ZECHARIAH, Zak-a-ry'-ah, Zak-a-ry'-as, Zek-a-ry'-ah, *memory of the Lord.*—1. A Reubenite. 1 Chron. v. 7. 2. A king of Israel: he reigned six months, and was murdered. 2 Kings xiv. 29. 3. Of the race of Korah. 1 Chron. ix. 21. 4. A Levite. 2 Chron. xvii. 7. 5. Son of Jehoiada, high-priest of the Jews, probably the same as Azariah: see 1 Chron. vi. 10, 11. 6. The eleventh of the twelve minor prophets, son of Barachiah: he returned from Babylon, A.M. 3484, about two months after Haggai had begun to prophesy. Ezra v. 1. 7. The son of Barachiah or Jeberechiah, of whom mention is made Isai. viii. 2. See 2 Chron. xxvi. 5. 8. A priest of the order of Abia, the father of John the Baptist. Luke i. 5, 12, &c.

ZADOK, Zay'-dok, *just, justified.*—The son of Ahitub, high-priest of the Jews, of the race of Eleazar. 2 Sam. viii. 17; xv. 24, &c.

ZAHAM, Zay'-ham, *crime, impurity.*—The son of Rehoboam. 2 Chron. xi. 19.

ZAIR, Zay'-ir, *little, afflicted.*—A city in Judea. 2 Kings viii. 21.

ZALAPH, Zay'-laf.—The father of Hanun, who repaired the wall of Jerusalem. Neh. iii. 30.

ZALMON, or SALMON, Zal'-mon, or Sal'-mon, *his shade, obscurity.*—A mountain in the neighbourhood of Shechem. Judges ix. 48; Psalm lxviii. 14.

ZALMONAH, Zal-mo'-nah, *the shade, your image.*—An encampment of the Israelites in the wilderness. Num. xxxiii. 41.

ZALMUNNA, Zul-mun'-nah, *shadow, image.*—A king of the Midianites. Judges viii. 5.

ZAMZUMMIMS, Zam-zum'-mims, *thinking, wickedness.*—Ancient giants beyond Jordan. Deut. ii. 20.

ZANOAH, Za-no'-ah, *forgetfulness, this rest.*—A city of Palestine. Josh. xv. 34.

ZAPHNATH-PAANEAH, Zaph'-nath-pa-a-ne'-ah, *one that discovers hidden things :* in the Egyptian tongue, *a saviour of the world.*—The name which Pharaoh gave to Joseph. Gen. xli. 45.

ZAPHON, Zay'-fon.—A city of Gad. Josh. xiii. 27

ZARAH, or ZERAH, Zay'-rah, or Ze'-rah, *east, brightness.*—The son of Tamar by Judah. Gen. xxxviii. 30. He had five sons. 1 Chron. ii. 6. See also ZERAH.

ZAREAH, Zay'-re-ah.—A village in Palestine. Neh. xi. 29.

ZAREATHITES, Zay'-re-ath-ites.—The posterity of Caleb. 1 Chron. ii. 53.

ZARED, Zay'-red.—A brook beyond Jordan, on the frontiers of the Moabites : it discharges itself into the Dead Sea. Num. xxi. 12.

ZAREPHATH, or SAREPTA, Zar'-e-fath, or Sa-rep'-tah, *ambush of the mouth.*—A city of the Sidonians, lying between Tyre and Sidon, on the coast of the Mediterranean Sea. 1 Kings xvii. 9, 10.

ZARETAN, Zar'-e-tan, *tribulation, perplexity.*—A place near the city Adam. Josh. iii. 16.

ZARETH-SHAHAR, Zay'-reth-shay'-har.—A city of Reuben, beyond Jordan. Josh. xiii. 19.

ZARHITES, Zar'-hites.—One of the Israelitish families numbered in the wilderness. Num. xxvi. 13.

ZARTANAH, Zar'-ta-nah.—A city of Palestine. 1 Kings iv. 12.

ZARTHAN, Zar'-than.—The same as ZARTANAH.

ZATTHU, Zat'-thew.—One that sealed the covenant with Nehemiah. Neh. x. 14.

ZATTU, Zat'-tew.—One whose children returned from captivity, to the number of 945. Ezra ii. 8.

ZAVAN, Zay'-van.—A descendant of Esau. 1 Chron. i. 42.

ZAZA, Zay'-zah, *belonging to all, going back.*—A son of Jonathan. 1 Chron. ii. 33.

ZEBADIAH, Zeb-a-dy'-ah, *portion of the Lord.*—A Benjamite. 1 Chron. viii. 15.

ZEBAH, Zee'-bah, *victim, immolation.*—A prince of the Midianites, whom Gideon thrust through. Judges viii. 5, 21.

ZEBAIM, Ze-bay'-im.—A place mentioned Ezra ii. 57.

ZEBEDEE, Zeb'-e-dee, *abundant portion.*—The father of the apostles James and John. Matt. iv. 21.

ZEBOIM, or ZEBOIIM, Ze-bo'-im, or Ze-bo'-e-im, *deer, goats.*—One of the five cities consumed by fire. Gen. x. 19; xiv. 2; xix. 25.

ZEBUDAH, Ze-bew'-dah.—The mother of Jehoiakim. 2 Kings xxiii. 36.

ZEBUL, Ze'-bul, *a habitation.*—Governor of the city of Shechem. Judges ix. 28.

ZEBULUN, Zeb'-u-lun, *dwelling, habitation.*—1. The sixth son of Jacob and Leah; Gen. xxx. 20: head of a tribe. 2. A city of the tribe of Asher. Josh. xix. 27; Judges xii. 12.

ZECHARIAH, Zek-a-ry'-ah.—See ZACHARIAH.

ZEDAD, Ze'-dad, *his side, his hunting.*—A city of Syria. Num. xxxiv. 8.

ZEDEKIAH, Zed-e-ky'-ah, *the Lord is my justice.*— 1. The last king of Judah, before the captivity of Babylon: he was the son of Josiah. See 2 Kings xxiv. 17, &c. 2. Son of Chenaanah, and a false prophet of Samaria. 1 Kings xxii. 11, 24. 3. A false prophet. Jer. xxix. 22.

ZEEB, Ze'-eb, *wolf.*—A prince of Midian. Judges vii. 25.

ZELAH, Ze'-lah.—A city of the tribe of Benjamin. Josh. xviii. 28.

ZELEK, Ze'-lek, *the noise of him that laps or licks.*— The name of one of David's thirty valiant captains. 2 Sam. xxiii. 37.

ZELOPHEHAD, Ze-lo'-fe-had, *the shade or tingling of fear.*—A person who died without male children, leaving five daughters, who received their portion in the Land of Promise. Num. xxvi. 33.

ZELOTES, Ze-lo'-tees, *jealous, full of zeal.*—Simon. Acts i. 13.

ZELZAH, Zel'-zah, *noon-tide.*—A village in the border of Benjamin. 1 Sam. x. 2.

ZEMARAIM, Zem-a-ray'-im.—1. A city of Benjamin near Bethel. Josh. xviii. 22. 2. Mount Shemer. 2 Chron. xiii. 4.

ZEMARITE, Zem'-a-rite.—A descendant of Canaan. Gen. x. 18.

ZEMIRA, Ze-my'-rah.—A Benjamite. 1 Chron. vii. 8.

ZENAN, Ze'-nan.—A city of Palestine, in the tribe of Judah in the valley. Josh. xv. 37.

ZENAS, Ze'-nas, *living.*—A doctor of the law, and a disciple of St. Paul. Tit. iii. 13.

ZEPHANIAH, Zef-a-ny'-ah, *the Lord is my secret, the mouth of the Lord.*—1. The son of Maaseiah, called the second priest. 2 Kings xxv. 18. He was put to death at Riblah by Nebuchadnezzar. Jer. xxxvii. 3. 2. The son of Cushi, a prophet of the Lord. See his Prophecy.

ZEPHATH, Ze'-fath, *which beholds, attends.*—A city of the tribe of Simeon. Judges i. 17.

ZEPHATHAH, Zef'-a-thah.—The valley in which Asa and Terah fought. 2 Chron. xiv. 10.

ZEPHI, or ZEPHO, Ze'-fy, or Ze'-fo, *that sees and observes.*—A descendant of Esau. Gen. xxxvi. 11.

ZEPHON, Ze'-fon, *that sees or observes.*—A descendant of Gad. Num. xxvi. 15.

ZEPHONITES, Zef'-fon-ites.—Children of Zephon.

ZER, Zer, *perplexity, tribulation, a rock.*—A city in the tribe of Naphtali. Josh. xix. 35.

ZERAH, Ze'-rah, *east, brightness.*—1. A grandson of Esau. Gen. xxxvi. 13. 2. A son of Simeon. 1 Chron. iv. 24. 3. King of Ethiopia, or of Cush, in Arabia Petrea, upon the Red Sea, who came against Asa, king of Judah. 2 Chron. xiv. 9, 10. 4. The great-grandfather of Achan. Josh. vii. 1.

ZERAHIAH, Zer-a-hy'-ah.—A Levite. 1 Chron. vi. 6.

ZERED, Ze'-red, *ambush.*—A brook in the land of Moab. Deut. ii. 13.

ZEREDA, Zer'-e-dah, *ambush.*—A city in the tribe of Ephraim, where Jeroboam, the son of Nebat, was born. 1 Kings xi. 26.

ZEREDATHAH, Ze-red'-a-thah, sometimes called ZARTHAN.—A city in the tribe of Ephraim, in which were cast the great works of brass that Hiram made for Solomon's temple. 2 Chron. iv. 17; 1 Kings vii. 46.

ZERERATH, Zer'-e-rath. — A country of Canaan. Judges vii. 22.

ZERESH, Ze'-resh, *misery, stranger.*—The wife of Haman, who advised her husband to destroy Mordecai. Esther v. 10, 14.

ZERETH, Ze'-reth.—A descendant of Judah. 1 Chron. iv. 7.

ZERI, Ze'-ry.—A singer in the temple. 1 Chron. xxv. 3.

ZEROR, Ze'-ror, *root, that straightens, a stone.*—1 Sam. ix. 1.

ZERUAH, Ze-rew'-ah, *leprous, hornet.*—The mother of Jeroboam. 1 Kings xi. 26.

ZERUBBABEL, Ze-rub'-ba-bel, *banished, a stranger at Babylon, dispersion of confusion.*—The son of Salathiel, of the royal race of David. Matt. i. 12; 1 Chron. iii. 19. He returned to Jerusalem from Babylon under the reign of Cyrus, A.M. 3468; and had the care of the sacred vessels. Ezra i. 11.

ZERUIAH, Zer-u-i'-ah, *pain, tribulation.*—The sister of David, and mother of Joab, Abishai, and Asahel. 2 Sam. ii. 18.

ZETHAM, Ze'-tham.—A treasurer of the temple. 1 Chron. xxiii. 8.

ZETHAN, Ze'-than, *their olive.*—A Benjamite. 1 Chron. vii. 10.

ZETHAR, Ze'-thar, *he that examines or beholds.*—An officer or chamberlain in the court of Ahasuerus. Esther i. 10.

ZIA, Zy'-a.—A descendant of Gad. 1 Chron. v. 13.

ZIBA, Zy'-bah, *army, fight, strength, stag.*—One of the servants of king Saul. 2 Sam. ix. 2, &c.   He was a friend of David, and put in possession of Saul's estates. 2 Sam. xvi. 1.

ZIBEON, Zib'-e-on, *iniquity that dwells, the seventh.*—A Hivite, whose daughter Esau married. Gen. xxxvi. 2.

ZIBIA, Ze-by'-a.—A descendant of Benjamin. 1 Chron. viii. 9.

ZIBIAH, Ze-by'-ah, *deer, goat, honourable and fine.*—The mother of king Jehoash. 2 Kings xii. 1.

ZICHRI, Zik'-ry, *that remembers, a male.*—One of the chief men of the tribe of Benjamin. 1 Chron. viii. 19.

ZIDDIM, Zid'-dim, *huntings:* in Syriac, *destructions.*—A city of Naphtali. Josh. xix. 35.

ZIDKIJAH, Zid-ky'-jah.—One that sealed the covenant with Ezra. Neh. x. 1.

ZIDON, Zy'-don, *hunting, fishing, venison.*—Gen. xlix. 13.   See Sidon.

ZIF, Zif, *this, that:* in Syriac, *brightness.*—The name of the second sacred month. 1 Kings vi. 1, 37.

ZIHA, Zy'-hah.—A Nethinim. Ezra ii. 43.

ZIKLAG, Zik'-lag, *measure pressed down.*—A city which Achish, king of Gath, gave to David, when he took shelter among the Philistines. 1 Sam. xxvii. 6.

ZILLAH, Zil'-lah, *shadow, which is roasted, the tingling of the ear.*—The wife of Lamech. Gen. iv. 19, 22.

ZILPAH, Zil'-pah, *distillation, contempt of the mouth.*—Leah's maid, whom she gave to Jacob. Gen. xxx. 9; xlvi. 18.

ZILTHAI, Zil'-thay.—A Benjamite. 1 Chron. viii. 20.

ZIMMAH, Zim'-mah.—A Levite. 1 Chron. vi. 20.

ZIMRAN, Zim'-ran, *song, singer, vine.*—A son of Abraham, by Keturah. Gen. xxv. 2.

ZIMRI, Zim'-ry, *my field, my vine, my branch.*—1. The son of Zerah. 1 Chron. ii. 6. 2. Son of Salu. Num. xxv. 14. 3. A general of Elah, king of Israel: he rebelled against his master, slew him, and reigned in his stead. 1 Kings xvi. 9, &c.

ZIN, Zin, or SIN, *buckler, coldness.*—A city south of Judea. Num. xxxiv. 4.

ZINA, Zy'-nah.—A Levite. 1 Chron. xxiii. 10.

ZION, or SION, Zy'-on, *a monument, sepulchre, turret.*—A mountain on which the temple of the Lord was built by Solomon, and where David built the city of David. Psalm xlviii. 2.

ZIOR, Zy'-or, *ship of him that watches, ship of the enemy.*—A city of Judah. Josh. xv. 54.

ZIPH, Ziff, *mouth, this mouthful.*—1. A city of Judah, about eight miles east of Hebron. Josh. xv. 24. 2. A city near Maon and Carmel of Judah. Josh. xv. 55.

ZIPHAH, Zy'-fah.—A descendant of Caleb. 1 Chron. iv. 16.

ZIPHION, Ziff'-e-on.—One of the sons of Gad. Gen. xlvi. 16.

ZIPHITES, Ziff'-ites.—Inhabitants of Ziph. 1 Sam. xxiii. 19.

ZIPHRON. Ziff'-ron.—One of the borders of the land of Canaan. Num. xxxiv. 9.

ZIPPOR, Zip'-por, *bird, crown :* in Syriac, *early in the morning, goat.*—The father of Balak. Num. xxii. 2.

ZIPPORAH, Zip-po'-rah, *beauty, trumpet.*—The daughter of Jethro, and wife of Moses. Exod. ii. 21.

ZITHRI, Zith'-ry, *to hide, overturned.*—A Levite. Exod. vi. 21.

ZIZ, Ziz, *flower, lock of hair :* in Syriac, *wing, feather.*—A cliff near which the Ammonites and Moabites marched when about to fight Jehoshaphat. 2 Chron. xx. 16.

ZIZA, Zy'-zah, *belonging to all, going back.*—A Simeonite. 1 Chron. iv. 37.

ZIZAH, Zy'-zah.—1 Chron. xxiii. 11. The same as ZINA.

ZOAN, Zo'-an, *motion.*—The capital of Lower Egypt, in the time of Moses; afterwards called Tanis. Num. xiii. 22.

ZOAR, Zo'-ar, *little, small.*—A city near Sodom, spared at the entreaty of Lot. Gen. xix. 22.

ZOBA, Zo'-bah, *an army, a swelling.*—A city of Syria. 2 Sam. x. 6.

ZOBEBAH, Zo-be'-bah.—A descendant of Judah. 1 Chron. iv. 8.

ZOHAR, Zo'-har, *white, shining, dryness.*—The father of Ephron, of whom Abraham bought the cave of Machpelah. Gen. xxiii. 8.

ZOHELETH, Zo'-he-leth, *that creeps or draws.*—A place near the fountain of Enrogel. 1 Kings i. 9.

ZOPHAI, Zo'-fay.—A person belonging to the family of Merari. 1 Chron. vi. 26.

ZOPHAR, Zo'-far, *rising early, crown:* in Syriac, *sparrow, goat.*—The Naamathite, one of Job's friends. Job ii. 11.

ZOPHIM, Zo'-fim.—A plain near Mount Pisgah. Num. xxiii. 14.

ZORAH, Zo'-rah, *leprosy, scab.*—1. A city of Judah. Josh. xix. 41. 2. A city belonging to Dan, and the birthplace of Samson. Judges xiii. 2.

ZOREAH, Zo'-re-ah.—A city of Judah. Josh. xv. 33.

ZOROBABEL, Zo-rob'-ba-bel.—See ZERUBBABEL. Matt. i. 12.

ZUAR, Zew'-ar, *small*.—The father of Nethaneel, a prince of the tribe of Issachar. Num. i. 8.

ZUPH, Zuff, *that observes, roof.*—1. A Levite, an ancestor of Elkanah. 1 Sam. i. 1; 1 Chron. vi. 35. Also the country of Zuph.

ZUR, Zur, *stone, plain, form.*—A prince of Midian. Num. xxv. 15.

ZURIEL, Zew'-re-el, *the rock or strength of God.*—The son of Abihail, a Levite. Num. iii. 35.

ZURISHADDAI, Zew'-ry-shad'-da-i, *the Almighty is my rock, splendour, beauty.*—A prince of the tribe of Simeon. Num. i. 6.

ZUZIMS, Zew'-zims, *the posts of a door :* Syriac, *departing money :* Chaldee, *strong.*—Certain giants who dwelt beyond Jordan, and were conquered by Chedorlaomer and his allies in Ham. Gen. xiv. 5.

THE END.

INSPIRATIONAL LIBRARY

Beautiful purse / pocket size editions of Christian Classics bound in flexible leatherette or genuine Bonded Leather. The Bonded Leather editions have gold edges and make beautiful gifts.

THE BIBLE PROMISE BOOK Over 1000 promises from God's Word arranged by topic. What does the Bible promise about matters like: Anger, Illness, Jealousy, Sex, Money, Old Age, et cetera, et cetera.

Flexible Leatherette . . . . $ 3.95
Genuine Bonded Leather $10.95

DAILY LIGHT One of the most popular daily devotionals with readings for both morning and evening. One page for each day of the year.

Flexible Leatherette . . . . $ 4.95
Genuine Bonded Leather $10.95

WISDOM FROM THE BIBLE Daily thoughts from the Proverbs which communicate truth about ourselves and the world around us. One page for each day in the year.

Flexible Leatherette . . . . $ 4.95
Genuine Bonded Leather $10.95

MY DAILY PRAYER JOURNAL Each page is dated and has a Scripture verse and ample room for you to record your thoughts, prayers and praises. One page for each day of the year.

Flexible Leatherette . . . . $ 4.95
Genuine Bonded Leather $10.95

Available wherever books are sold.

or order from:

Barbour and Company, Inc.
164 Mill Street   Box 1219
Westwood, New Jersey 07675

If you order by mail add $1.00 to your order for shipping.
Prices subject to change without notice.

CL-2